THE COMPLETE BOOK OF RACQUETBALL

by STEVE KEELEY

Endorsed by:
U.S. Racquetball Association
National Racquetball Club

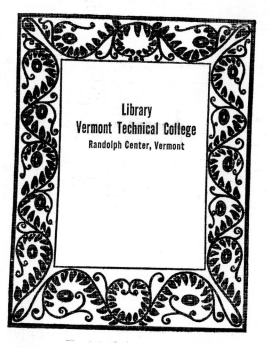

DBI Books, Inc., Northfield, Illinois

staff

Editor
Charles Drake

Photographers
Sequence Illustrations
by Joe Thein, San Diego

Tournament Photos by Arthur
and Dick Shay, Chicago

Graphic Designer
Mary MacDonald

Production Manager
Wanda Sahagian

Associate Publisher
Sheldon L. Factor

Cover photo of Steve Keeley and
Richard Wagner by Arthur Shay.

2 3 4 5 6 7 8 9 10

ISBN 0-695-80651-3   Library of Congress Catalog Card #75-37355

PREFACE

This book is designed to benefit *every* racquetball player, from the greenhorn beginner to the seasoned veteran. No aspiring player is immune from its instructional benefits. Specifically, the text is divided into three separate parts: I. "Racquetball before entering the court," II. "Racquetball for the novice and intermediate player" and III. "Racquetball appendices."

Part I provides a brief journey through the history of the game, the most complete rundown on racquetball equipment ever published, and an overview of the basic rules governing the sport.

Part II lays the foundation for an individual who is about to, or has recently, embarked upon the sport. It is concerned with the *basics*, which encompass strokes, and the offensive and defensive shots required to make the game an enjoyable and competitive experience. This portion of the book is especially rich in illustrations, supporting the cliche that a picture is worth a thousand words. The reader will also discover countless on-the-court drills and shot exercises here, a necessity for the truly ardent racqueteer. In short, "Racquetball for the novice and intermediate player" presents a cut-and-try excursion through the game's essentials.

The first two parts are the meat of this book, sufficient food for thought for any racquetball player. In addition there is section III, the appendices—a listing of the official rules, a glossary of the familiar terms commonly utilized in the racquetball dialect and a photo portrait of a typical tournament. In addition the summaries of the instructional chapters have been recapped for easy use.

At the onset, this book was to have covered the most subtle techniques, shots and strategies utilized by players of advanced and even championship caliber. However, when the sum: text, photographs and diagrams were brought together upon completion, the result was mammoth. Therefore, the originally intended single book was split into *two* autonomous texts. I emphasize that both *The Complete Book of Racquetball* and the planned second book, *Racquetball: For Advanced to Champion Players* are complete, whole entities in themselves.

The second book is oriented toward the advanced player who has satisfactorily mastered all aspects of the first book's how-to-do-it chapters and who desires to strengthen his game through sophisticated techniques. *This* test provides a "fun" learning process which includes a generous smattering of strategy tips: kill shot placement, conserving energy, anticipation, the offensive theory of playing, pre-tourney psych-up, plus a word on off-the-court conditioning. As the player progresses up through the ranks of club hacker to "C" to "Open" player, he discovers this progressive evolution relies mainly upon expanding his *mental* approach to the game. In a nutshell, where the first book deals with the execution of the basics, the second will offer an in-depth study into the cerebral aspect of racquetball.

It is important to note that each chapter in this book is preceded by a *summary* of the important points which are to follow in that particular chapter. The value of this listing of introductory tips cannot be overemphasized. While studying the chapter's more in-depth explanations, use this outline to keep the most significant points in focus. Review each chapter after the initial perusal by checking the opening capsule summary to see if you can recall the expansions made within the chapter. Also employ the introductory synopsis as a ready-reference *after* having completed the book. For your convenience the summaries of the instructional chapters have been collected at the end of this book into an easily removable "pocket guide."

Tribute has already been paid to the importance of visual presentations of strokes, court positioning, etc. The photographs alone, many of them rapid-swing sequences, make this book an invaluable pictorial record of the proper racquet swing. The text is copiously strewn with diagrams, drawings, and illustrations—apply these not separately but in conjunction with the written descriptions. When the book directs the reader to refer to Figure "X", you are urged to do so immediately in order to correlate the words *with* the picture. A fuller understanding of the concept being presented will be gained.

One final appealing word to the wise enthusiast: becoming proficient in any sport has three requisites. First, one must know *what* to do, and this publication, hopefully, fulfills that need. Second, one must *practice* the activity presented over and over until the movement becomes second nature. Practice here is meant to suggest solo drilling in the court; a weekend hacker does not become a Serot, Schmidtke, Brumfield, or Strandemo without hours of solitary drilling. Third, the serious racqueteer must fuse what he has learned and that which he has practiced by *playing* the game itself. And that is where the fun comes in.

• • • • •

Dedication

This is dedicated to Loveday, who begat Mule,
who begat Brum, who begat this author.
Thusly evolved the dubious ancestry of this book.

• • • • •

CONTENTS

PREFACE   3

KEY TO DIAGRAMS   6

section I   RACQUETBALL BEFORE
               ENTERING THE COURT

chapter one   HISTORY   9

chapter two   EQUIPMENT   22

chapter three THE GAME   42

section II   RACQUETBALL FOR
               THE NOVICE AND
               INTERMEDIATE PLAYER

chapter four   FOREHAND   63

chapter five   BACKHAND   89

chapter six   PASS SHOTS   105

chapter seven DEFENSIVE SHOTS   123

chapter eight BACK WALL PLAY   154

chapter nine   OTHER SHOTS   177

chapter ten   SERVICE   201

chapter eleven SERVICE RETURN   236

section III   RACQUETBALL
               APPENDICES

chapter twelve OFFICIAL RACQUETBALL
               RULES   251

chapter thirteen GLOSSARY OF TERMS   261

photo essay   PORTRAIT OF
               A TOURNAMENT   273

collected summaries A POCKET GUIDE TO
               RACQUETBALL   281

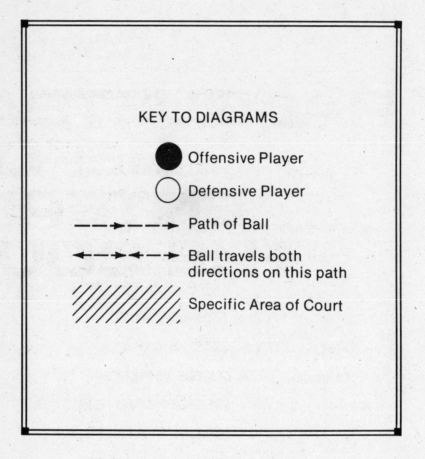

KEY TO DIAGRAMS

● Offensive Player

○ Defensive Player

— ▸ — ▸ Path of Ball

◂ — ▸ ◂ — ▸ Ball travels both directions on this path

▨ Specific Area of Court

section I
RACQUETBALL BEFORE ENTERING THE COURT

CHAPTER 1 SUMMARY

I. **History of paddleball**
   A. Championed by Earl Riskey
   B. In early days game was not standardized
   C. Evolution: Paddletennis on the handball court, to paddletennis on the court, to paddleball
   D. Ball metamorphosis: Tennis ball, to sponge rubber ball, to tennis ball core, to the Pinkie, to the Pennsey Purple ball
   E. First champion in 1930 was Harvey Bruss
   F. First national tourney in Madison in 1961
   G. Listing of national paddleball champions
   H. Paddleball is dissipating, being replaced by racquetball

II. **History of Racquetball**
   A. Joe Sobek excerpt on history from *Racquetball* magazine
   B. History of the game's official name
   C. First national tourney in 1969 in St. Louis; Bud Muehleisen premiere champion
   D. Formation of I.R.A. by Bob Kendler
   E. Listing of national racquetball champions

III. **The present and the future**
   A. Present racquetball status: "Alive, active, doing well"
   B. Professional racquetball
      1. Split of old I.R.A. into new I.R.A. and N.R.C.
      2. 1973 N.R.C. pro tour
      3. 1974 and 1975 pro tours by N.R.C. and I.R.A.
      4. $10,000 prize money per stop

   5. Top money winners: Brumfield, Serot, Strandemo, and Keeley
   C. Sport is booming among amateur masses
   D. San Diego is racquetball mecca
   E. Future prognosis is outstanding

GENERAL HISTORY

The history of racquetball takes thickest roots in its kissin' cousin sport of paddleball. And from what seed did paddleball sprout? Well, from many seeds. This antedates my court career, but the historical information is nonetheless available. Therefore, let us turn back the pages of time to those years before even paddleball existed. From those long gone days we shall move forward chronologically through the era of the wooden paddle. Then, finally, to the top of the family tree where racquetball now roosts in brilliant blossom.

Prior to delving into the ancestral past of racquetball, be forewarned that the following text may reveal close, almost emotional attachment between this author and the historical account. For, in a way, I was a small component of that history—beginning in 1967 and extending to present. For most people, the sports of paddleball and racquetball are only the toy departments of their lives. However, for me the games were and still are the entire warehouse of my existence.

HISTORY OF PADDLEBALL

Let us commence spinning this somewhat passionate yarn with a true anecdote. It was more instinctive curiosity than intelligent thinking which prompted Earl Riskey to step gingerly into the dingy Ann Arbor, Michigan, court to match wooden paddles against the footballer, now transformed into a wildly flailing paddleballer. Riskey's stalwart opponent gripped the paddle as though it were a tenpin, shifted the football helmet to more comfortably accommodate his ten-gallon cranium, adjusted the cumbersome chest guard so as to lessen the bind on his overgrown pectorals, and clattered the shin guards together to signal readiness to receive service.

Such were the beginnings of *paddleball*, first introduced to the world by the forementioned curiosity seeker who was up against that equipment-burdened ogre. The name was *Earl Riskey*. Now, this was before this era of newfangled court sophistication and etiquette. Yes, this predated these modern days of antiseptic dress whites, precision-balanced aerodynamic racquets and a game which terminates with a kiss and handshake within the service box. Back in those days of yore, the tennis shoes often doubled as street shoes. They were either solid black or all white in color. Some upstart players, heaven forbid, even sported hightop ground grabbers. And undershirts were "in" as court frock.

The paddleball paddle.

Back then, the game of paddleball, as Riskey described it, often consisted of batting a tennis ball around a squash court using a wooden paddle. Stuff that gross incongruity into your vacuum-sealed can of balls, you modern era theorizers and advocates of angles and hinders. In short, standardization then of anything was not standard.

When, a few years back, I wrote Earl Riskey seeking contributions to an anecdote book on paddleball and racquetball, I received an unexpected five-page singlespaced typewritten list of court stories. In this lengthy correspondence Earl related everything from playing "cutthroat doubles" (six players on the court at once!) to playing the game (what game?) with two balls: a black one and a pink one. In this latter pastime, the black ball was served and then the pink sphere was immediately served into the same area. The balls had to be played in precisely that order—black then pink, black then pink.

Out of these painful growing stages a "regular" game did eventually emerge. The true origin of paddleball dates back into the late 1920's. That's right, your parents' (grandparents?) generation of the stockmarket crunch, the chiropractor's dance dream in the Charleston, and when "Oh, you kid!" came rolling off hep tongues. Tennis players living during this grandiose period discovered they could improve their tennis games by utilizing indoor handball courts for practice during the drawn winter months of inclement weather. This activity evolved into what was (logically) called "paddletennis on the handball court."

As an avid athlete in the category of Jack-of-all-sports, Earl Riskey promoted this tennis-handball incorporation. Soon a viable national paddletennis association was formed. Riskey then furthered interest in the sport upon becoming associated with the Department of Athletics at the University of Michigan at Ann Arbor. He was instrumental in helping the game up the next evolutionary step: paddletennis in the handball court took on handball rules and its name was subsequently shortened to an official "paddletennis on the court."

With the arrival of the 1930's, wooden paddles were introduced into the court realm, replacing the much longer, hard-to-bring-around tennis racquets. Later on, rope thongs, to be placed around the wrist for safety, embellished the crude wood weapons. The official rules were printed up and distributed. Then things really started to germinate. Quick as one could say "Did you ever see a freak ball?" the game took on the nomenclature "Paddleball." And paddleball it is termed today.

Still, by this time the popular YMCA and campus

Glass-walled courts allow hundreds to view the professional players in action.

sport of paddleball was standardized in theory only; realistically it was more multi-standardized. Riskey used to tramp to the intramural building handball courts during the 1930's armed with handball gloves, a tennis racquet, a paddleball paddle and a squash racquet, along with a comparable arsenal of balls. He knew not with whom or in what activity or combination of activities he would be competing.

Let us take a historical side trip in order to explore the parallel development of the *ball*. As alluded to in the preceding paragraph, the criterion for what type of ball to use often depended upon what type of ball one happened to have with him at any given game. For sure, the evolution of the paddleball would have made Darwin wince.

A regulation tennis ball was employed during the very early stages of paddleball. This sphere proved to be much too heavy and, besides, nobody wanted to use a ball borrowed from another sport. The tennis ball was supplanted by a sponge rubber ball, which may have been hunky-dory for Rover to fetch, but which again was too heavy to stimulate a lively game.

So Riskey experimented. He soaked tennis balls in gasoline to remove the fuzzy cover. Smelly erosion thus yielded a core, and this lighter tennis ball core was much bouncier in the court. In addition, it was borrowed neither from another sport nor from the neighbor's Doberman Pinscher.

The sphere metamorphosis seemed completed . . . except for color. The dark core was hard to visualize in a poorly-lit court; and I can personally vouch for the cave-like visibility of the Ann Arbor "dungeons." In 1950, the famous (renowned to us veteran paddle-ballers, anyhow) Pennsylvania "Pinkie" ball came into being. Though the name sounded more like a gay wrestler from the Quaker state, the Pinkie was awarded full recognition as the regulation ball. Now paddle devotees proudly swatted around the game's latest innovation, a ball of their very own. Actually, the Pinkie was simply a finished and buffed tennis ball center which, due to ultra-high internal pressure, bounced with even greater vigor than today's racquetball. Bounced high, heck—that's an understatement. I used the Pinkie a few times in the old days and could whack the thing as hard with my clunkier wooden paddle as the 1970's photon producer Steve Serot is able to hit the present day racquetball with his tightly strung racquetball racquet.

What next, after the superball Pinkie? As the game and its number of participants expanded, an outfit called the Pennsylvania Rubber Company acknowledged a potential market by manufacturing a dark greyish sphere with a hole in it. The hole once and for all time eliminated the familiar catcalls, "Hey, buddy, where's the dog you stole that ball from?" The hole also relieved the high internal pressure which had caused the ancestral Pinkie to whiz around the court at rocket velocity. The ball maturation was complete.

Thus surfaced the end product of generations of ball evolution: tennis ball, to sponge rubber ball, to tennis ball core, to the Pinkie, to today's official Pennsey Purple ball.

That is a 50 year focus on the random evolution of the paddleball. Meanwhile, as if by spontaneous generation, the *first paddleball champion* of any kind was crowned. According to Earl Riskey, the king was a stud named Harvey Bruss. The date was 1930, and the location was the University of Michigan. But of what consequence is a champion of a sport boasting so few participants? This was not the case for long, as thousands of sports-minded folks began flocking to the courts. The paddleball king started picking up a multitude of followers.

World War II was a shot in the arm for paddleball, meteorically increasing the number of wooden armament partakers. Paddleball was selected as one of the activities for the United States Armed Forces Conditioning Program at Ann Arbor. There thousands of men in the military forces acquired the game skills, and from this springboard the sport propagated rapidly from sea to sea. After World War II ended, colleges and YMCA's together with various clubs and centers added paddleball to their activity list.

Another game booster sharpened into focus. *The first paddleball national tournament* was held in Madison, Wisconsin. It was December, 1961. To put this date into proper perspective, 1961 was approximately a year after this author transcended social naivete by claiming his Boy Scout Tenderfoot badge. And 1961 was about 6 years before I, as a tenderfoot freshman at Michigan State University, first began myopically loping about the intramural courts on pretzel legs, doggedly endeavoring to keep the damn paddleball lower than 10 feet on the front wall with my forehand, and praying simply for any kind of solid paddle contact every time the thing came to my backhand. A spastic on two size nines and a cloud of dust.

So, 6 years prior to my first court capers, a redhead, crew-cut, All-American type named Paul Nelson was crowned the first paddleball singles national champ. He raked over 11 other clods in the singles field en route to this berth. There were doubles at that tournament also—12 teams worth—and an unknown dynamic duo out of Detroit captured that premiere championship.

It was an auspicious beginning. Since 1961, a national tournament has been held annually, though you may have missed the write-ups in *Sports Illustrated*. I have jousted against most of the characters in the following list of paddleball champions, and have entered the paddle or racquet court at one time or another against all of the singles champs.

There is a question being circulated in whispered tones about the dank university locker rooms where the few surviving paddleballers slink following their workouts: Does paddleball have a viable future, or is it going the way of the market crash, Charleston and "Hey, you kid!"? There has been considerable talk of the paddle game dying (being dead), yielding to the more glamorous, more easily played sport of *racquetball*. Racquetball! The mere mention of the "sissy" sport puckers up the ire of any hard-core wood paddle man; this is the reaction I sense each time I visit my old hangout, the MSU intramural courts.

Yes, paddleball is on the wane. Except for a few isolated hang-by-the-fingertips locations in Michigan, Wisconsin, and other sections of the Mid-Northwest, the game has all but dissipated. Even on the courts within these remaining paddleball hotbeds, one more frequently hears the hollow "twang" of ball against string in lieu of the solid "plunk" of compressed ball against laminated wood.

I did not intend to conclude on such a melancholy note for the paddle people. The goodby waves and tear sheddings are unnecessary and, to the diehards, unacceptable. The paddleball prognosis may be less than favorable, but the wood gang still gathers once a year for its national tourney, and the good ole Pennsylvania Rubber Company continues to pump out the official Pennsey Purple for this dedicated bunch.

Nor was the preceding chronicle meant to belittle paddleball's replacement—racquetball. The "sissified" sport is here to stay, so let us close the book on paddleball and page on into the history of racquetball.

HISTORY OF RACQUETBALL

The 20' x 20' x 40' fun and frolic called *racquetball* has expanded like a ball of yeast gone amok since its

NATIONAL PADDLEBALL
CHAMPIONSHIP WINNERS

OPEN SINGLES

1961	**Paul Nelson** Madison, Wis.
1962	**Paul Nelson** Madison, Wis.
1963	**Bill Schultz** Madison, Wis.
1964	**Paul Nelson** Madison, Wis.
1965	**Mobey Benedict** Ann Arbor, Mich.
1966	**Bud Muehleisen** San Diego, Cal.
1967	**Paul Lawrence** Ann Arbor, Mich.
1968	**Bud Muehleisen** San Diego, Cal.
1969	**Charles Brumfield** San Diego, Cal.
1970	**Charles Brumfield** San Diego, Cal.
1971	**Steve Keeley** E. Lansing, Mich.
1972	**Dan McLaughlin** Ann Arbor, Mich.
1973	**Steve Keeley** E. Lansing, Mich.
1974	**Steve Keeley** San Diego, Cal.
1975	**Dan McLaughlin** Ann Arbor, Mich.
1976	**Steve Keeley** San Diego, Cal.
1977	**Steve Keeley** San Diego, Cal.
1978	**R.P. Valenciano** Flint, Mich.

OPEN DOUBLES

1962	**John Blanchieu** **Maurice Ruben**
1963	**Bob McNamara** **Dick McNamara**
1964	**Bob McNamara** **Dick McNamara**
1965	**Harold Kronenberg** **Galen Johnson**
1966	**Harold Kronenberg** **Galen Johnson**
1967	**Harold Kronenberg** **Galen Johnson**
1968	**Bud Muehleisen** **Charles Brumfield**
1969	**Bud Muehleisen** **Charles Brumfield**
1970	**Bob McNamara** **Bernie McNamara**
1971	**Craig Finger** **Paul Lawrence**
1972	**Dan Alder** **Evans Wright**
1973	**Dan Alder** **Evans Wright**
1974	**Steve Keeley** **Len Baldori**
1975	**Dick Jury** **R.P. Valenciano**
1976	**Steve Keeley** **Andy Homa**
1977	**Dick Jury** **R.P. Valenciano**
1978	**Dick Jury** **R.P. Valenciano**

MASTERS SINGLES

1974	**Harold Branster** Flint, Mich.
1975	**John Shaw** Adrian, Mich.
1976	**Al Hosner** Vicksburg, Mich.
1977	**Al Hosner** Vicksburg, Mich.
1978	**Al Hosner** Vicksburg, Mich.

MASTERS DOUBLES

1968	**Larry Fitchett** **Chuck Austin**
1969	**Harold Kronenberg** **Bill Pier**
1970	**Nik Caramehas** **Charles Austin**
1971	**Steve Galetti** **Rod Grambeau**
1972	**Rod Grambeau** **Steve Galetti**
1973	**Harold Kronenberg** **Audrey Olsen**
1974	**Steve Galetti** **Rod Grambeau**
1975	**Steve Galetti** **Rod Grambeau**
1976	**Harold Branster** **Lee Middleton**
1977	**Gayle Mikles** **Herbert Olsen**
1978	**Gayle Mikles** **Herbert Olsen**

There is a fine line of distinction between the avoidable and unavoidable hinder in racquetball. Strandemo vs. Keeley.

conception in the late 1940's or early 1950's (depending upon whose history version one believes), since its subsequent gestation period of perhaps 20 years, since its eventual true birth with the occasion of the premiere Nationals in 1969, and since its successive 5-year developmental process leading to the first professional tour in the fall of 1973. That is the history of racquetball in a one-sentence nutshell.

To be more specific, the *Homo sapien* has always

been fascinated by any spherical object—which has come to be known as the *ball*. And ever since the first semi-intelligent ape swung down from the branches for good and discovered he could wiggle his thumb better than his hairy cousins still incarcerated up in the trees, man has felt some innate compulsion to grasp something in order to hit something else. It is only natural that racquetball should come into being.

I suppose the foregoing could be called our game's

genesis. By way of continuing from this point of origin, an excellent review of the history of racquetball appeared in *Racquetball* magazine. This is presented below, in part. The text is in the form of a direct quote by **Joe Sobek**, generally revered as the "Father of Racquetball." Sobek claims to be the one responsible for first getting the court sport started utilizing a strung racquet. A tennis pro at Greenwich, Conn., at the time this article appeared in *Racquetball* magazine, Joe Sobek offers the following account concerning the beginnings of racquetball.

"In 1950, I left my normal occupation as a tennis and squash pro for the confinement of a desk job. My answer to the lack of physical activity was supplied at our local Greenwich YMCA. However, there were problems as to what activity I could participate in conveniently. Handball was too painful for my hands, but paddleball was interesting because of its similarity to squash.

"After a short time of enjoying paddleball, I felt that a strung racquet would be far superior to a dead wooden paddle. I designed a racquet with the same weight and measurements as the paddle, but with the additional advantage of a strung hitting surface.

"My first order was for 25 racquets, which a manufacturer agreed to make, although he would lose money on such a small specialty order. The new racquet opened up a new game. Its resilient strings created all kinds of new shots and my friends and I were very pleased.

"However, soon we were faced with another problem. The ball we were using was a nondescript ball that had lain on their shelves for a long time. When we exhausted their supply, there were none to replace them. Finally, after canvassing all the sports stores within a reasonable distance, we asked our friends who traveled to distant cities to do the same.

"At this point, I decided to find the manufacturer of this play ball. I succeeded and ordered a minimum order of 150 dozen. Unfortunately, I was stuck with the balls because they were too lively and completely unsuitable for play. I had to wait two years before the ball lost its compression and would match the old play ball we had been using.

"During this waiting period, I approached one of the country's most reputable rubber ball manufacturers and they agreed to try to meet my rigid specs. After much time, heartache and expense, the present official ball resulted.

"With a fine quality racquet and ball, paddle racquets—now Racquetball—became a sensation in Greenwich. As people left Greenwich for other cities, they introduced the game to their new Y and the next thing I knew there would be a request for equipment.

Although I was not equipped, or in the business, to handle their requests, I felt an obligation to do so because I was responsible for the game.

"Because the largest play is in the four-wall court I had to address myself, when it came to rules, to this court. Some felt the rules should be the same as handball, others thought—because of the racquet—it should follow squash, others made their own house rules.

"I decided there must be uniformity in rules if the game was to grow. Hence I organized a committee and compiled the present rules. I also formed the National Paddle Racquet Association to control the rules and promote the game.

"That's how it all started."*

Joe Sobek was not the sole steersman in this literary excursion through historical racquetballdom. There was another helmsman known affectionately as "the Mule." **Dr. Bud Muehleisen** has been scampering around racquetball courts for as far back as anyone I know. As an ex-doubles partner of this author and long-time court devotee, Mule once gave me this historical description of the game. It happens to jibe closely with Sobek's story. I asked him how racquetball got its name.

"About 25 years ago, I guess, a fellow named Joe Sobek shortened a tennis racket and brought it with him to a handball court. Sobek's idea eventually became the game as we know it today.

"When it was decided to hold a national tournament in the late 1960s, of course we couldn't have a championship in a sport without a name, so some of us began offering suggestions. We tried calling it paddleball, but that was already a separate sport. Then we tried 'racket tennis,' and then 'paddle tennis.' Finally Bob McInerny (a San Diego-based tennis pro) came up with the French spelling of 'racquetball.' So there you have it—a 25-year-old sport with a 5-year-old name."

The sport with its own name went bigtime. In 1969 the *First International* (that is, United States plus Canadian players participated) *Racquetball Tournament* was organized. Faint tremors forecasting a sports BOOM spread practically unheeded across the country with the occasion of this monumental event, the genuine birth of racquetball. The site for the first nationals was the Jewish Community Center in St. Louis. (Familiar and favorite stomping grounds for this author—the St. Louis JCC is a present day mecca for racquetball buffs, as well as a prolific pro-

---

Racquetball, Vol. 3, No. 3, May, 1974, Stillwater, Okla., "Hall of Fame", pp 3-4.

ducer of the game's hardest hitters: Steve Serot, Jerry Hilecher and Marty Hogan.)

At this tournament, the *International Racquetball Association* was established through the resources and leadership of Chicago business entrepreneur **Bob Kendler.** The call letters "IRA" and the name Kendler were one and the same in the minds of a legion of court followers. Just as he had virtually kept the "ugly sister" sport of handball alive throughout its waning years, Bob Kendler nurtured this brand new babe by bringing together many of the splinter rac-

quetball groups, formerly spread asunder across the nation.

A newborn sport was now on shaky but willing legs. The first National Racquetball Champ was crowned. He was a San Diego dentist by the name of Bud Muehleisen, a mild-mannered, soft-spoken man who toted a big stick. Bigger sticks succeeded the Mule. Since racquetball's glorious inauguration in 1969, national tourneys have been held annually throughout this United States. The years, locations and victors are presented herewithin:

NRC AND USRA NATIONAL CHAMPIONS

MEN PRO

1975	Charles Brumfield
1976	Charles Brumfield
1977	Davey Bledsoe

WOMEN PRO

1975	Peggy Steding
1976	Peggy Steding
1977	Shannon Wright

MEN AMATEUR

1975	Jay Jones
1976	Ben Koltun
1977	Jerry Zuckerman

MEN AMATEUR DOUBLES

1975	Mike Zeitman / Davey Bledsoe
1976	Dave Charlson / Roger Souders
1977	Dave Charlson / Roger Souders

MEN SENIORS

1975	Deryck Clay
1976	Joe Gibbs
1977	Jim Austin

MEN SENIORS DOUBLES

1975	Ed Creagh / John Mooney
1976	Jim Austin / Chuck Hanna
1977	Jim Austin / Chuck Hanna

MEN MASTERS

1975	Sam Koanui
1976	Bob McNamara
1977	Bud Muehleisen

MEN MASTERS DOUBLES

1975	Jim White / John Fazio
1976	Carl Loveday / George Brown
1977	Bob McNamara / Chuck Jackson

MEN GOLDEN MASTERS

1975	Jim DiVito
1976	Stan Berney
1977	Carl Loveday

MEN GOLDEN MASTERS DOUBLES

1975	Jim DiVito / Sam Rizzio
1976	Cal Murphy / Stan Berney
1977	Jim DiVito / Sam Rizzio

WOMEN AMATEUR

1975	Ruth Knudsen
1976	Sarah Green
1977	Karin Walton

WOMEN DOUBLES

1975	Peggy Steding / Jan Pasternak
1976	Jennifer Harding / Camille McCarthy
1977	Jan Pasternak / Linda Siau

IRA HONOR ROLL OF CHAMPIONS

OPEN SINGLES

1977	Jerry Zuckerman
1976	Joe Wirkus
1975	Wayne Bowes
1974	Bill Schmidtke
1973	Charles Brumfield
1972	Charles Brumfield
1971	Bill Schmidtke
1970	Craig Finger
1969	Bud Muehleisen

OPEN DOUBLES

1977	Steve Trent Stan Wright
1976	Gene Gibbs Bob Fraut
1975	Charles Brumfield Craig McCoy
1974	Steve Strandemo Dave Charlson
1973	Charles Brumfield Steve Serot
1972	George Rudys Mike Luciw
1971	Mike Zeitman Ken Porco
1970	Bob Yellin Don Wallace
1969	Mike Zeitman Allan Hyman

WOMEN'S SINGLES

1977	Karin Walton
1976	Sarah Breen
1975	Peggy Steding
1974	Peggy Steding
1973	Peggy Steding
1972	Jan Pasternak
1971	Jan Pasternak
1970	Fran Cohen

WOMEN'S DOUBLES

1977	Barb Tennessen Ev Dillon
1976	Kathy Williams Sue Carow
1975	Janell Marriott Jennifer Harding
1974	Peggy Steding Ann Gorski
1973	Peggy Steding Ann Gorski
1972	Jan Pasternak Kimberly Hill

JUNIOR SINGLES

1977	Jeff Larsen
1976	Bob Adam, Jr.
1975	Marty Hogan
1974	Jerry Zuckerman

SENIOR SINGLES

1977	Jim Austin
1976	Bud Muehleisen
1975	Bud Muehleisen
1974	Bud Muehleisen

MASTERS—45 SINGLES

1977	Bud Muehleisen
1976	Bob McNamara
1975	John Halverson
1974	Bill Sellars

MASTERS—40 SINGLES

1973	Bud Muehleisen
1972	Bud Muehleisen
1971	Giles Coors
1970	Glenn Turpin
1969	Marlowe Phillips

MASTERS—45 DOUBLES

1977	Gene Grapes Dr. Al Schafner
1976	Dr. William Sellars Richard Walker
1975	John Fazio Jim White
1974	John Fazio Jim White

MASTERS—40 DOUBLES

1973	Bud Muehleisen Carl Loveday
1972	Marlowe Phillips Joe Zelson
1971	Marlowe Phillips Milt Harris

GOLDEN MASTERS—55 SINGLES

1977	Floyd Svenson
1976	Ike Gumer
1975	Fred Vetter
1974	Ike Gumer

GOLDEN MASTERS—55 DOUBLES

1977	Carl Loveday Don Green
1976	Ike Gumer Irv Zeitman
1975	Don Green Cal Murphy
1974	James DiVito Stan Rizzio

GOLDEN MASTERS—50 DOUBLES

1973	Gene Grapes Sam Caiazza

SENIOR DOUBLES

1977	Bob McNamara Bud Muehleisen
1976	Bob McNamara Bud Muehleisen
1975	Myron Roderick Bud Muehleisen
1974	Bud Muehleisen Myron Roderick

JUNIOR DOUBLES

1977	(Not held)
1976	Hank Marcus Jeff Larsen
1975	Hank Marcus Jeff Larsen
1974	Bob Adam, Jr. Mark Domanque

Racquetball is played standing, sliding and flying. Keeley vs. Serot.

THE PRESENT AND THE FUTURE

A state of affairs report on racquetball in North America *today* might read like the daily log we kept on the cows at the large veterinary hospital back in my university days: "The animal appears alive, active and doing well." Accurate figures concerning the number of player participants, racquets purchased and balls sold are difficult to come by, conflicting in nature and increasing daily. Suffice it to say, the game once played by a helmeted ogre with chest protector and shin guards has arrived with somewhat more than a meek "hello."

Today there are even *professional* racquetball tours which are saying "hello" to major cities across the country. Engendered by the split of the original International Racquetball Association in 1973, two new groups began. These were the "new" International Racquetball Association (IRA) and the National Racquetball Club (NRC). The new IRA remained amateur, but the avant-garde NRC initiated the first pro circuit in the fall of 1973. The reins of the run-away NRC coach were, and are, fondled by a familiar figure along the racquetball road—Bob Kendler.

The NRC-sponsored tour was a courageous start, yet fell short of some goals. Six out of a predicted 12 pro tournaments were actually staged that opening season of 1973.

The following years, 1974 and 1975, both the NRC and the IRA sponsored separate pro tours, each of which faired fairly. (In addition, both organizations hyped numerous amateur events.) Both money tours boasted about eight yearly stops each, usually at the racquet hotbeds. Las Vegas, Detroit, Chicago, Minneapolis, San Diego, St. Louis, Houston and many others witnessed racquetball at its absolute finest. They dug what they saw and invited the two tours back for future seasonal stops.

The normal prize money at the professional tourney was modest by some standards, but incentive enough for many court crazies. In 1974, the total pot at each stop amounted to around $10,000, with $1,500 going to the first place winner. The top four money earners in 1974 (Charles Brumfield, Steve Serot, Steve Strandemo and Steve Keeley, though not necessarily in that order) garnered over $10,000 each, a far cry from playing for trophies and T-shirts. These days, as someone has appropriately stated, the pros proclaim, "Volley for show and shout for dough!"

But it is among the nonprofessionals that the sport is especially booming. Among that mass of three-times-a-week fun seekers, over 2 million court buffs vie for too few courts. Over half a million play for trophies and T-shirts in amateur tournaments. New courts are popping up faster than dandelions in spring-time, but the hungry horde of hackers devour court time at a startling rate.

San Diego is exemplary of the growing pains being experienced by many racquetball-rabid cities. Indeed, San Diego presently is *the* mecca of racquetball. The hottest of racquet hotbeds, where it is said a player may go and improve his game 100 percent simply through osmosis. Come learn to be a pro in six easy lessons!

It must be admitted that this sunshine capital of Southern California boasts many of the game's VIPs. The hometown heroes include such bubblegum card collector's delights as Muehleisen, Loveday and Brumfield. Other supereminents of first star magni-tude have immigrated to the chosen city: Serot, Wagner, Drake, Strandemo, Alder, Baldori and this author.

San Diego, among all the racquetball cornerstones, is a kind of brilliant light toward which all serious court moths are drawn, racquet tucked under wing. Those buffs who reside elsewhere prefer a different analogy. They say San Diego is the core of the rac-quetball apple and all the fat worms eventually find their way there. Moths and worms alike, they are overflowing the 125 courts in the area.

Although San Diego may be the only place in the country where the pros make love to their racquets and the amateurs consider their racquets less a court weapon than an exotic pet to be cradled and pam-pered, symptoms of similar zaniness are surfacing in all the 50 states and Canada. So, the *future* of the game? An assured positive prognosis. If the outlook for ol' paddleball appears to be in the dying ember stage, the future for its successor, racquetball, is that of a potential blaze.

chapter two
EQUIPMENT

CHAPTER 2 SUMMARY

I. Introduction—"court equipment ain't what it used to be."

II. Shoes and socks

III. Shorts and supporters

IV. Shirt and warm-ups

V. Sweatbands and gloves
   A. Sweaty palm is due to emotion and perspiration from arm
   B. Use one or two wristbands
   C. Use of the glove
   D. Most sticky sprays and powders are ineffective
   E. The mini-towel is universal solution to the racquet slippage dilemma
   F. Headbands effectively combat the "beady forehead syndrome" and hair-in-eyes problem

VI. Eyeguards and safety lenses
   A. Highly recommended—the singular major injury common in racquetball is related to the eye
   B. Test protective efficacy with "roll test"
   C. Test range of peripheral and vertical vision
   D. Superior solution is safety lenses. Ensure that present glasses are safety lens equipped
   E. Contact lenses okay if are soft type

VII. The racquet
   A. Descendant of the wooden paddle—history
   B. Three price ranges
   C. Question of which frame material to buy: plastic or metal?
      1. Plastic frame summary
      2. Metal frame summary
   D. Question of racquet length: standard or extra length?
      1. Standard length summary
      2. Extra length summary
   E. Question of racquet strings
      1. Material: usually silicone coated, braided monofilament nylon
      2. A quality racquet usually has quality string
      3. Tension: optimal range is 26-34 pounds. More specifically, 28-30
      4. Novices often prefer tightly strung and veterans more loosely strung tensions.
      5. String will settle in first week of play, i.e., lose 2-4 pounds tension
      6. Strings usually not guaranteed
      7. Restringing: acquire full restringing rather than patchwork. $5 to $8 for quality nylon
   F. Question of grips: rubber or leather?
      1. Rubber grip summary
      2. Leather grip summary
   G. Grip size
      1. Racquetball stroke more comparable to golf than tennis stroke

2. Tennis grips usually oversized for racquetball
3. Try out a small grip; it may be built up with tape
4. Overriding factor is comfort
H. Miscellaneous racquet information
1. Test run tentative racquet prior to purchase
2. Mail in guarantee card

3. Most court faults due to strokes rather than racquet itself

VIII. The ball
A. Two problems at present
B. Pepping up pooped spheres; two methods

IX. The court

EQUIPMENT

The court equipment these days just ain't what it used to be. Fortunately! Let us introduce today's line of racquetball accouterments by first focusing momentarily on the not-so-distant past. Prepare for a quick look-see at yesteryear's court frock and primitive weaponry. Following this, we shall progress to the more serious business of what is proper on the racquet court today.

The number one personality of the kindred sports of paddleball and racquetball has been, is and probably will be for some time—Charlie Brumfield. The first time I ever came into contact with this dual-sport champ was at the National Paddleball Tournament in Fargo, N.D., in 1970. I was lazing around the facility practicing not looking nervous on the morning of opening play and, with nothing better to do, decided to watch some of the tourney hopefuls warm up. Most of the court tadpoles I saw that morning were but very green grass ripe and waiting to be chewed into cuds by very hungry court veterans. But then I peered down into one of the 20' x 20' x 40' cement boxes and beheld a person whom I later discovered was the incumbent national singles champ, the preeminent Charles Brumfield.

How does one react to such a treat? Judge for yourself. From bottom to top, Brum appeared to be modeling dirty laundry rather than tournament togs. Chas sported those baggy, off-white gym socks which you generally keep scrunched to the rear of your underwear drawer for emergency use only. The socks sagged dejectedly about his boney ankles, forced to cling to his broad flat feet by a pair of low-cut black Converse tennis shoes—the kind they used to make kids wear in grade school gym class. The soles of these pathetic ground grabbers begged *audibly* for repair, for whenever Charlie walked the loose soles plopped. And flopped. His tennies, complete with black laces, thus functioned effectively as a pair of weird sounding podiatric cow bells and signaled the champ's presence wherever he trod.

Above the socks and shoes, via quarterhorse legs, were his gym shorts. They were emblemless things which just said "blah." Their color hinted that they might have once been white prior to sharing hot wash water with a clothing article of a dark red hue. So tightly did the pink shorts grasp Brum's massive thighs, I could not envision how he ever slithered into them. As such, his tournament shirt—the plain white undershirt variety—was untucked at the belly end and hung loosely on his frail upper torso.

Above a prominent clavicle, sparse chest hairs—suggesting ensuing entrance into manhood—converged upward into a dark beatnik style goatee. And upside from the semi-beard, perched atop an inquiring nose, were the thick, black-rimmed glasses most often identified as the sure trademark of a kindergarten child prodigy. A piece of dandruff-laden medical tape secured these coke-bottle-lensed spectacles about Charlie's shaggy cranium. Topping off this unlikely looking athlete there roosted a Coors' beer visor with brim turned toward the ceiling. It was the kind of visor the bank teller wears on "Gunsmoke" just prior to being shot and robbed.

Shaggy socks, black tennies, pinkish shorts, mini-undershirt, beard, spectacles and visor: I witnessed Charlie Brumfield roll ball after ball off the bottom board of the front wall with machine-gun rapidity, howitzer power and scoped-in precision.

The attire has changed dramatically since the paddleball days of 1970; if not so much from a utilitarian standpoint, then at least on the grounds of not creating such an eyesore.

Racquetball is an uncomplicated sport for which to outfit oneself when compared to many other activities. Provisions include the playing uniform: shoes, socks, shorts, supporter, shirt (and optional warmups, sweatband, eyeguards and gloves), as well as the racquet, ball and court. Let us consider each of these items individually in quest of, if not swinging the meanest racquet in town, at least presenting the image of a suave jock-frocked court veteran.

SHOES AND SOCKS

You can skimp on the shorts, forget the headband and play jockless if desired, but do not go second class on the *gym shoes*. Brumfield's soles plopped when he walked and it is a wonder his ankles did not crack when he changed directions. Proper fitting, quality shoes are essential to safe frolic on the court.

Without becoming lost in a jungle of brand names and styles, suffice it to say that whatever your reputable shoe dealer recommends for the basketball player's feet is generally just the ticket for the serious racquetballer. Both sports require a good deal of pivoting and pushing off, thus necessitating a fairly thick sole with plenty of overall support. Do not try to lope around the racquetball court shod in a pair of thin-soled track shoes. Nor would your footsies greatly appreciate the $4.98 superstar specials with treads that transform the hardwood floor into an ice skating rink.

A word on high top tennis shoes. Although out of vogue at present due to their Clydesdale appearance, the old high-rising "wrestling tennis shoe" is tops for superlative ankle support. No low-cut tennie will do the job as well as these. I stand on a couple of feebly-constructed ankles myself and I used to injure one or the other about every 2 months for the first 3 years of my court career. Then I changed to high tops and have had few ankle problems since. Despite their tutti-frutti come-on and slightly heavier weight, high-cut tennis shoes are a must for any player who experiences the woeful propensity toward ankle sprains and strains.

Prior to stuffing your two feet into your two newly acquired Buster Browns, do not forget to put on the *socks*. Furthermore, anyone who can afford two pairs of socks should wear them (simultaneously) to avoid blisters and to ensure a tight shoe fit. (When purchasing your tennies in the first place, allow for the space occupied by the extra pair of socks.) In addition to providing a tighter shoe fit, I find that this double thickness of socks absorbs more moisture which in turn allows me to play longer without that step-and-squish syndrome setting in. In conclusion, the Brumfield style of ankle-drooper socks are acceptable if one equates the chic with the grubby look. (Figure 2-1.)

SHORTS AND SUPPORTERS

When it comes to tutus and jockstraps, I can only

Fig. 2-1—Shoes? Heavy duty and high tops for ankle problems. Socks? Two pairs prevent blisters.

Fig. 2-2—"...bloomers impede your elephantine locomotion."

recommend the former out of intuition and the latter out of experience. Whatever, do clad yourself in jock/jill straps prior to entering the glass-walled court.

And then cover either of these up with a pair of gym *shorts*. (Girls and women may opt for the tennis style skirt.) Your shorts should act neither as leg tourniquets, as was the case with the 1970 Mr. Brumfield, nor as bloomers to impede your elephantine locomotion. I prefer the double knit nylon shorts over others because this material does not absorb perspiration and cling to the thighs. (Figure 2-2.)

SHIRTS AND WARM-UPS

As with the playing shorts, *the shirt* worn on the racquetball court should not fit as though it were a second sun tan. These can bind as a straight jacket binds, so save the tight fits for muscle beach. Just as bad is the size extra large T-shirt on the size extra-small torso. These tent like items hinder the wearer's movement as well as hindering the opposition's view of the ball as it breezes by one's over-frocked body. The assortment of shirt materials and styles is endless. I like the cotton shirt because it ''breaths'' better than most other materials. As for style, the sleeveless ''handball'' shirts are okay if your deltoids demand revealing and if your nose does not run a lot.

Warm-ups are a must only for the fashionable court aficionado who wants to make the scene flaunting groovey outside threads. Besides hiding your pampered body, the sweats also serve to keep your body warm. I favor 100 percent stretch nylon warm-ups due to their wrinkle resistence and washability. However, the nylon does not keep you warm as toast on a cold court as would, say, wool. If you plan to wear warm-ups *while* playing (e.g. bottoms for leg protection during rambunctious double games), then nylon is the key: you won't overheat, the blood washes out easily and the knees do not sag after a few uses like your old pajama bottoms.

As far as I am concerned, store-bought sweats are a luxury to be afforded by the affluent or sponsored player. Prior to my sponsored days of recent years, my tournament warm-ups consisted of a longjohn underwear top. (Figure 2-3.)

SWEATBANDS AND GLOVES

Sweatbands include *wristbands* and *headbands*. Both obviously function to keep the sweat where you do not want it to lurk in damp hinderence. Depending upon how copiously one perspires, sweatbands perform anywhere from satisfactory to might-as-well-let-it-drip. Let us first consider wristbands and gloves, then headbands. (Figure 2-4.)

Fig. 2-3—Shirts and warm-ups.

Fig. 2-4—Stomp out sweat!

Racquet slippage is the bad penny which keeps coming back. A majority of the racquet populace, from the court fledglings to the top pros, are victimized by this malady. To discuss its cure, one must first understand the mechanics of racquet slippage.

Supposedly, the palm of the hand does not perspire due to the same stimulus which turns on the sweat glands within other body areas of the skin. Rather, *emotion* activates palm perspiration. (Thus arose the common phrases "clammy palm" and "sweaty palm" when one is subjected to emotional stress.) I concur with this concept from reading in various literature and from personal experience; my hand sweats mostly during tense, important matches. "But," you ask, "if my palm isn't spittin' out the sweat, where's it all coming from?" Most of the perspiration trickles down from your arm. Due to the positioning of the hand at the termination of the arm and because the arm most often hangs toward the floor from the shoulder socket, gravity is the culprit responsible for sending the rivulets of sweat toward the palm. You can effectively dam this by using a wristband. Some players use two of them, which looks gaudy but seems logical.

An acceptable alternative to the wristband is the *glove.* A glove may be worn on the racquet hand for any one of three purposes. First, and more commonly, it is utilized by the player who sweats profusely and subsequently often loses his grip on the racquet while swinging. A glove alleviates this problem satisfactorily. Secondly, women and others may wish to prevent blisters and calluses. A third reason for the glove, especially among four-walled tenderfeet, is that it acts as a confidence builder. Do not chuckle at this. These players insist that when they don their super-grip, genuine imitation kangaroo hide grip grabber, it is tantamount to Clark Kent slipping into his cape and blue tights. The glove, in other words, is their five-fingered placebo.

Is the glove effective? Yes, it does reduce racquet slippage arising from a sweaty handle/palm; but if you become involved in a barnburner of a match, be prepared with plenty of dry glove replacements. And yes, do wear the glove if you think it adds something to your grip, game or ego. For sure, following mastery of the basics (strokes and strategy), racquetball is very much an "inner" or mental game where the power of positive thinking emerges momentously. Employ such mental crutches whenever possible.

The basic objection to doing the five-finger wiggle into a racquetball glove is that the "extra skin" reduces whatever innate feel for the racquet one had in the first place. Glove manufacturers may refute this claim. Others express this sentiment when they say,

"I seem to lose my 'touch' on the ball when I wear a glove." Experiment with and without a glove to decide if it is your bag.

Most companies dealing in a line of racquet products also offer selections of gloves specifically designed for our sport. There are many styles to choose from, but most professional players favor the type with an "elastic-grip" strip adjustable band around the wrist as opposed to the old fashioned buckle type. Be sure to buy a product which is washable.

The more common racquetball glove is full-fingered, although some players believe they can "feel" their racquet better without anything covering their fingers. For them there is the half-finger glove style, which exposes the fingers starting at the first joint. Another half-finger style is more daring in that it is cut off almost to the palm. Handball gloves serve as a poor substitute in racquetball. The handball glove is primarily concerned with hand protection and moisture absorption, so it is usually thicker, heavier and does not allow for that delicate hand-finger sensitivity on the racquet.

Obviously, the racquetball glove should be as a second skin. The leading manufacturers of these products agree that the key to an ideally functioning racquetball second skin is its weight, which must be kept as light as possible without sacrificing quality and durability. Leather is the solution. There are a few cloth gloves on the market but I am told by those in the know that they do not do the job. Leather can be cut to a sheer thinness, stays soft, lasts longer and is an excellent moisture absorber. Therefore, check to see that your intended glove purchase has a palm made of top-grade deerskin or calfskin. Again, the back of the glove may be terrycloth or a nylon elastic material.

There is an old adage admonishing that the mittened kitten catches no mice. But if you do opt to go with the funky finger look, make it leather and make it snug.

A sidenote concerning the issue of racquet slippage: There is a line of powders and sprays hyped by various manufacturers for their effectiveness in eliminating the sweaty hand situation brought about by perspiring in "all" sports. This claim is as ludicrous as the universal deodorant which keeps one's armpits sweet smelling and dry even during the rigors of running a marathon race across the Sahara Desert. These sticky grip applications are generally not suited for racqueteers, but were designed with the baseball batter or gymnast in mind, where sweat does not flow so freely.

Personally, I use the half-finger glove but, I did not always do so, and yet I had absolutely *no* prob-

Fig. 2-5—Secure top half of the mini-towel in your shorts.

Fig. 2-6—Wrap bottom half of the mini-towel around the handle and within your palm.

lem with the racquet handle squirting out of my hand amid droplets of perspiration. I call the alternative remedy which I chanced upon a couple years ago the *mini-towel*. Rip or cut up a discarded bath towel into approximately 4-inch by 10-inch strips. Tuck one end of a resulting towelette into your gym shorts (on the right side by the hip bone if you are right-handed, left side if a southpaw). A hint for males only: guys, if you tuck the material solely under your gym shorts, it is bound to frequently fall out at inopportune times. Therefore, secure an inch or so of the towelette under the waistband of your suporter and it will remain intact until shower time. (Figure 2-5.)

Now, with mini-towel in place, when your hand becomes sweaty as a pitcher of iced tea on a hot summer day, simply lay the racquet handle onto the flappy part of the towel, wrap the loose end of the material over the damp rubber or leather grip and then twist the material around the handle a few times with your own hand. Note figure 2-6. Not only does

the towel absorb the sweat hanging out on your palm, it also completely dries the surface of the racquet handle after just a couple of firm turns. Many court dwellers have tried this anti-perspiration ruse, found it preferable to sweatbands and gloves, and now recommend it as vociferously as I.

Whether one employs a wristband, glove or mini-towel, the sweaty palm syndrome must be conquered for the sake of the stroke. But what of the "beady forehead syndrome," the scourge of the hairless everywhere. This ailment arises when the cranial sweat glands crank into overdrive, perspiration beads unite to form progressively larger droplets in the wrinkles of the forehead, the droplets are jolted into overflow by a body tremor such as a dive for a fall-off, and the sweat cascades down into the eyes.

Older gents sporting the haircut-with-the-hole-in-the-middle look are especially susceptible to this wet curse. I have witnessed more than one lollipop head emerge from a humid court rubbing his eyes in salty

Who is best dressed: Strandemo with turban headband and turtle T-shirt, or Keeley with mini-towel, batman goggles and spaghetti hair?

pain and dripping sweat from ear to ear as though he had just stuck his head into a spittoon. Who has not felt the sting in the eye and lost a point because of it?

Bushy eyebrows, of the shaggy dog type, alleviate this problem somewhat. In fact, if God had had racquetball on His mind upon creating Adam, He would have replaced the presentday pair of smaller eyebrows with a singular forehead brow which extends continuously from one temple to the other. Alas, He saw this was not good and the *headband* was invented. It does effectively blockade the stream of sweat flowing from furrows to eyes during a heated match, although like the wristband the headband eventually reaches a saturation point and must be replaced by a dry one.

The headband may also serve a second purpose. At one time I wore a headband concocted out of a dis-

carded jock strap. The reason for this was to corral a wild head of hair which hampered my vision. Whichever crops up as your motivation, the color coordinated headband adds a flare to anyone's court outfit, as well as being perched up there for utilitarian purposes.

Headbands may be store-bought, often in combination with a set of wristbands. Or they may be fabricated out of rope, shoelaces, handkerchiefs, ripped towels or a properly snug supporter with the hangy-down portion removed.

EYEGUARDS AND SAFETY LENSES

At times, the ancient sports adage "keep your eye on the ball" is taken too literally in racquetball. The worst injury I know of, which arises with fair frequency within the 20' x 20' x 40' cement arena, involves the eyes. These lesions range from the inconsequential "guided muscle" type of black eye to the serious detached retina. I once sustained a racquetball eye injury which fell somewhere between these two extremes. In this instance, my tournament competitor rushed a lob serve that was falling to a potential landing area just behind the service short line. I glanced back to see what was happening as the lobbed ball descended and WHOMP! my stalwart rival volleyed the service out of the air. He pulled the sphere cross-court and, from perhaps 3 feet away, drilled it into my left baby blue.

Past personal experiences, especially the traumatic type, are the strongest motivations for action; I heartily encourage the use of *eyeguards*. Usually constructed of aluminum tubing or plastic, these protectors fit over and shield the eyes from those screaming rolloffs off the cornea. Most of the eyeguards in vogue today make the wearer appear as though he were auditioning for a Batman role, but fortunately most of them work. To *test* any particular pair for protective efficacy, don the masklike contraptions and roll the ball along under and around the protective frame (figure 2-7). Even when the sphere is pushed in firmly, there should be no ball-to-eye contact.

The only justifiable criticism aimed against eyeguards is that they interfere with one's side vision. If you have witnessed a player sporting a pair of the forementioned goggles, you may have seen him swivel his head about on his shoulders as the ball whizzed back and forth in the same manner that a ventriloquist's dummy shakes his head in an energetic negative reply. Such unnatural head movement is required to retain constant visual contact with the ball during a game. Therefore, if you are in the market for a pair of eyeguards, select a style which offers the *widest range of vision* (as well as providing ample eyeball safekeeping). The maximum extension of this field of sight can be ascertained by putting the eye shields on and by using the index fingers as focal points to roughly measure how far to either side the guard frames allow your eyesight to extend. This is demonstrated in figure 2-8. Test the vertical vision allowance similarly.

One may easily blink off all of this rigmarole of testing the shielding efficacy and of determining the range of vision simply by purchasing *safety lenses* from your optometrist. Safety lenses are regular glasses, except the shatterproof lenses function for protection rather than visual assistance. Note: You four-eyed court stompers are in luck. All your life you've hated your gaudy goggles; well, now the

Fig. 2-7—Eye guard protection test.

Fig. 2-8—Testing the peripheral...

...and vertical visual allowance.

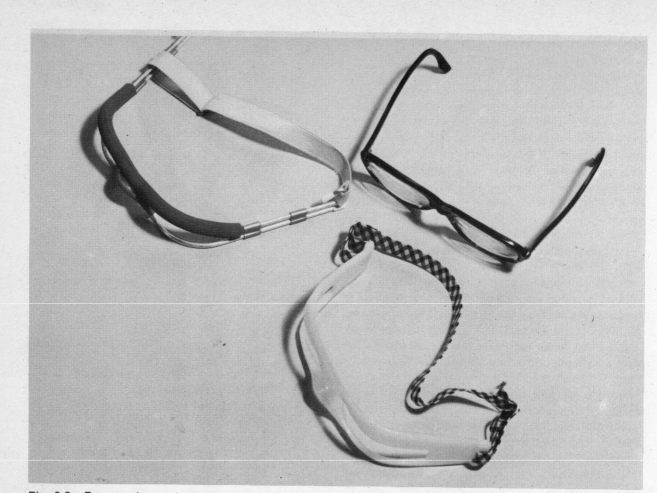

Fig. 2-9—Eye guards may look like anything from normal glasses to Halloween masks.

loathed specs are "in." Assuming your present corrective lenses are shatterproof (most of them are, but, to be sure, check with the eye doctor who prescribed them), no supplemental eye precaution is required. Incidentally, contact lenses do not afford much protection on the court but do not present additional danger if they are the *soft* type. (Note eye protection models in figure 2-9.)

If the reader scoffs at the foregoing and one day does indeed get hit in the eye with a ball or racquet, rather than saying, "I told you so," I encourage you to rush to an ophthalmologist or hospital for immediate examination. You would be surprised at all that junk that can jar loose and jingle around within your eyeball when it is shaken up a little—it is remarkably similar to vigorously shaking up a dried gourd. Remember, the chance of permanent damage to the eye increases with the passage of time following the incident.

Do as I say and not as I did, and let us complete the introductory anecdote to this section. As we left the scene of the accident, my left eyeball was almost

hanging from the socket by a few strands of whatever holds the eyeball in orbit. I had just been struck from point blank range by a fast-flying orb and I can only rationalize that this trauma affected my decision to try to finish out the tournament match rather than hustling down to the hospital. Having won the first game, I now dropped the second game subsequent to the injury—my depth perception was that of a Cyclops and every time (out of habit) I served the ball into the left rear corner, I was obliged to do a 180 degree neck twist in order to keep sight of the sphere with my "good" right eye. Having split the first two games, I wised up in the third and started serving to my opponent's forehand—the right rear corner. Thus I had only to rotate my head slightly to see what was shakin' back there with the service return. In addition, I terminated every rally as soon as possible with an attempted killshot.

It was a routine win. The match was mine but the tournament was not. I hastened to the hospital following the 21st point of game three and kind of melted into myself as the ophthalmologists voiced their disapproval at my postponement of treatment. I had to forfeit out of the racquetball tournament and I suppose I deserved the pain which plagued that left eye for the next few days. I was lucky, in the same way that the little kid who jumps from a tree and only breaks an arm and a leg is lucky. The vision in the afflicted eye was nill for 2 days and then gradually returned over the next 2 weeks. Then I was back on the court serving my lob serves a little bit deeper and looking like an escapee from a costume ball, but nonetheless contentedly protected by a pair of funky eyeguards.

THE RACQUET

The court nut of 1970 and earlier was by no means as well equipped in the department of armaments as is today's four-walled habitué. Reflect for a moment on that outlandishly attired character seemingly from the Looney Tunes who was warming up to defend his national singles title in Fargo, N.D. If Charlie Brumfield's raiment was not suggestive of the ten best-dressed honor roll, at least his wooden hitting implement was congruent with his eccentric threads.

Brum's paddle looked like some abandoned weapon out of the Neanderthal era. It was an unwieldly thing, more suited to bringing down an unfriendly troglodyte than a simple rubber sphere. There was the thick wooden handle, made fatter by layers of white tape. Indeed, this was one of Charlie's revered Loveday autograph paddles, and the tape was there for deeper reason than building up the grip. Carl Loveday, who had been instrumental in bringing Chas through his formative paddleball years, autographed the handles of certain paddles owned by Brumfield just prior to tourney time. Charlie, of course, carefully preserved the mint sacred name with layers of sheltering tape. Sweat and palm grime on Loveday's hermetically sealed signature would have been dreadfully sacrilegious! No wonder I saw this champ clutch his Loveday model tenderly to his concave chest the way a baby fondles a rattle.

On the lollipop end of Brumfield's paddle, above the bulky grip with the underlying secret inscription, the face of the paddle hung dejectedly. Magic marker cross-hatches had been drawn in on both sides of the face so the paddle appeared to be one step up from an inch-thick checkerboard glued to the end of a corpulent popsicle stick. Both of these magic markered hitting surfaces were undergoing speedy erosion, or necrosis, or both. That is, the laminated plywood was splitting off everywhere, leaving large craters which Chas had filled in and patched up with liberal amounts of medical tape. As paddles go, this one was

a farce. But I reiterate: Brum rolled off a steady stream of bottom boarders with the thing.

It is agreed that the wooden paddle is a far cry from *any* type of strung racquet, yet the racquets of the late 1960s were still ridiculously prehistoric. With their small hitting surfaces, short handles and thick wooden rims, the early racquets hardly resembled their future evolutionary end product. That end product is on the market now. Today, even the budget minded twice-a-week hacker may purchase a quality racquet for an agreeable sum. Sporting goods stores display a wide spectrum of models with prices ranging from about $5 to $50.

Wooden rimmed racquets fall into the lower price grouping, from approximately $5 to $12. I do not recommend these for *any* level of play. There are numerous reasons. The thick frames are cumbersome, giving rise to frequent "wood shots." These wooden clunkers are usually shorter in length than racquets composed of non-wood material, which greatly reduces stroke power through loss of leverage. Finally, the strung hitting surfaces on these products are very inconsistent when compared to a similarly priced plastic or alloy racquet. Therefore eschew the wooden framed abortion of the 1960s, which swings like a ten-pin and frequently hits like a butterfly net.

To my way of thinking, the finest quality racquets fall into the $18 to $28 price range. Select from myriad models constructed of *fiberglass* [*plastic*] *or metal* [*alloy*]. The leading racquet manufacturer, Leach Industries of San Diego, at one time offered a line of less than a half-dozen racquets. Increased demand spawned a crayon-box selection and now that same company puts out virtually a model for everyone, and then some. A few people I know actually collect racquets like stamps, and are even able to point out the vintage years for certain models.

Besides the $5 to $12 wooden and $18 to $28 plastic/metal court weapons, there are a few racquets which cost $30 to $50. Generally speaking, these *expensive models* support the adage "a sucker is born every minute." This Rolls Royce line of goods caters to the potential purchaser's ego, in that the buyer mentally grooms himself with false thoughts of "the more money I spend, the better I'll play." The gold stars, extra layer of sheen and hand-crafted carrying case are usually not worth the extra $25.

When you enter a store and are about to plop down 20 bucks or so for a new racquet, you are likely to be confronted with a vast array of products that would perplex a Chinese puzzle maker. Approach the situation logically. Some *questions* which immediately pop into mind are:

1) Which material: plastic or metal?
2) Which length racquet: the regular (more popular) length, or the extra long style for added power?
3) What about strings: material and tension?
4) What about grips: material and size?

Let us deal with each of these pertinent inquiries individually, maintaining the faith that there is at least one racquet under $30 which will fulfill the reader's strictest requirements.

First, a brief explanation of terms. In the following paragraphs I use the word ''fiberglass'' synonymously with ''plastic.'' Actually, the plastic racquet consists of two specific materials: nylon and glass (fiberglass). The nylon base gives the racquet softness and flexibility. To this base material the fiberglass is added to increase weight and strength. The amount of fiberglass added is usually between 10 percent to 50 percent; the higher the glass content the more brittle the product.

Too, I interchange the words ''metal,'' ''alloy,'' and ''aluminum,'' in the upcoming text. To be more specific, most metal racquets at present are constructed of aluminum. The important thing to remember is that various grades of this metal alloy may be used in manufacturing racquets.

This leads us into the pros and cons of the *plastic vs. metal* racquet controversy. If the reader wishes to skirt the technical details, this choice boils down to a simpler question: Which of the two materials feels more *comfortable* to the individual racquet wielder? To whom details are a concern, the concept of frame material is more intricate.

As a general guideline, the *plastic* rimmed weapons provide superior flexibility. Fiberglass proponents are quick to point out the pole vaulting analogy. Fiberglass vaulting poles, they claim, bend or flex tremendously and subsequently whip back to augment propulsion of body over bar. Similarly, the highly flexible plastic racquet ''gives'' upon contact with the ball and ultimately snaps back more to enhance stroke power. A converse way of explaining this phenomenon is to tell you that when ball contact occurs, a metal frame vibrates much more than a plastic one. This excess vibration absorbs energy (into the racquet and hand) rather than imparting energy back to the sphere. Power is lost. Accordingly, plastic is the key to power.

Plastic exponents go farther in saying that since the ball is on the strings of a fiberglass racquet longer (due to the flex), more touch or ''feel'' is procured. Thus, plastic is also the key to control.

On *paper,* all of the above sounds logical to me, but I'll leave it to the sit-down technicians to belabor the issue.

Metal racquets, on the other hand, wear much better than their somewhat destructable counterparts. Breakage with aluminum models is minimal, whereas it is not unusual to stroll through a court club and spot a dejected novice holding a fiberglass racquet sporting the snapped-frame look. His court implement is as useful as a 22 rifle with a square-knot tied in the barrel. It is sad but true that the court neophyte, who usually possesses an anesthetic feel for the many angles and walls intrinsic to our sport, is bound to clobber the plaster wall rather than the rubber orb a few times, during his early performances. Therefore, the metal racquet is highly recommended to such upstarts.

To sum up the frame material quandry, use whatever knocks 'em dead. Avoid the wooden rims. Beginners prefer metal but once a player becomes good enough and breakage becomes less of a problem he often switches to fiberglass. Among the supereminent racqueteers on the pro circuit today, the general attraction is to plastic. (Of the top 16 players at present, I estimate that 75 percent of them swing plastic.)

Whether one chooses from the metal or fiberglass lines, the next question to commonly crop up is ''What *length* racquet should I use?'' For the sake of those who write those boring rules in the rear end of every instructional book, let us take a quick peek at the official regulations. They dictate that the racquet head must not be greater than 9 inches wide nor greater than 11 inches long. Plus, the maximum handle length is 7 inches. Furthermore, the sum of the length plus the width of the racquet is not supposed to exceed 27 inches, which is interesting if not redundant.

Continuing with the rule interpretations, every racquet is required to have a safety thong, which is that hangy-down band of rope, leather or nylon worming its way out the handle end of every legitimate racquet. This thong is not there to finger play baby-in-the-cradle with during time-outs; utilize it during play by fully encircling the wrist of your racquet hand. (Note: the thongs on many factory-fresh racquets are sometimes insecurely tied. You will discover this when the knot slips after the first few swings and the next thing you see is your opponent wearing a forced grin the width of your racquet head —9 inches, by regulation. Avoid this chagrining situation by tying a square knot yourself in the thong of a newly purchased racquet.)

Leaving the rules, it is common knowledge that there are *two lengths* of racquets being marketed

Fig. 2-10—The extra-length racquet (top) provides more leverage but less control.

now: the standard and extra length models. It is my feeling that there is no sensible place for the extra length implement on the court today. (See figure 2-10.) True, the added inch of handle/throat provides the advantage of boosting the swing power (for some players); nonetheless, because of the extreme liveliness of the balls employed for play, this bolstering zip is often a detriment rather than an aid. As an old tennis coach once screamed into my good ear from a racquet length away, "It's not how hard you hit it, PEA-BRAIN! It's WHERE you hit it!"

If this is not justification enough, read on. The overriding disadvantage of the longer racquet is that it is harder to bring around on the stroke downswing. Prove this to yourself just by swinging the two different length racquets without hitting the ball. Too, the excess inch seems to hamper the wrist breaking process during ball contact. (It will be explained in later chapters why the breaking of the wrist is imperative for both the forehand and backhand strokes.)

The most convincing summarizing statement is that 90 percent of the game's professionals scoff at the extra leverage provided by the added length and instead opt for the regular span racquets.

The issue of *strings* is next on the list of perplexities which often confront the potential racquet buyer. Racquetball racquets, unlike tennis rackets, are almost always strung with nylon. Catgut strings are shunned in the four-walled sport because the gut is more susceptible to corrosion from perspiration. In a game such as racquetball, where sweat drips to saturate clothing and then flies in asunder directions with every vigorous movement, the strings must be water resistant. Nylon serves this purpose perfectly. Although catgut is stronger than nylon, the super strength material is not necessary since racquetball racquets are strung at a much lower tension than in tennis. In addition, gut is more expensive than nylon.

Nylon may be monofilament or multifilament. In racquetball the single filament nylon is utilized almost universally. Multifilament (many strands of nylon filaments wound to produce a stronger string) is impractical due to its increased diameter and weight; its use is generally confined to the more tightly strung tennis racket.

Look at the strings in your own or prospective racquet. We have already established that they are probably monofilament nylon. But there are various grades of this string. Basically, a telltale sign of a cheaper nylon is one which has been painted. The clearer the nylon, the better. Clearness is indicative of a nonblemished material, and this is desirable. Do not confuse the substandard painted nylon with braided material. The red, blue or other hue string intertwined with the clear nylon is strictly for decorative purposes and does not signify a blemished material.

Do not worry a heck of a lot about the strings in your new racquet. Racquet quality usually dictates string quality. If the product is one from the medium

Metal racquets play
well and are not prone
to breakage.

Fiberglass racquets
may break but the
"pros" prefer them.

or better price range and if the manufacturer is reputable, the racquet's string will be satisfactory—probably silicone-coated monofilament nylon with a twist of decorative braid.

From the utilitarian standpoint, I would be more concerned about your racquet's string *tension*. The large racquet manufacturers put 'em out strung at 30-32 pounds. It makes no difference whether the frame is metal or fiberglass when discussing tension. For either material, I recommend a maximum of 34 pounds and a minimum of 26 pounds. A tension higher than 34 will mean board-like stiffness each time you hit the ball, while less than 26 will feel as though you are swinging a butterfly net. To narrow this range down, if you don't know a racquet from a racket then take my word that the ideal string tension is 28-30 pounds. (As shall be expanded upon, this tension will loosen slightly with play.)

That group of novices known as the "blind flailers" often prefer a very tightly strung court weapon. These uninformed players are convinced they can bash the ball harder with their cutting boards simply because the sphere tings off the strings after only the shortest pause for contact. The experienced veterans who string their racquets at the lower end of the tension scale (26-28) know better. They hit the ball just as hard with an equal output of effort. In addition, the decreased tension means there is more flexible hitting face. This allows the racquetball to stay on the strings longer, thereby enhancing touch and control. I know this theory is valid from personal experience and from viewing stop-action photographs of sphere-string rendezvous.

Whatever string poundage you prefer, remember that after six or eight hard hitting games the strings will have gradually "settled in." That is, they will have loosened up by 2 to 4 pounds. Thus, your 27 pounds of tension will have been reduced to about 24 pounds after a week of playing every other day. View this loss of tension optimistically in that each pound loss, up to a certain point, means additional control gained.

What if your strings develop a break before the settling in process has even had a chance to transpire? In this rare instance, return the racquet and explain the situation. A new set of quality strings should last 60-90 days. If you play every single day or if you are one of those random rippers whose sole purpose in entering the cement arena is to pulverize every shot, anticipate a broken string every month. No racquet manufacturer guarantees their strings for any amount of time. But, as alluded to in the infrequent occurrence above, if your strings break during the racquet's initial games, most companies will oblige the owner with a replacement or new strings.

That brings us to *restringing*. There is always a place to obtain this service, whether it be from the manufacturer, a sporting goods outlet, or the little old lady down the street who is a badminton freak with a fetish for needle and thread. The little old lady probably does just patch jobs (single string replacement) and has never heard of racquetball, so avoid her. Tell your restringer that you want an entire string job, as opposed to patchwork. Otherwise, one-half of your repaired racquet may hit like a brick and the other half like a fish net. You have been educated on the concept of various nylon grades, so be sure to agree upon the quality of string to be employed prior to leaving your coveted rubber smasher. A reasonable price for a complete racquet restringing is $5 to $8.

We have discussed the racquet in some detail regarding frame material, length and strings. That leaves the *grip*. Do you want to hang onto a rubber or leather covered handle? These are the normal options available on stock racquets from the factory. Of course, all serious racquetballers undergo the "perverted handle phase," an unavoidable stage in one's court career manifested by compulsive tendencies to experiment with one's handle. My experience with this innovative era was marked by fat handles and thin handles, tape grips, reverse tape (sticky side out) grips, sandpaper grips and no grips at all.

Since my recovery from the "phase" I have stuck with the rubber grip. The major criticism leveled at this material is that it gets wet (and therefore slippery) after 5 minutes of energetic snortin' and stompin' round the court . . . unless a glove is worn. As indicated earlier, I overcome this slippage problem via the mini-towel and never experience any difficulty. Another criticism aimed at rubber grips, and it is

Fig. 2-11—Rubber or leather handle regrip kits make it easy to replace worn or torn grips.

just as valid a one, is that the material wears down faster than leather—for this, there is the regrip kit (see figure 2-11).

Actually, there is rubber and cork-filled rubber being used on racquet handles. The cork-filled material is nice to feel in that the cork provides a tacky touch, but it tears more easily; on the other hand, there is the regular rubber grip, which wears somewhat better without the cork. This comes in various quality grades but the subject is even more drab than a discussion of the perverted handle phase.

Leather grips are therefore superior to rubber in two ways: most players are able to grab longer without slippage, and leather wears longer. Leather's main disadvantage is that the grips are slightly more expensive.

A lengthy discourse on the grades of leather is not that titilating either. Suffice it to say that there are your true leathers and your synthetic (vinyl) leathers. The latter ones are considered inferior because the imitation material does not retain its tackiness over an extended period of time. Of the true leathers, the smoother is usually the higher quality. Excess decorative designs, fancy ribbing or numerous holes often serve to disguise blemishes.

The question of *grip size* is a more difficult and significant one to handle than that of grip material. The best way to preview this quandry is to refute one of the *biggest misconceptions* prevailing among racquetball enthusiasts today. The kinesis of the racquetball stroke is much more suggestive of the golf stroke than the tennis stroke. I will listen objectively to any arguments which refute this fact and then tell the hamburger to stick it in his gym bag. As will be expounded in later chapters, our sport is a *wristy* game, similar to the flexible golf swing and alien to the rigid tennis motion. My best, hardest hitting pupils have been former golfers. Charles Brumfield, who needs no introduction among racquetball aficionados, does not even play golf regularly but is able to drive the little white sphere over 300 yards. Steve Strandemo is another top-notch professional player who employed golf as a springboard into the court world. Steve started out with all the mechanical talent and aptitude for racquetball as a jock-frocked crustacean larva. He moved to San Diego and played golf almost daily, utilizing just a five-iron to develop his racquetball wrist and stroke form. Now he is a part-time champ, well metamorphosed past the larval stage.

All this exemplary ballyhoo is just to exaggerate the importance of the wrist breaking on the stroke . . . which is directly affected by the grip size. Your hand will be twisting, your wrist extending and flexing with every stroke—you need a smaller grip size than you might think. Do not enter the sporting goods store and ask for a 4⅝ grip size simply because that's what your tennis game demands. I am told that tennis grips start at 4⅜ and increase in size. In racquetball, 90 percent of the male and female court dwellers have hand sizes best suited for about 4⅛ grip. Young players or small-handed females may prefer a slightly smaller size.

Depending on the racquet model and its manufacturer, grip sizes may be cataloged as small, medium and large, or by the familiar tennis system of measuring down to the ⅛-inch. The leading racquet manufacturer has simplified its production as well as the consumers options by putting out one standard grip size—the one which fits 90 percent of the racquetball population. (There is also a line of "junior" racquets designed for players with lesser strength as well as

smaller fists.) This company's policy is that anyone possessing an overly large hand can easily build his racquet grip diameter by removing the grip, adding a few layers of tape to increase the thickness and then reapplying the grip.

Allow me to temper the preceding hard-line expose by saying that just as orangutans can swing from sundry sized branches, so can the human hand adapt to a range of grip sizes. Charlie Brumfield at one time hustled a bet using a plastic bleach bottle and I, on a lark, once ripped off a decent game of paddleball employing a hard-soled oxford for a paddle. We were not that concerned with grip sizes, but it must be taken into account that we both knew how to properly apply the wrist into the stroke, whatever the hitting implement. You can adapt, within tolerances, but it is logical to get hold of the ideal grip in the first place so adaptation is not necessary.

Use a grip size that feels comfortable, and then opt for a size smaller; it is relatively easy to build up a handle but difficult to shrink it down. Better yet, have a knowledgeable person examine your hand as it grasps the grip in question. Or, find a veteran with the same hand size and try out his racquet. Or, test run racquets having different handle diameters.

The reader should now feel secure, if not omniscient, in purchasing a spanking new racquetball racquet. There are a couple of miscellaneous items to keep in mind prior to trading a fistfull of dollars for a fistfull of racquet. First, I strongly suggest that you borrow and try out on the court (with a few shots or, preferably, with a game) the particular racquet model which you are contemplating obtaining. In doing this, you can familiarize yourself with which frame, weight, grip, tension and so on feels best. This realistic test run of the borrowed racquet(s) will spare you the familiar embarrassing situation of vicariously swinging away in the center of the store in trying to imagine yourself wielding the same racquet on a real-life court.

Second, once you finally walk out with new racquet in hand, do not forget to mail in the guarantee card enclosed with most manufacturer's models. Fiberglass racquets are frequently guaranteed against breakage with normal use for three months. Metal models are similarly protected for up to a year.

The third and final bit of counsel mildly distorts the nice tidy racquet image presented hitherto. Sad to say, the perfect racquet makes not the perfect player. In 90 percent of all cases of substandard play, the court foibles are the result of improper technique rather than a rotten racquet. (But, the rest of this book should remedy that.) Should your perfect new racquet seem spastic in your hand at first, give it at

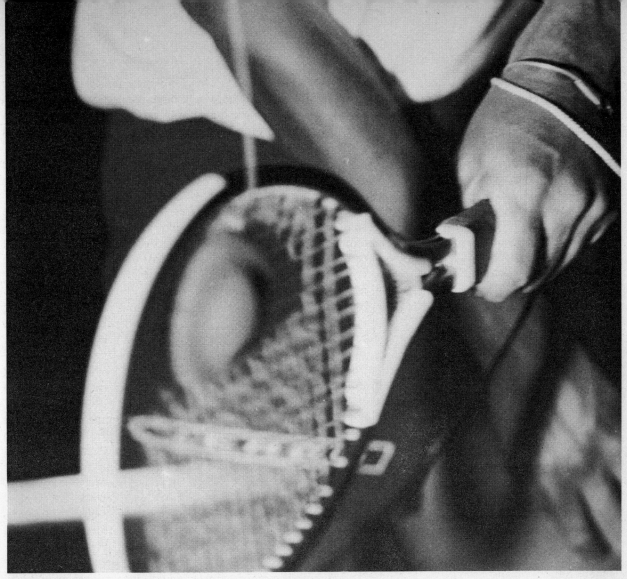

Stop-action photo at the precise moment of racquet and ball rendezvous.
Note compression of ball and "give" of racquet strings.

least a couple weeks of play to matriculate as a permanent fixture on the end of your gun hand.

In the old days of equipment innocence, one often acquired his court armament by hand-me-down perpetuation. However, the modern era player with his form-fit supporter and hand-knit headband, can afford to be more finicky in choosing a racquet. With the luxury of wide selection today, it is only common sense to consider, scrutinize and then pick the one with which you plan to smite thousands of killshots in the months to come.

THE BALL

In dealing with the history of paddleball and racquetball, Chapter One traced the rough evolutionary road over which the game's ball has bounced. I hope that the end of that long road has not been reached yet be-

cause the racquetballs being spewed out to the hungry playing public are grossly substandard in relation to racquetball's other equipment. There are two problems with the present day stockpile of spheres: breakage and inconsistency.

In a recent issue of *National Racquetball* magazine I alluded to the issue of ball breakage in a somewhat sarcastic article entitled "The Genesis of Racquetball." In this I wrote, "And God spoke again, 'Behold!' And from the nothingness there appeared a hollow rubber sphere which bounced once...bounced twice . . . and spliteth into two. And God said, 'This is not good.' The sun rose and the sun fell twice more and it was on the fifth day that the Lord concocted a divinely round ball which He personally sanctified for one week or ten games, whichever cometh first."

God knew what he was talking about when He muttered, "This is not good." He had probably ex-

The most popular racquetball is manufactured by Seamco.

So much for the two Achilles tendons, breakage and inconsistency. Now let us take another invigorating peep into the rule book. According to regulations, the standard racquetball is 2.5 inches in diameter, weighs a hefty 1.4 ounces and bounces 67-72 inches high when dropped from a height of 100 inches in a constant environmental temperature of 76 degrees F. Only Einstein could appreciate the beauty of this jive; the rest of us know if we have a good ball by just smacking it a couple of times.

If the ball under scrutiny is slightly dead, it is possible to liven it up. (Note: rather than attempt to revive the *really* dead cow pucky bouncers, bequeth the languorous things to the neighbor's dog.) To increase the ball's liveliness, its internal pressure must be increased. This can be accomplished by one of *two* methods: one way is to ask a doctor friend to take time out from ruptured spleens and terminal hangnails to pump 3-10 cc of air into the underinflated pneumatic orb using a small (26 gauge or smaller) needle and syringe. This method is very effective for pepping up a pooped sphere. I know of more than one instance where a tournament director spent hours pumping up hundreds of slow racquetballs prior to the tourney's opening day. (Note: it must be emphasized that the equipment required for this shot in the sphere is illegal except in the hands of qualified personage such as an M.D., D.V.M., or D.D.S.)

The alternate means of hyping the internal pressure of the racquetball is through the application of *heat*. Place the slow-moving ball under hot water or into a sauna for a few minutes. Presto! The air within the rubber globe will expand and what emerges is a very revitalized racquetball.

I hasten to point out that the treatment in the two above procedures is sometimes worse than the cure, in that the amplified internal pressure may increase the likelihood of the ball breaking. But a short-lived bouncer is better than a long-lived dud.

THE COURT

Racquetball is played upon a standard handball court, which is increasingly becoming better known as the standard racquetball court. It measures 20' x 20' x 40'. The design is simple enough to justify the use of the more descriptive term, "oversized cement chicken coop."

Some racquetball courts have less than the popular four walls, especially the outdoor varieties of the game. One-wall outdoor racquetball is played in the northeastern section of the country, though the game is on the wane. Three-wall outdoor racquetball finds its greatest following in Southern California where many of the grade and high school playgrounds are

perienced the lamentation Himself of the stupid sphere breaking after just a couple of good smites. Unlike God, the ball manufacturers do not guarantee their product for a certain number of days or games. To be fair, it must be admitted that these companies say they are striving to produce a more durable product.

By the way, send new but broken balls with some or all of the *logo* writing still intact back to the manufacturer or place of procurement and ask for a free replacement.

The other rub that plagues us racquetball consumers is equally as frustrating as the breakage problem. The balls today are consistently inconsistent. Two balls taken from one can do not necessarily indicate close geneology. Often one will bounce like a superball and the other will kind of plop like a cow pucky. When purchasing racquetballs at a court club, YMCA or similar place, ask if it is first possible to hit a couple of ceiling balls by way of a test run for consistency and bounce. In this manner you will not waste money buying duds. Furthermore, if you plan to participate in tournaments or leagues, attempt to discover prior to said event which brand of ball is to be used. Practice with it accordingly.

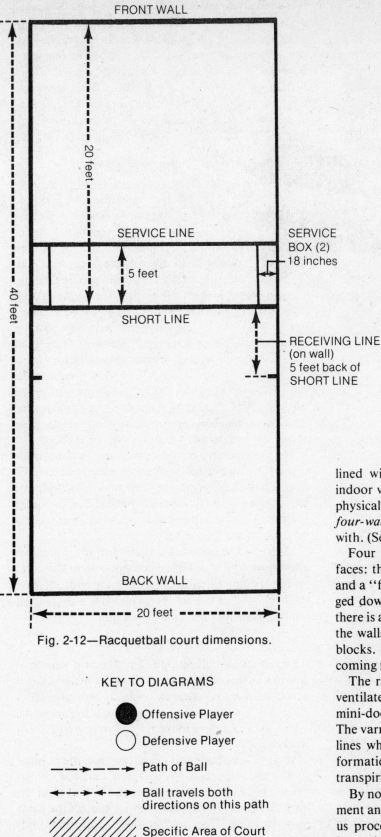

FRONT WALL

20 feet

SERVICE LINE

SERVICE BOX (2)

18 inches

5 feet

SHORT LINE

RECEIVING LINE (on wall) 5 feet back of SHORT LINE

40 feet

BACK WALL

20 feet

Fig. 2-12—Racquetball court dimensions.

KEY TO DIAGRAMS

● Offensive Player

○ Defensive Player

- - -► Path of Ball

◄- - -►◄- - -► Ball travels both directions on this path

///// Specific Area of Court

lined with the playing areas. It is the four-walled indoor variety of racquetball which is the rage of the physical fitness minded populace today. And it is this *four-walled* sport that this book specifically deals with. (See figure 2-12.)

Four walls? Actually, there are *five* playing surfaces: the front and back walls, the two side walls, and a "fifth wall"—the ceiling. Without getting bogged down with architectural details, suffice it to say there is a cement or, more often, wooden floor, while the walls and ceiling are usually plaster over cement blocks. Prefabricated panels and glass are also becoming more popular as court wall materials.

The racquetball court is lighted from the ceiling, ventilated (hopefully), and the entrance/exit is via a mini-door most often located in the rear court wall. The varnished floor is sectioned off by a few painted lines which outline specific playing areas. More information on the court in relation to the activity transpiring on it is covered in the next chapter.

By now the reader must agree that the dress, equipment and court really "ain't what it used to be." Let us proceed to incorporate this chapter's guidelines into what this book is all about: racquetball—the game!

THE GAME

CHAPTER 3 SUMMARY

I. The teaser
   A. Brief overview of racquetball
   B. An individual sport
   C. One-time test run is a hooker
   D. Racquetball's mass appeal all-encompassing
   E. Common denominator—healthy fun

II. The game
   A. The serve
      1. Must hit front wall first
      2. Must carry past short line but not to back wall
      3. Concept of faults—two successive faults cause a side-out
      4. Side-out also results when serve does not initially hit front wall, or if serve touches server's body on the fly
   B. The serve return
      1. Return must be made before ball hits floor twice; ball may be taken on fly
      2. Any combination of walls or ceiling is permissible on return
   C. The volley
      1. Is the alternate hitting of ball by players
      2. Shots must be made before ball hits floor twice; ball may be taken on fly
      3. Any combination of walls or ceiling is permissible
   D. The exchange
      1. Terminates the volley
      2. Occurs when either player:

      a. Lets ball hit floor twice prior to hitting
      b. Lets his shot hit floor en route to front wall
   E. Point scoring system
      1. Each exchange results in a point or side-out
         a. Exchange in favor of server is a point
         b. Exchange in favor of receiver is a side-out
      2. Only server may score points
      3. One game is to 21 points
      4. Best two out of three games is a match
      5. At 20-20, the next point scored wins that game

III. Additional suggestions
   A. Hinders—disruptions of play: two types
      1. Unavoidable hinders
      2. Avoidable hinders
   B. Ball out of court: two circumstances
      1. After ball hits front wall: a simple hinder
      2. Before ball hits front wall: a point or side-out

IV. The chocolate freak

V. Doubles
   A. Methods of court coverage
      1. Half-and-half
      2. Front-and-back (I formation)

B. Center court exchange—the team not hitting the ball has the right to front court positioning

C. Keys to doubles strategy
   1. Center court control
   2. Patience
   3. Ceiling rallies
   4. Kill shots—side wall-front wall
   5. Cross-court pass to the left
   6. Strong serves and serve returns necessary
   7. The inner game
   8. Isolation factor

D. Eschew the madness

VI. Basic singles strategy
   A. Strategy on the service
      1. Low and high zones of ball contact
      2. Variety is the spice of service
      3. After serving, retreat along diagonal toward corner at which one served

   4. Watch the ball during play
   B. Strategy on the service return
      1. Strategy revolves around center court position
      2. Usual return is a defensive shot
      3. Take the serve on the fly if possible
   C. Strategy on the rally
      1. Know your own and your opponent's capabilities
      2. Use of complementary shots
      3. Offensive vs. Defensive play
      4. Three different hitting areas on the court
      5. Kill shot strategy and areas of shooting
   D. Strategy on miscellaneous situations
      1. Game plan formulation prior to game
      2. Warming up: Stretching and circulation stimulants
   E. Summary

THE GAME

From its dubious beginning with a tennis racket and sponge rubber ball, *the game* has arrived. And in the last 6 years a racquetball mania has stormed this country by gigantic bounces. Accustomed to being a known figure in an unknown sport, at least these days it is heartening that when I tell someone I am a professional racquetball player, I no longer receive raised eyebrows crowning a blank stare and the return reply, "What's racquetball?"

Still, there remain perhaps a few off-the-beaten-court folks who have not even heard of racquetball. This is excusable. Many other people have accepted the term "racquetball" as a household word but are as yet puzzled about the activity: isn't that supposed to be the new deal where you use a hacked-off tennis racket to bash a superball around a handball court? Isn't it true that the sport is slated to be in the next Olympics? And do you mean there's *really* a pro tour where players can win heaps of money? To answer these inquiries: Yes, sort of. No. Yes and No.

The questions fly more rapidly than a front line rally. Hopefully, this chapter will shoot back some solid answers. It is presented both as an enticement and as an introduction to the fantastic court realm of garbage serves, pinch shots and overheads. I will first provide a brief "teaser"—a comprehensive overview of the game. This is by no means designed to be a complete rundown; that will follow later in this chapter.

THE TEASER

Racquetball is played in a box-like area by two (singles), three (cutthroat) or four (doubles) participants. This book deals mainly with the most popular variation—*singles*. The two singles players alternate striking a pneumatic rubber ball around the enclosed concrete box, hitting with something that resembles a small-headed, shortened tennis racket.

Each competitor's prime objective is to hit the sphere where the other guy isn't, thus winning points. Points accumulate on either side until 21 is reached by one player and that contest is terminated. This one game takes from 15 to 45 minutes to play, depending upon the pace, style and quality of competition. A player accomplishes the task of hitting the ball where the other guy isn't by employing a mixture of finesse, power, hustle, and court savvy. What's more, procuring points often means rambunctiously jockeying for court position, grunting with intense effort and . . . gradually . . . becoming very aware of the opponent's sweat.

Unlike many sports, here one must go both ways—offensive and defensive—with no coach other than the whimsical gallery, no trainer other than the guy in the crowd whose college major is veterinary medicine, and no pinch players. It is one of those activities mundanely dubbed an "individual sport."

If the damp image pictured above does not seem all that teasing, just give it a try. The one-time test run is a hooker for most. I believe this is the reason for racquetball's meteoric rise in participant numbers over recent years. After just a single court outing, you will walk away convinced that you are spastic beyond repair, but also that you are rabidly enthused about your newfound pastime. Spasticity to the wind! You'll want to try it again. After two or three outings, racquetball will become your narcotic. You'll buy a cheapo racquet, subscribe to a racquetball magazine, and weird words like "super-pinch" will creep into your everyday conversation. Then, for some, racquetball will evolve into a full-time gig: while *on* the court you will become so intensely wrought-up by the game that the hassles of the other world will dissipate into nonexistence; and while *off* the court you will spend a great deal of time wrought-up in vicarious games against Serot, Brumfield and other superjocks you read about in that racquetball magazine subscription.

Racquetball has more mass appeal than any sport short of tiddlywinks and jacks. It is an activity with a flexible pace that enables a person of average, or even below average coordination and reflexes, to attain a rousing physical *and* mental workout in an hour. Racquetball does not require the pain of running, leisurely hours of golf nor the skill and strength of tennis. I have instructed an 8-year-old upstart no taller than a racquet and a half, a 60-year-old grandmother looking for an alternative to day-long television addiction, professional football players seeking a quick, intense workout, a "recovered" polio victim whose lack of visual depth perception and puppy-like reflexes drove his tennis instructor to tell him to "give up tennis and try another sport," male and female students bent on keeping their carcasses squared instead of rounded at the corners, and—in short—a conglomeration of curiosity seekers who dared to take that initial step through the court door.

These diversified racquetballers discovered a common denominator—healthy fun. And if that isn't a titillating tease, nothing is.

THE GAME

It is simple to partake of the promised healthy fun if a few fundamentals and rules are learned. This is the purpose of the remainder of this chapter. In the foregoing hypothesis, it was hinted that the basic racquetball requisites include a court, some simple rules, a ball and a couple of racquet-wielding players. These combined components yield perspiration and a final game point. Now let us expand upon these notions.

The essential rules of the game are as follows: (A complete listing of official regulations can be found at the end of this book.) The game includes: the serve, the serve return, the volley, the exchange and the point scoring system. After an explanation of these we shall continue with brief dabblings in other related areas of significance.

First, the ball must be *served*. The server stands in the service zone, drops the ball to the floor and swats it on the *first* bounce. The ball must travel *directly* to the front wall and then rebound *beyond* the short line before touching the floor. Note figure 3-1. After the served ball caroms off the front wall, it may strike *one* of the side walls—but it must bounce posterior to the short line before hitting a third wall on the fly.

Try though he may, sometimes the novice screws up the service in one of a number of ways: 1) If, as mentioned in the preceding paragraph, the served sphere strikes three walls prior to bouncing on the floor, this is deemed a "fault" and one more serve attempt is allowed. 2) If the served ball ricochets off the front plaster but does not carry past the service short line, this is also called a "fault" and the server has one more try. 3) Similarly, if the well-smote sphere carries to the back wall on the fly *without* first bouncing to the floor, a "fault" is called by the receiver. 4) If the ball hits the front wall and then the ceiling it is a "fault." 5) If the server steps out of the service box while serving it is a "foot fault."

What if the served ball does not strike the front wall *first*? This is an embarrassing experience which results in a horse laugh and a "side-out." A "side-out" means that the server loses his serve to the receiver—without a second attempt at a legal serve. Therefore, a "side-out" may occur if the ball put into play by the server initially hits the floor, either side wall or the ceiling. Review the preceding paragraph quickly and be aware that if two "fault" serves are made in *succession*, a "side-out" results and the players exchange position. This two-in-a-row "fault" scheme is analogous to the double fault in tennis. There is one other instance where a "side-out" and *two* horse laughs come about. This occurs when the served ball collides with the server's cumbersome carcass en route to the horse laughing receiver.

That covers the serve. If you have the "faults" confused with the "side-outs," look over the outline for this chapter. Gaze again at figure 3-1. Understand it now? Then we are prepped to fortify our rudimentary racquetball know-how with a consideration of the *serve return*. The receiver must stand at least 5 feet back of the short line, and cannot hit the ball until it passes the short line. Basically, the person

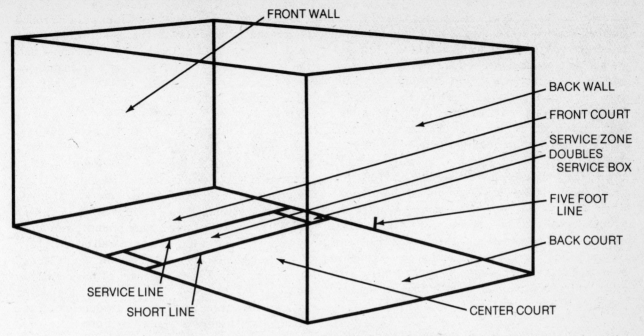

FRONT WALL

BACK WALL
FRONT COURT
SERVICE ZONE
DOUBLES
   SERVICE BOX
FIVE FOOT
   LINE
BACK COURT

SERVICE LINE
SHORT LINE

CENTER COURT

Fig. 3-1—The racquetball court. In this book the term "anterior" refers to toward the front wall, while "posterior" denotes a directional movement toward the back wall.

receiving service must return the ball to the front wall before it hits the floor *more than once*. The serve may legally be taken on the fly, but the instant it touches the floor for a second time the volley is ended and a point is chalked up for the server.

The receiver may use *any combination* of walls or the ceiling in returning the ball to the front wall—as long as the sphere gets there before touchdown with the ground. Unlike the serve, the return of service shot may initially strike the side wall, or ceiling, or, of course, the front wall. At the risk of redundancy, I emphasize that the serve is required to hit the front wall *first*; the return is only required to hit the front wall *eventually* before bouncing on the floor.

If the service receiver does not return the served ball before it bounces to the floor twice, or if his shot does not reach the front wall prior to hitting the floor, then the receiver is said to have lost the "exchange" and the server is awarded a "point." These terms will be more explicitly defined momentarily.

Following the serve and the serve return, the *volley* ensues. The volley is the *alternate* hitting of the ball by the two singles players. Thus, the server must chase down the receiver's return and hit it to the front wall before the sphere hits the ground *twice*. If he accomplishes this, then it is his rival's turn to pursue the elusive orb and propel it to the front wall in perpetuating the volley. Remember that during the volley, as with the service return, the ball may be

taken out of mid-air on the fly. Too, the ball may initially strike any playing surface or surfaces—back wall, side walls and/or ceiling—but it must carry to the front wall before bouncing on the floor.

Therefore, play continues with the take-a-turn volley until the *exchange* occurs. Essentially, this translates that someone goofed and the rally is terminated. The exchange transpires most frequently when one of the players either: 1) Allows the ball to bounce twice on the floor prior to hitting; or 2) One of his shots hits the floor before reaching the front wall.

That brings us along in our quest for court savvy to the *point scoring system*. Points, when tallied, are done so on the exchange. Only the *server* can win points. If the receiver wins the exchange, he is awarded a "side-out" rather than a point. In the case of a "side-out," the receiver exchanges positions with the server and thereby wins the right to garner points. The racquetball point system is similar to that of volleyball in that only the serving person (team) is awarded points, as opposed to the ping pong scoring method where a point is scored on every rally despite who serves.

The players each continue to accumulate points until one of the two reaches that magic *21 points*. Twenty-one signals a "game," the end of that particular court battle. If the game becomes tied at 20-20,

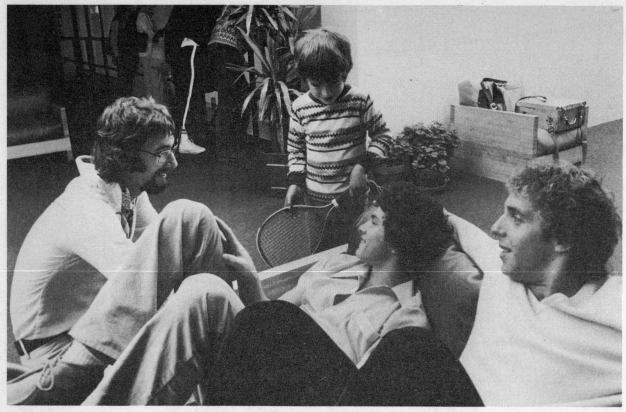

Anyone can play racquetball. The champs and a future court king.

the winner of the next point captures the game; there is no overtime or win-by-two points rule as in ping pong or tennis. The best two out of three battles in racquetball makes up the war. That is, in tournament play or friendly competition the first player to take two 21-point games wins the "match."

That is a simplistic view of the regulations governing the sport of racquetball. But sometimes game play is interrupted. I have had tournament matches "disrupted" due to time-outs (legal and illegal), lost tennis shoes during play, diarrhea runs to the bathroom, drinks dropped onto the court due to gallery intoxication, and a body dropped onto the court due to a participant's heart attack. This termination of the volley—any pause of regular play—is termed a "hinder." There are two types of "hinders": The unavoidable and the avoidable. The *unavoidable hinder* is a simple discontinuance of play which, after the lull, resumes with a reversion to the status quo. No "side-out" or "point" is awarded. The unavoidables most commonly come about when:

1) The ball strikes an object or irregular part of the court which causes it to take an erratic bounce.

Such objects may include light fixtures, door knobs, towels or equipment stuffed into a court corner, and large cracks or protuberances in the walls or floor. For the sake of avoiding later argument that is sure to come about, discuss *prior* to the start of the game what actually is to constitute a court hinder.

2) One player hits the ball toward the front wall but it strikes the opponent's body en route and on the fly. Even if the ball would not have made it to the front wall in the air, this is still a hinder and the play goes over. (If the ball touches your body when it is your turn to hit it, you lose the exchange.)

3) One player physically collides with his rival as an unavoidable result of pursuing the ball, or when one player does not make body contact (but would have) but is hindered from getting to a shot by the opponent's physical presence.(Note: If you feel you may collide with or hit the other guy with your racquet or ball, hold up and call a hinder. He may return the favor someday.) Thus, body contact is *not* required for an unavoidable hinder. On the other hand, neither is body contact *necessarily* a hinder. For example, if Player X runs into Player Y, but X would not have reached the ball even if

Y had not been blocking his way, no hinder can legitimately be called. You may wish to reread this facet of the unavoidable hinder upon considering the soon-to-come description of the avoidable hinder.

4) One player's body blocks or partially blocks the other person's view of the ball such that the latter is unable to see to make a satisfactory shot. This is also called a "screen" ball. For example, a "screen serve" takes place when the served sphere ricochets off the front wall and passes close enough to the server's body to obstruct the receiver's view. This is not a "fault" but merely a hinder on the serve and play goes over. In friendly play the receiver calls all "screen" balls whether they occur during the volley or on the serve; in tournaments this decision is up to the referee, though the service returner or screened player may petition the ref for an uncalled visual hinderance. Along this line of play, a ball which passes *between* the legs of one of the players is *not* an automatic hinder. Again, it is a play-over only if one participant is hampered from seeing or swinging at the ball.

5) A "backswing hinder" occurs. This means that one player makes racquet contact with another player's body during his backswing. This is an automatic hinder if called immediately and, incidently, is the *only* hinder the player may legitimately call himself in a tournament—the referee is responsible for all other hinder decisions.

6) The ball breaks during play.

Those are the unavoidable hinder situations. *Avoidable hinders,* on the other hand, result in a point or "side-out," depending upon whether the offender was serving or receiving. Avoidable hinders are usually not called in friendly play but the reader should familiarize himself with the situations under which they could be called. An avoidable hinder occurs when:

1) One player does not move sufficiently to allow the opponent his shot. The interpretation of this rule is subjective.

2) One player moves into a position which obviously blocks the opponent's return shot to the front wall.

3) Deliberate pushing off or shoving occurs during the volley.

Let us leave the hinder confusion and focus on what happens when the ball goes out of the court. The sphere's flight path may carry it up, up and over the back or side walls under one of two circumstan-

ces: 1) *After* the front wall return. Any ball returned (or served) to the front wall which on the rebound or on the first bounce goes into the gallery is just a hinder (unavoidable) and the play goes over. 2) *Before* the front wall return. Any ball not returned to the front wall, but which caroms directly off a player's racquet into the gallery (whether or not it touches a side, back wall, or ceiling), is a "side-out" or point against the player who smacked the ball outa there.

That is the game of racquetball in a literary nutshell. Please forgive any lackluster or complexities in the foregoing reading. It is not difficult to put the myriad rules and regulations in practice; it is just difficult to put them into words. It is easier done than said . . .

. . . for most people. Then again, there are a rare few for whom the opposite is true. This puts me in mind of a certain young man whom I once instructed in racquetball. On behalf of this individual, it is only fair initially to point out that he was a court greenhorn in every sense of the word, having never participated in anything more strenuous than sitting down to and getting up from the dinner table.

But to put it bluntly—and pity should be no reason for sugar coating the bare facts—the guy was a klutz. He swung a mean club foot and a horrendous racquet stroke. I have never witnessed a funkier backhand, and his forehand packed the same languid wallop as catnip, watered-down yogurt or a bad franchise hamburger. Be thankful, reader, you were not created in the image of this poor player.

So, how does one go about teaching racquetball skills to a person with the physical adeptness of an inebriated slug? I spent a lot of time with him on the rules. He was terrific on remembering the rules, which is fortunate because it gave us a common denominator for communication throughout our series of *six* lessons. I swear, he must have studied the rulebook I gave him by the hour. He is one of the few individuals to correctly answer my "final exam" question: "You are playing in the finals for the national championship. It is the third and final game with the score tied 20-20 and you are serving. You are one point away from victory, one point away from defeat. You enter the service box and nervously bounce the ball once . . . twice . . . three times. Just as you are about to bounce it an additional time for the serve, it hits you like a bolt of lightning! If you bounce the ball one more time you will have violated the maximum three-bounce rule on the service and your opponent will be awarded a 'side-out.' That is the dilemma. What is the solution?"

Quicker than you could say "21st point on a freak

ball,'' my pupil piped back the correct answer: ''You call a time-out.'' This is one of the few times throughout our six lesson series that I felt a tinge of pride rather than shudder of sympathy for the chocolate freak.

Chocolate freak? Yes, that is what I called him in my own mind because that is what he resembled. *Potbellied* and lots of *zits*. When he walked, he waddled . . . and when he smiled, he popped. He tried hard, but just did not have it. I recall that early in each lesson, after just a couple of racquet swings, his gamey armpits told me his inferior carcass simply was not accustomed to this rigorous activity. My student was truly an all-pro sweater and honorable mention panter. After the six-lesson torture concluded, I didn't know whether to offer the chocolate freak my condolences, an emergency enema or a large tube of acne cream.

But he was dynamite on the rules and regs.

DOUBLES

A word on doubles, in my opinion, that catastrophic mutation of the real game. And a word of advice, again from personal experience: Eschew the madness. A fair amount of past doubles practice and tournament play qualifies me in reporting that no more than two people should occupy one court at one time. Especially if one or more of the participants is a chocolate freak or similarly handicapped biped. It should be posted above every racquetball court entrance, like the fire hazard sign: Capacity Two Persons.

Doubles is a complex game which requires more patience, strategy and racquet control than singles. Watch four good players on the court at the same time. Since successful kill shots must be right on to be winners, the percentage method of play is a waiting game. Typically, there is a drawn out ceiling ball rally interrupted by a mishit ceiling shot. One team attempts to administer the coup de grace; if the kill is a roll-off the rally ends, and if the ball comes up it is re-killed.

For those brave souls or those players forced into doubles play due to the common too-many-players-for-too-few-courts syndrome, there are two styles of court coverage most frequently used in doubles. The *half-and-half* method is by far the more widely used. Here, each player of one team is responsible for covering that hardwood acreage to either side of an imaginary line drawn down the center of the court. (Figure 3-2.) Realize that this line is only an aid to decrease ''waffle faces'' and that it may be crossed at any time by either teammate. Assuming both players

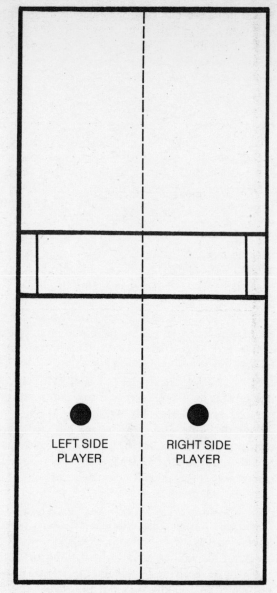

Fig. 3-2—The doubles half-and-half or side-by-side formation.

are right-handed, the one with the superior backhand usually takes the left side. A shot coming directly down the middle of the court, for example off the backwall, is the left side player's responsibility since this would be a forehand shot for him. With a righty-lefty duo, the half-and-half style is tailor-made because both players are able to employ their stronger forehand strokes the majority of the time. The southpaw plays the left side and the person wielding the better backhand takes shots down the middle.

The other common doubles court coverage method is the *I formation*, also called the front-and-back style. Here, an imaginary line is drawn from side wall

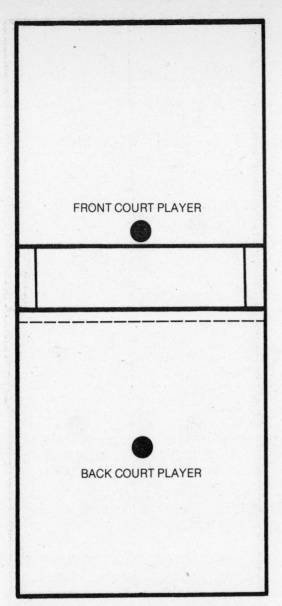

FRONT COURT PLAYER

BACK COURT PLAYER

Fig. 3-3—The doubles front-and-back or I formation.

singles, control of the mid-court terrain is the key to doubles success. Vying for domination of that important area is sometimes a subtle cat-and-mouse ploy, at other times it is a violent elbowing slugfest. There is a means of maintaining order at that center court epicenter of activity, and though it is logical and straightforward many players have a heck of a time executing the mechanics of this method.

Simply stated, if a player of Team 1 is about to hit the ball then the opposing Team 2 has the unwritten right to occupy the front (center court) position. After Team 1 makes the shot, it is Team 2's turn to do the hitting. Therefore, Team 2 relinquishes the front position to Team 1. The rally continues with this perpetual exchange (on the right and left sides of the court) of the optimal front position by both members of both teams. (See figures 3-4a and 3-4b.) It was mentioned earlier that a professional doubles contest often consists of drawn out ceiling ball rallies. The ceiling exchange is simple in itself, but look for a more complex exchange of positions in center court after *each* shot. The smooth give-and-take interaction, or slipping in and slipping out of station with each shot, resembles a four-man ballet when ideally performed.

I am constantly amazed by two things in the realm of racquetball these days. First, I am amazed at the total lack of beautiful young women dressed solely in jill-straps on the courts after midnight. Second, I am amazed at the total lack of strategy employed in doubles matches. The first of these dilemmas I have no control over but the second perhaps I can remedy.

It has been hinted that *center court control* is imperative in doubles. It is admittedly tiresome, but in this event one must remain alert, aggressive and on the move even during the relative "ceasefire" of a chronic ceiling exchange. Too, *patience* is not only a virtue but also a necessity in doubles. A three-quarter set-up in doubles is no longer the 100 percent plum ball that it is in singles because there are two nerds up there waiting to gobble up and spit back anything but a perfect bottom boarder.

Stay patiently to the *ceiling,* broken up once in a while by an around-the-wall ball. (These shots are covered in later chapters.) When you do try to smite a kill, it is a percentage maneuver to go for the *side wall-front wall shot.* This "pinch shot" carries the ball low to the center of the front wall where it is less likely to pop up or be covered by either member of the opposing team. (See figure 3-5.)

Against a team composed of two right handers, the *cross-court pass to the left* (V-ball) is a bread-and-butter ploy. (Figure 3-4a.) The right side player should remain aware of this percentage V-ball at all

to side wall at about midcourt, with the front player being responsible for shots in the anterior half of the court and his back court counterpart taking balls in the posterior half. (Figure 3-3.) Again, that dividing line is only imaginary and teammates will often find themselves crossing it to cover for each other. Those teams choosing this formation are frequently composed of a back player with a good ceiling game and accurate kills, and a front player who is jackrabbit quick and an aggressive court coverer.

Whichever of the above two formations is utilized, the problem in doubles usually revolves around the *center court control exchange.* Even more so than in

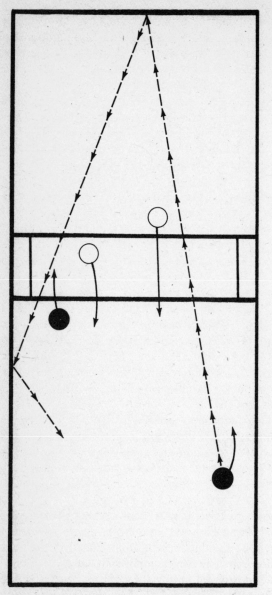

Fig. 3-4a—Beginning of the front court position exchange: Right side offensive player (● right side) takes the shot. The opposing team (○'s) are occupying front court.

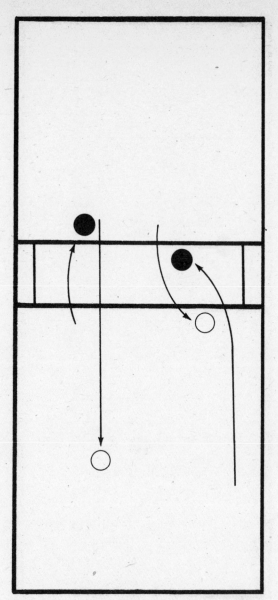

Fig. 3-4b—The exchange is completed: Now the situation is reversed with the left side ○ retrieving the ball and his partner also relinquishing his front court position. The two opposing players (●'s), now awaiting a return shot, have moved into the vacated front court.

times, mixing his returns off set-ups with this shot and kills. Against a righty-lefty combo, the cross-court pass is no longer such a threat because the left side player would be returning such a blast with a farther reaching, stronger forehand stroke. The V-ball is still applicable, but vary its use with a wider angle pass (this will tend to jam the player) or drive down the center of the court (which presents itself to both players' backhands). (Figure 3-6.)

Strong serves and serve returns are musts if a team wants to enter the big leagues of doubles play. On the service, one may employ any of the serves talked about in Chapter 10, with one caution: On the high level services (garbage, high-Z, lob) take care that your initial shot is not rushed and pulverized on the fly by the opposing team. If you choose to serve up a garbage, lower the altitude of the serve to prevent the volley return.

On the service return, take the ball *on the fly* on any high level serve. This is more easily done in

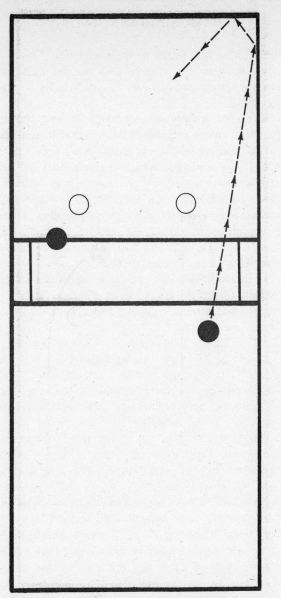

Fig. 3-5—The pinch kill shot (forehand or backhand side) is often more effective in doubles than a straight in kill. Ball goes to middle court away from both defensive men.

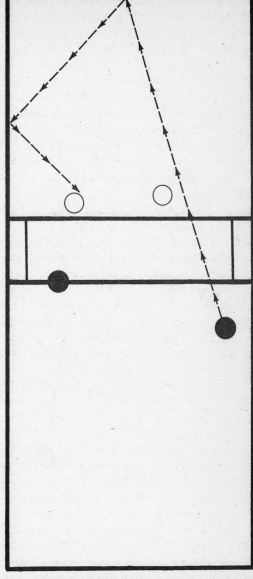

Fig. 3-6—The wide angle pass shot which jams the left side defensive player.

doubles than singles because each team member has only one half of the receiving area to handle.

In doubles especially, there is an "outer game" and an "inner game." The strategic explanation heretofore has dealt solely with the outer game, or the physical maneuvering and shots. The *inner game* of racquetball concerns the mental aspects of play. The inner game pervades doubles. There is a high school locker room adage that "enthusiasm creates momentum," and this is very apparent with a doubles

team. It is astonishing what a little hustle and desire by one teammate will do for the other. It is infectious, engendering a double "hot streak" by a team. Often an encouraging word or even a well-timed mild admonishment aimed at a teammate will mark the turning point of a match.

Doubles players sometimes use an *isolation strategy* in their game, whereby one of the opponents is singled out to receive the brunt of the attack. The chosen one is badgered with serve after serve, ceiling ball after ceiling ball, shot after shot, until he wilts to the varnished hardwood, physically and mentally spent. Meanwhile, the team utilizing the isolation factor reaps a fringe benefit. As the chosen player is being worn down, his ignored partner experiences the doldrums of boredom and complete inactivity. The latter player often slips into a haze of disinterest or observation hypnosis. If and when he is finally hit a shot, the inactive player is so "cold" or out of the groove that he blows it. This often elicits vocal exasperation from his teammate who has been flailing about like a tangled-up puppet. Dissention among the ranks cracks the team.

How to choose which player to isolate? The major prerequisite is in picking the weaker of the team members. Too, often a team will select the left side player to nag with continuous sphere assault, assuming he is a right-hander. At other times it is wise to isolate the opponent who is having a hot streak by directing the majority of balls to his partner. Finally, if you ever come across a doubles duo composed of a chocolate freak and his teammate, do yourself a favor and run the pimples and pot-belly off the freak.

As a parting note on doubles, allow me to re-emphasize my opening sentiments. The two-on-two situation puts me in mind of a small group of dancers jabbing hips and gyrating pelvises on the dance floor to the musical command of an acid rock band's heavy beat. You look at that mass of ducking, dipping bodies and say to yourself, "There *must* be a common denominator of rhythm somewhere within all that movement, but I sure as heck can't pick it out." Most doubles is exactly that: unorganized rhythm grooving to the whims of a high velocity sphere. Instead of hip jabs there are racquet jabs, and when contact is made it isn't a meeting of tender caress but rather the clash of racquet on tender flesh.

Even when the four participants are veteran court virtuosos of multi-years experience, it is often movement and strategy without synchrony: a quartet of autonomously functioning carcasses double teamed in questionable combat. And when the teams are less accomplished than the learned virtuosos of which I speak—for example, club hackers out for a good time—the combat is even more questionable. Too many times I have witnessed knee-ed knees and waffled faces among novices by the time the music is over. Red circular pock marks—welts, as they are termed in the racquetball vernacular—are the most obvious manifestations of the greenhorn doubles disease. These red badges of courage (?) are no fun.

I strongly feel doubles is a fool's tango. Eschew the madness.

BASIC SINGLES STRATEGY

Let us now skip along to merrier music. Ignore the sirens beckoning to doubles and consider a safer and more sporting song: *Singles* . . . and the basic strategy of singles.

The term strategy in racquetball connotes the skillful employment and coordination of tactics and shots for the purpose of playing ball to one's fullest potential. The following strategic summary does not delve deeply into the cerebral game; rather, it provides fundamental guidelines for such things as when to hit what shot and why to take up what position. A much more concentrated study of these racquetball stratagems is considered in this book's sequel, *Racquetball: For Advanced to Champion Players.*

In the following, we shall deal with basic strategy under four sub-headings: On the Service, On the Service Return, On the Rally and a section on the miscellaneous situations.

STRATEGY ON THE SERVICE

Chapter 10 covers the serve in detail and the reader will discover helpful strategic tips on serving there. However, a few additional points should also be highlighted. (Note: If you are not familiar with some of the terms utilized below, such as "garbage serve," definitions may be found in the glossary at the end of this book.)

First, realize there are two levels (altitudes) to serve from: the low zone and the high zone. That is, one may wish to contact the service ball within the *low zone,* which is mid-calf to knee high. This level includes the drive serves and the low Z-serves. Or one may wish to put the ball into play within the *high zone,* which is mid-thigh to chest high. This level encompasses the garbages, lob and high Z-serves.

The idea behind the service level is that any serve struck from the low zone is generally done so in an attempt to elicit a *weak return.* For example, an accurate low hard drive serve to the backhand will likely force a feeble return. The server administers the coup de grace to the set-up and the rally ends in a total of three shots. True, serves initiated from the low zone are more effective than those initiated from the high zone, but there is a problem of compensation: it is much more difficult to pinpoint the course of the low serves. That low drive serve may just as easily rebound off the back wall for a plum ball and the rally ends in a total of two shots.

On the other hand, any serve struck from the high zone is generally done so in an attempt to simply put the ball into play *without making an error on the*

Two-time national champ Schmidtke knows Bledsoe is back there some-where—But where? This situation probably resulted in a hinder play.

serve. For example, a capable biped should be able to serve accurately nine out of ten garbages to the backhand. There should be no such animal as a misdirected garbage serve. But, by a reverse rationalization from the preceding paragraph, this particular serve (service high level) does not frequently elicit a weak set-up on the return. The rally is likely to carry on a number of shots.

Besides the two levels of service, the reader should be aware that variety on the serve is usually desirable. Changing serves leads to confusion within the receiver's mind and keeps him guessing. Most of the professional players have three or four staple serves which they vary seemingly at random throughout the match. Your service repertoire should include at least two from each of the two serve zones.

To justify my own service regime, allow me to hedge a tad on this "variety is the spice of service" concept. Someone once said, in retrospect (after learning the hard way), "always change a losing game and never change a winning game." This quotation applies especially to the serve. Against an unknown opponent in the early stages of the game, it is wise to experiment and explore your rival's skills through service variety. Once you discover which serves and shots are most strategically sound, badger him with those particular ploys.

It will be discussed later in greater detail that most serves should originate from approximately the center of the service box and that most are directed at the competition's weaker stroke, his backhand. It will also be pointed out in some length that a specific serve may be used to force the receiver to come back with a specific service rebuff. Therefore, your selection of serves will hinge upon what type of game you wish to force upon your opponent.

The wet-behind-the-ears court dunce is often in a quandary as to where to go after putting the ball into play. As often as not, the inexperienced player will either sashay randomly around the service box like a dog looking for a spot to lie down, or he will make a sleepy retreat to the nearest sidewall. Wrong! After hitting the ball, the server should back two or three steps out of the service box *toward the rear corner at which he directed the served sphere.* In other words, most serves go to the backhand or left rear corner. The server, originally stationed in the center of the service zone, should follow an imaginary diagonal line toward the left rear corner. This is diagramed in figure 3-7.

The amount of *distance* to retreat along this diagonal depends on the accuracy of the serve. A satisfactory garbage serve allows the server to tread posteriorly along the hypotenuse a good four or five

steps. An inept drive serve which rebounds off the back court plaster for a set-up forces the server to play it tighter; he should back up one or two steps, or not at all.

This backpeddling leads us to watching the ball. WATCH the ball, whether on the serve or during the rally. This observation of the orb will aid you in anticipating the other guy's shots, in following the general direction of play and in helping cut down the number of those photon shots to the ol' kidneys which instantly reduce the staunchest, macho he-man to a sniveling boob.

STRATEGY ON THE SERVICE RETURN

As with the serve, the reigning factor concerning the service return is *center court positioning.* For now, we shall roughly define center court as that area indicated in the diagram, figure 3-8. As in chess, whoever dominates center court the majority of the time will emerge the eventual victor.

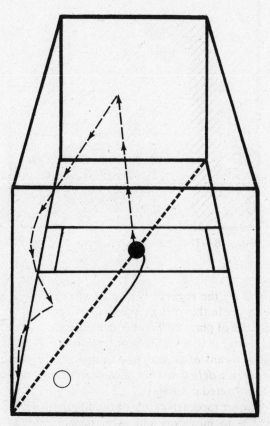

Fig. 3-7—Retreat of the server: ● has just served a garbage serve to the backhand side and is retreating along the imaginary diagonal. If it is a good serve he may trace the dotted line 4-5 steps; if it is a poor serve he may not back out at all.

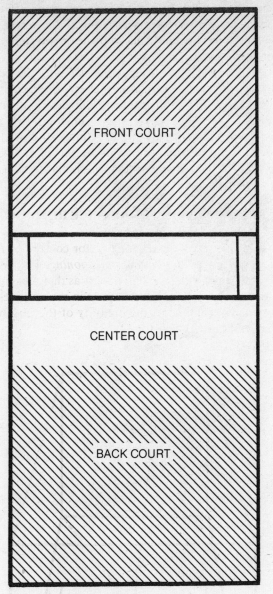

Fig. 3-8—The three court areas.

fly? Do this by "reading" or observing the server's habits and idiosyncrasies. He may step toward the right front corner when about to serve to the forehand side, or he may lick his nose when about to serve up a garbage. Too, you can anticipate the type of expected service by checking out at which of the two serve levels the server contacts the racquetball. If he drops the ball knee high and bends deeply at the waist prior to swatting, prepare for a low drive or low Z. However, if he stands in the service box like Frankenstein at attention and is about to contact the sphere shoulder high, then get your receiving rear into gear and rush up to take the ball out of the air.

In summary, a one-sentence guide to returning service might be; if the ball can be taken below the knees then one may smite it offensively, but if the ball must be taken above the knees then pamper it defensively. And repeat over and over the following while awaiting service: "Better to return with perfunctory patience than pretentious pizzazz."

STRATEGY ON THE RALLY

The typical novice match features caterpillar brain, that splendid physical specimen (simian musculature and rattlesnake reflexes, runs wind sprints in the soft sand for relaxation), against goggle eyes, that brawnless brain bank (straight A's in computer science and head honcho of the debating team, peruses the dictionary for relaxation). Where Mr. Caterpillar Brain is adept physically, Mr. Goggle Eyes is most inept. And where old four-eyes is adept mentally, the insect brain is most inept.

Their court battle is a classic confrontation of compensation. Mind over matter, or matter over mind? If the reader identifies with either of these characters, there is some strategic advice available. The essence of strategy on the rally is to be cognate of your own capabilities and foibles, to know your opponent's capabilities and foibles, and then to hit the shots that you have found through experience to be the most effective in procuring points. With the two court sports described above, caterpillar brain would find it beneficial to play a running, hustling, driving, power game to maximize his physical prowess. Goggle eyes might better utilize systematic logic and finesse through superior positioning and serve and shot selection.

The cornerstone of any strategy during the rally, whether applied by beginner or veteran, is the use of *complementary shots*. This is a sweet way of saying "Hit the ball where the other guy ain't!" For instance, if one of your shots causes your rival to run forward and to the right to retrieve, the (next) com-

Because the receiver is located in deep court and the server in the virtual epicenter of center court at the onset of play, the number one objective in returning service is to exchange court positions. The most logical means of accomplishing this goal is through the use of a *defensive shot,* a subject which is meticulously covered in Chapter 7.

Another racquetball rule of thumb on the return of serve is to move up and take the ball *on the fly* whenever possible. Your volley shot need not be a *thread-the-needle* pass or kill because the server will still be off in limbo land by the time your ball zooms past him.

How to anticipate in order to take the ball on the

Center court control is a perpetual mental and physical struggle. Serot shoots for killshot with Hogan coming up fast to cover.

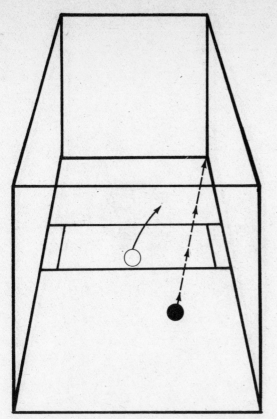

Fig. 3-9a—The offensive player hits the ball into the front right corner, and the defensive man retrieves.

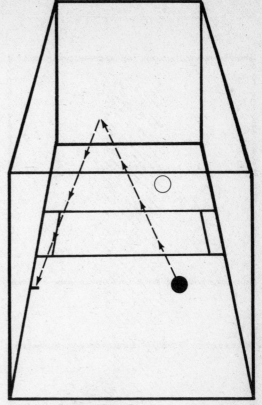

Fig. 3-9b—●follows up his last shot by hitting the complementary shot, a drive to the left rear corner.

plementary shot would require your rival to run back and to the left. In other words, your present shot should be the complement of your last one. (See figures 3-9a and 3-9b.)

Another important facet of rally strategy involves the concept of *offensive vs. defensive play*. Remember that the aggressive player is the better player, with a few guidelines. If you are stationed in front or center court with your competitor lingering in back court, now is the time to administer an offensive thrust via a kill shot. Contrarily, if you are presented with a set-up in back court and your opponent is in center court position, strategy usually demands you to go defensively with a ceiling ball or perhaps a quasi-defensive pass shot. This idea of shot selection and defensive vs. offensive play will be considered further in chapters within Section II.

It can be seen, then, that certain shots are usually attempted from different areas of the court—depending on one's degree of shot making proficiency. The offensive (hitting) player may be presented with a ball in one of three areas (figure 3-8). The set-ups in front court usually should be put away (killed). The set-ups at mid-court are handled aggressively, de-

pending on the defensive player's position. The set-ups in back court usually are returned defensively.

Everybody wants to kill the ball . . . which is not a bad desire at all. Chapters 4 and 5 deal with the stroke techniques of bottom boarding the ball, as well as touching on kill shot strategy. Assuming one *can* kill the ball, *where* does one do so? Figure 3-10 roughly outlines the basic areas for killing the ball. (Obviously, you need not kill every set-up from within any given area.) This diagram is a lesson in oversimplification but is helpful in one major aspect: When attempting the celebrated perfect roll-off, the killer should direct most forehand kills to the forehand corner and most backhand kills to the backhand corner. Also note figures 3-11a and 3-11b.

By way of summary, the beginning to intermediate player should keep three strategic items in mind during the rally: (1) Know your own and your opponent's capabilities and apply the basic shots accordingly. If during a volley you are at a loss for the correct choice of shots, either (2) go with the complementary shot, or (3) adopt the offensive vs. defensive logic.

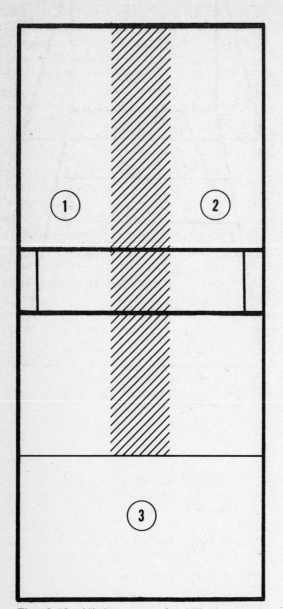

Fig. 3-10—Hitting areas for kill shots: 1) Most kills go into the front left corner. 2) Most kills go into the front right corner. ▨ Overlapping shaded area—kills may be directed toward either front corner. 3) Backcourt—do not attempt a kill shot if opponent is in center court position.

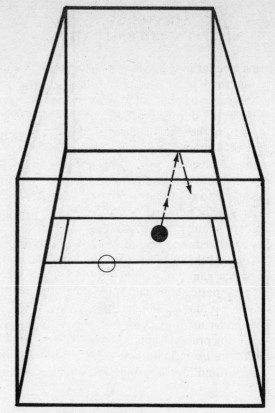

Fig. 3-11a—Straight-on kill to place ball away from opponent.

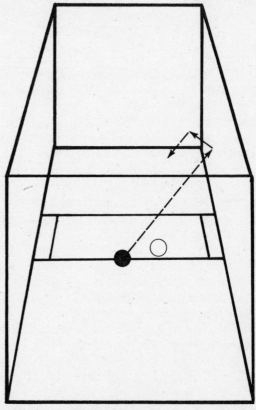

Fig. 3-11b—Side wall-front wall kill to place ball away from opponent.

STRATEGY ON
MISCELLANEOUS SITUATIONS

The first pointer in this synopsis of strategic tips involves the *game plan*. It is a good idea to formulate some semblance of a plan of attack prior to the opening serve (even during practice games). All that is being asked of the reader is that he think a mite *prior* to game time about what he intends to do. Organize this strategic blueprint while driving to the courts or as you climb into your supporter.

This is not to say that the prearranged game plan must be strictly adhered to. A pre-match strategy which proves faulty once actual play commences can always be altered. This was alluded to earlier with the explanation of changing a losing game and maintaining a winning game.

After composing your game plan for the upcoming battle, there is another important item to tend to. Be sure to limber up your body well. Before you even start swatting practice shots you must loosen up. To me, *warming up* includes two things: (1) stretching the tendons and muscles, and (2) getting the blood circulating. Stretch out the major muscle groups with 5- to 10-second exercises such as toe touchers, arm rotations, hamstring stretchers and trunk rotations. Do not bounce when performing these movements (a constant progressive stretch is better) and do not rotate at helicopter speed. Now that you are stretched out, get the blood gurgling by jogging in place, jumping jacks or similar heart starters. Your entire warm-up need not last more than 5 to 10 minutes, and this interim is a ripe time for formulating the game plan.

Basic strategy is born out of thinking and being tuned into the here and now of service, service return and rally racquetball. If the foregoing discussion of basic strategy seems to take up points rather quickly and then drop them just as rapidly, then this chapter's purpose has been served. You have the border pieces of the puzzle fit together now and although you may not be able to envision the picture, the instructional chapters of Section II will provide all the center parts and the whole picture will gradually piece together.

section II

RACQUETBALL FOR THE NOVICE AND INTERMEDIATE PLAYER

chapter four
FOREHAND

CHAPTER 4 SUMMARY

I. **Forehand grip**
   A. **Handshake grip**
   B. **"V" positioning**
   C. **Trigger finger**
   D. **Heel-in-butt**

II. **Forehand stroke**
   A. **Basic three elements**
      1. **Pendulum swing**
      2. **Wrist cock set position**
      3. **Step forward**
   B. **Set position—wrist cock**
   C. **Point of contact**
      1. **For passes—knee high; for kills—ankle high**
      2. **Away from body**
      3. **Off lead heel**
   D. **Break wrist upon contact**
   E. **Level follow-through**
   F. **Hit ball with 80 percent effort**
   G. **Killing the ball—same stroke; ankle high**
   H. **Baseball sidearm swing**

III. **Forehand drills**
   A. **Practice is mandatory**
   B. **Exercises**
      1. **Drop and hit—3 positions**
      2. **Set-up and hit—3 positions**
      3. **Drop and kill**
      4. **Set-up and kill**
   C. **Obtain feed back**
   D. **Stave off boredom**

INTRODUCTION TO STROKES

Possibly the only thing more frustrating than teaching the basic racquetball strokes is learning the basic racquetball strokes. It is a teeter-totter learning process. One day you will do no wrong and every powerful swing will be in perfect imitation of top pro Steve Serot. The very next day you will not be able to hit the front wall with the ball. Let us patiently examine the proper strokes in racquetball.

First, what is a *proper stroke*? Here it is defined as the swing most easily assimilated by the novice with the fastest results. Admittedly, there is more than one way to propel a compressed ball with a strung racquet, and the reader is encouraged to experiment on his own using the *model* swings presented as the basic building block. Do not deviate far from our model, however.

The stroke will first be explained in words. Then a series of sequence photographs with correlating text will be given. If studied closely these sequence frames and captions should prove highly beneficial. Following this a series of stroke drills will be presented. Finally, if only to assure the reader that the forehand and backhand models outlined in this book are indeed the swings utilized by the top players in the sport, pictures of two of the top-notch in action are provided.

THE FOREHAND GRIP

You will quickly learn that the proficiency of the forehand is limited by the correctness of the grip. The

Fig. 4-1

Grasp the racquet throat
with the off-hand.

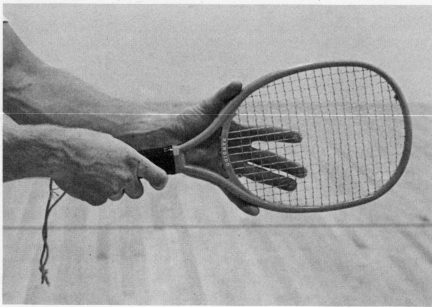

Shake hands
with the handle.

right grip allows maximum power and control; the incorrect grip severely cramps one or both of these experiences. The idea of the ideal grip is as difficult to grasp via words and illustrations as is trying to learn to tie shoelaces without actually having shoelaces in hand. Therefore as you peruse the following explanation simultaneously *act out* the concept with a racquet.

If you can shake hands with a stick you have a good chance of being able to hold a racquetball racquet correctly. The basic forehand grip is the handshake grasp with the addition of a "trigger finger." Pick up the racquet at the throat area (where the handle joins the face) and hold it in front of your body at navel level—with the left hand if you are right handed or the right hand if you are a southpaw. The string face of the racquet should be perfectly perpendicular (not parallel) with the floor. Now grab hold of the handle using your dominant hand as though you are shaking hands, as figure 4-1 indicates. The palm of your hand should be in approximately the same plane as the face of the racquet. Stated in different words, your palm should be contacting one of the two flat surfaces of the basically rectangular handle.

All that is required now is a few minor *adjustments*.

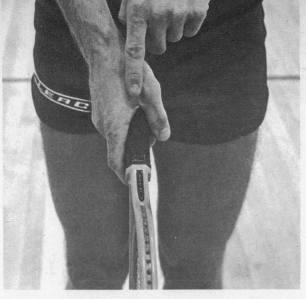

Fig. 4-2

The *V-juncture* lies
on the handle's topmost
surface.

Fig. 4-3

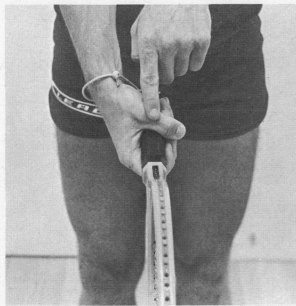

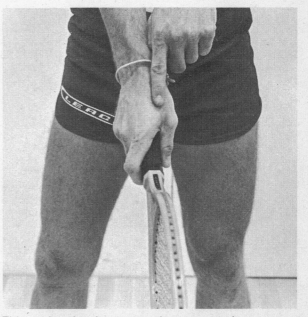

This twisted grip closes the racquet face too much.

This twisted grip opens the racquet face too much. Compare the V-juncture in this and the photo on the left with the proper grip in Fig. 4-2.

Check to see that the handle is properly rotated within your hand. To do this visualize an imaginary straight line drawn along the top-most flat surface of the racquet handle. As you follow this line along the upper-most surface from the throat of the racquet toward your hand, it should exactly intersect the "V" formed by the juncture of the bases of the thumb and index finger. Note this intersection in figure 4-2. Comprehension of the "V" area juncture will be necessary in the next chapter when the switch from forehand to backhand grip is performed. If the "V" is now properly placed over the center of the upper-most surface plane, you are assured of attaining maximum power and accuracy out of your forehand stroke. If you are grasping the racquet improperly with the handle twisted within your hand, you will discover your ensuing hits to be less than solid. In considering a twisted grip, one of two unwanted possibilities will result. If the racquet face is too open (top slanted backward), the ball will be sliced and hit higher than intended. If the face is too closed (top slanted forward), you will likely drill the ball into the floor unless some abnormal anatomical adjustment of the wrist is made during the swing. Figures 4-3 and 4-4 demonstrate these two faults due to improper open and closed grips.

Fig. 4-4

Improper closed racquet face directs the ball into the floor.

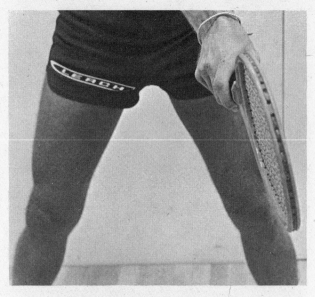

Improper open racquet face causes slicing of the ball.

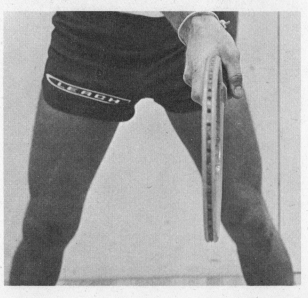

With the ideal grip, the racquet face is *parallel* with front wall at point of contact.

Fig. 4-5

The "trigger finger" grip.

A slight space between
the first two fingers allows
better racquet control.

Fig. 4-6 The thumb falls between the first two fingers.

We are ready for the next adjustment. Extend your index finger about ½-inch toward the racquet throat, as figure 4-5 points out, such that a small space appears between the first and other three fingers. This is commonly termed the "trigger finger" grip because of the resemblance to shooting a pistol. It allows your hand to cover more of the racquet handle resulting in enhanced control of the swing. Almost all seasoned players utilize the "trigger finger" technique for additional touch. This minute finger extension also automatically places your index finger just ahead of your thumb on the handle, as figure 4-6 portrays.

Next adjustment. How high up on the handle should you grasp the racquet? The butt of the rac-

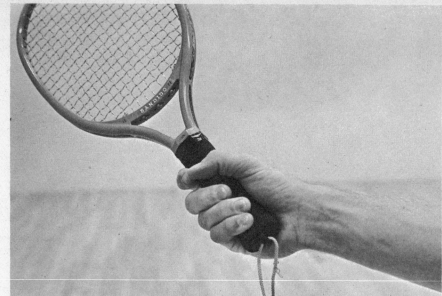

Fig. 4-7

Butt of the racquet
goes against the heel
of the hand.

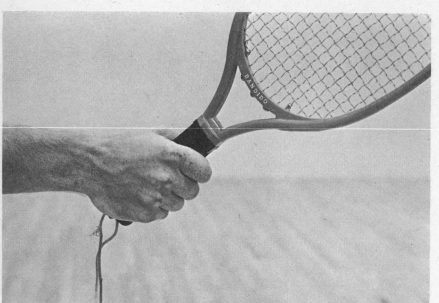

Fig. 4-8

Improper fist grip.

quet (the bump at the end of the handle) should be placed against the heel of the hand. That is, the rounded terminal bump should rest against the fleshy portion of your lower palm. This is clearly illustrated by figure 4-7.

If all of the above points have been accomplished correctly, you are presently gripping the racquet just as most of the professionals do. The only difference is that you have taken 10 minutes to perform this task while experienced veterans grasp their weapons confidently without thinking in a split second. Anything is easy if one knows how. If possible, have a knowledgeable person check out your grip. If it is judged

true to form then practice grasping your court weapon over and over until it becomes as natural as shaking hands.

There are a few common errors which should serve as an adequate summary of the forehand grip. First, many beginners feel compelled to take hold of the racquet with a clenched *fist* grip, as though eager to perform a few mean forehand swings on their worst enemies. Do not hold the handle with a fist; the "trigger finger" spread grip provides much improved leverage and control. Take note of this mistaken grip in figure 4-8.

Another typical error occurs when novices tightly

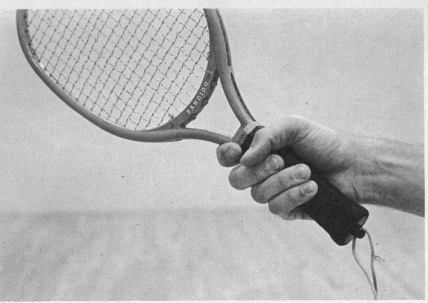

Fig. 4-9

Improper "ping-pong" grip with handle grasped too high.

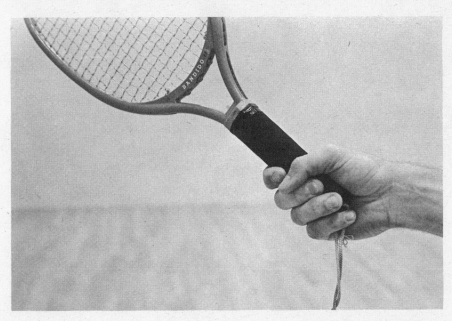

Improper "eagle claw" grip with handle grasped too low.

affix their phalanges to the handle as though it were a rope from which they were dangling over an abyss. Incorrect again. When about to smack the racquetball with forehand or backhand the degree of *grip tightness* will obviously depend upon the strength of the individual, but a good rule of thumb is to grasp the handle firmly and with authority, just as when you shake hands when warmly greeting a person. Of course, the grip should relax slightly after the player strikes the ball, and it tightens with confidence again when the player sets up to wallop the next shot.

One other grip mistake characterizes court club competition across the country. Many people experi-

ence difficulty in remembering where on the handle to hold the racquet. "How high up do I grab this thing?" they plead. Another rule of thumb to apply here is "butt-in-heel" as alluded to earlier. For some peculiar reason the inexperienced female tends to hold the racquet up too close to the throat, something akin to wielding a ping pong paddle. In making this error, these girls are unknowingly losing a large amount of their potential power. Male players are not immune to grip problems. Give a guy a racquet for the first time and he will as often as not grab it at its very end, with the racquet butt in the center of his palm and his little finger grasping more air than

Fig. 4-10

The pendulum swing...

emphasizes smoothness...

and fluid movement.

handle. This "eagle claw" grip admittedly increases the whip of the swing and, therefore, the stroke's power, but it simultaneously cuts down on control. Notice the grips in figures 4-9. Strive for the happy medium—"butt-in-heel."

If you have conquered the forehand grip, you are well on the way to mastering the backhand grip as well, as will be taken up in Chapter 5. Now, let us get into the swing of things.

THE FOREHAND STROKE

"Front foot pointed, back foot planted, shoulder down, head up, racquet back!"

"Watch where you're hitting this thing!"

"Shift your weight to the balls of your feet!"

"What do you mean, where are the balls of your feet?"

"Racquet back farther."

"Farther. Now swing!"

"Great follow through—now we'll give you two more strikes."

It can be confusing, can't it? Compared to tiddly-winks, it is difficult, but compared to tennis it is

Fig. 4-11

The wrist cock set position.

The wrist breaks at the bottom of the pendulum downswing.

easier—and much more fun, as racquetball proponents are quick to point out. But to have fun you have to be able to hit the ball, preferably at least a couple of times in a row. If you are game, read on.

To get into proper position for the forehand stroke begin by standing facing the right side wall if you are right handed, or the left wall if you are a southpaw. (For simplicity sake the following description assumes the reader to be right handed. For you lefties, all "rights" should be changed to "lefts" and vice versa in the oncoming reading.) As you face the right side wall, your feet should be about shoulder length apart, your weight mostly on the balls of the feet and the knees slightly bent. Grasp your racquet with the correct forehand grip and you are ready to swing. *Without* using a ball perform the following *three basic motions* which comprise the forehand swing.

One—The Pendulum Swing. As figure 4-10 displays, swing your racquet from a starting backswing position to a finishing follow-through, then swing back to the backswing position and so on until you attain a continual back and forth rhythm. This is termed the

pendulum swing because of its resemblance to the mechanical motion of a freely swinging pendulum weight on a grandfather clock. Again, we are emphasizing smoothness and rhythm of stroke, not wrist snap or ball contact, etc. The physical motion of the pendulum swing closely correlates to that of a golfer's swing, only the racquetballer obviously does not use his left hand to pull the racquet through. This is Step One en route to the three step forehand formula.

Two—The Wrist Cock Set Position. It was indicated in step one that the player is to initiate his pendulum downswing at some nebulous point hereinabove termed the "backswing position." To pinpoint this exact starting position of the backswing, one should begin with the racquet behind the head with a *fully cocked wrist*. That is, in preparing to start the downward pendulum swing the racquet should be drawn back in close approximation to the right ear with the elbow bent at about a 90 degree angle. Note this set position in figure 4-11. With your arm placed in this manner and the wrist in an extended cock, complete the pendulum swing and follow-through. The all important wrist cock will be expanded upon soon. Now

Fig. 4-12

A healthy step forward...

transfers body weight to the front foot...

and *power* to the ball.

you are ready to add the final step to the forehand pendulum.

Three—The Step Forward. In order to ensure forward body momentum concurrent with the stroke, you must step into the swing. The size of the step will vary with the leg length of the individual. As a basic guideline, pretend you are a batter stepping forward to swing a baseball bat at an oncoming pitch. The length of your racquetball stride will compare closely to this step within the batter's box. As you step forward, your left toe should point in the general direction of the right front corner of the court. In fact, through experience you will discover your front foot usually leads the shot, pointing to where you are aiming the ball. The lead foot step begins as soon as the racquet downswing from the wrist cock position commences. Your left foot should become planted in the new anterior spot at about the same instant the racquet swings past the left ankle. Refer to figure 4-12 if you still have questions on the step forward.

Thus we have the pendulum swing, to which is added the wrist cock at the top of the backswing, to which is added the forward step. These elements make up the three elementary building blocks of the forehand. (And, as will be learned later, the backhand too.) If ever during the course of undertaking the forehand swing the reader becomes smothered in details or otherwise confused, simply erase the hodgepodge of instructional garble clouding your mind and commence anew with the three basics. Now let us embark upon a more inclusive sojourn into this trio of forehand essentials. Keep in mind that we are still swatting just air, or at an imaginary ball. The actual ball will come into play soon, however.

Racquetball's forehand stroke begins with the *set position:* body in athletic position as described previously, racquet back and ready to begin the downswing and the wrist fully cocked. Watch any veteran racqueteer in a game situation and you will observe the first thing he does in preparing to hit a ball is to assume the set position. And he accomplishes this *quickly*, as soon as he realizes whether the ball will be

The Harlem Globetrotter of racquetball, Charlie Brumfield, demonstrates his forehand set position: knees slightly bent, torso rotated, weight on rear foot and wrist
cocked. Don't forget the wrist thong.

Fig. 4-13

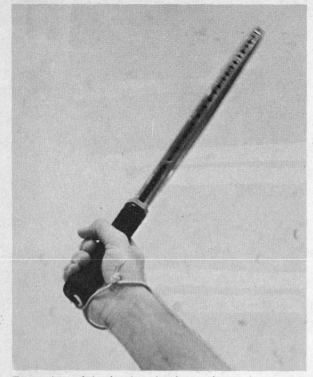

Front view of the forehand wrist cock.

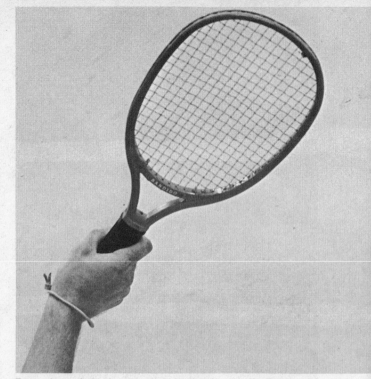

Rear view of the forehand wrist cock.

coming to his forehand or backhand. Now for the wrist cock portion of this set position. Have you ever wondered why the emaciated shrimp, who hangs around the YMCA gym hitting the ball for hours and then stands around unnoticed in some corner fermenting until the next court opens up so he can resume practicing, is able to blast the ball so much harder than you? His secret strength is really no secret at all—nor is it strength. This scrawny dude with the carrot sized biceps generates the power for his strokes from his supple *wrist*.

The best way to explain what is meant by the wrist cock is to simulate a baseball bat or golf swing at the top of the set positions. The right wrist on your racquet handle is laid back, or extended, in a cocked position as indicated in figure 4-13. This laying back of the tendons crossing the wrist puts you in legitimate position to initiate the downswing. The wrist is maintained fully cocked *during* the downswing until the head of the racquet reaches a point about six inches in back of our imaginary ball. Just as the racquet strings are about to explode upon the ball the *wrist breaks*, or snaps. This is shown in figure 4-14. And therein originates the majority of the power behind the racquetball swing.

There are two tests to demonstrate this point to yourself. The first is to take your racquet in hand and

Fig. 4-14

The *wrist breaks* forcefully precisely at the point of contact.

perform a normal swing without a wrist snap at the point of contact. That is, imitate the stiff-wristed tennis stroke. Listen for any audible swish as the racquet swings past the front foot. You will be disap-

Fig. 4-15

The "*swish*" occurs as
the wrist snaps at the
potential point of
ball contact.

Fig. 4-16

The racquetball may be hit hard...   by using only...   the power of the WRIST.

pointed for all you can hear is a gentle hissing noise as the strings pass harmlessly through the air. By comparison, now swing again, this time snapping your wrist at the bottom of the downswing. You will hear a loud, satisfying SWISH sound which indicates the racquet is traveling at a much greater speed at the potential point of contact, which signifies increased power when you start to hit an actual ball. The second test to convince the disbelieving reader that the power necessary to propel photon shots lies in the wrist and subsequent wrist snap, is a demonstration which Bud Muehleisen is fond of performing in clinics. Muehleisen, racquetball's premier National Champion, is a swinging testament to the power of the wrist. Drop a ball off the front foot and hit it at this point using *only* a full wrist cock and very little follow-through, in other words, do not take a back-swing, downswing or step into the ball. Surprise! The ball steams off the racquet as though repelled by a strong magnet. There, in the wrist, is the power. After this, all that is really necessary is adding a bit of timing in putting together the wrist snap with the re-mainder of the swing. (Note: utilizing the wrist as the main energy source eliminates hitting with the arm muscles. If your shoulder or upper arm is sore fol-lowing a workout then you probably are not employ-ing enough wrist action. See figures 4-15 and 4-16 for visual representation of these two tests.)

Fig. 4-17

Close-up of the *wrist break*...

which takes place at the bottom of the downswing...

which is off the lead foot.

You have now assumed the set position with the wrist fully cocked. You are prepared to begin the *downswing*. Do so in the pendulum movement, listening for the swish sound as you break your wrist at the potential point of contact. We have referred frequently to the "point of contact" without really defining this important area. The point of contact is where the wrist snaps, which for now is at a position knee high off the floor and 3 feet out from the lead (left) leg off its heel. The preceding is a whopper of an instructional sentence, packed with significant details. Let us examine it more thoroughly, referring often to figure 4-17 to correlate words with pictures.

The forceful wrist snap must occur exactly as the racquet strings strike the ball. Where is this point of contact in relation to the floor? It is *knee high* for now, until we start talking about kill shots. Where is this point of contact in relation to the body? The ball should be struck off the *heel* of the front foot. How close to the body should one contact the ball? Do not crowd yourself with a racquet swing that comes too close to your body, as this author once did in his tennis days of old. Neither is it correct to swing the racquet so far away from the body that the hitting arm is hyperextended in order to reach the distant ball. The ideal distance from the body that the ball should be struck is a compromise between these two extremes, or about 3 feet away from the body for the average height person.

At the risk of muddling the reader's mind with detailed technicalities, let us touch briefly on a couple of additional points concerning the downswing. As you move from the top of the backswing through the follow-through your *hips should turn* naturally with your general body motion. That is, your pelvis starts facing and parallel with the right side wall as you draw your backswing. (The pelvis may even be cocked slightly in the direction of the back wall.) As you swing the racquet downward and forward the hips should rotate to assume a position facing more toward the front wall, as demonstrated in figure 4-18. An anology might be helpful here. The pelvic twisting motion is very similar to that employed by the golfer swinging at a golf ball or batter coming around to hit a baseball. Charles Brumfield's potent forehand form stems largely from his extremely powerful lower torso. Although his upper body region consists basically of a concave chest to which are attached two chopstick arms, Brumfield's buttocks and upper thighs are blessed with massive musculature for quick dips and bends, twists and turns. Get a little hip into your swing for magnified power.

Another natural by-product of your downswing is *transfer of weight*. During the backswing most of the

76

Fig. 4-18.

In the set position, the hips and shoulders rotate slightly...

they begin to uncoil with the step forward...

they continue to "de-rotate"...

and thus bolster swing power.

Fig. 4-19—The forehand at racquet-ball contact. Note especially where the majority of body weight rests.

player's weight is on the rear foot. Weight transfer from rear to lead foot ensures the desired anterior motion of body momentum, which in turn is imparted to the ball in the form of increased power. See figure 4-19.

We have thus far accomplished the backswing set position, the downswing and contact with our imaginary ball. All that remains is the *follow-through,* which is relatively easy compared to what the reader has just waded through. The follow-through is the result of a good swing. If your stroke is true to form then your continuation of swing after striking the ball will naturally follow in the proper groove. Remember that you are not on a tennis court. Therefore, for the safety of your opponent and for a better strike your follow-through should not consist of a wide, roundhouse movement. Rather it should be more compact, low (about knee to waist high) and end up straight away from your body at about a foot and a half distance. Note figure 4-20. Keep a few helpful hints in mind: do not terminate the swing after contacting the ball, but follow through; do not roll the wrist over the ball, top spinning it as in tennis.

(Sidespin is more appropriate, as will be pointed out momentarily.) Do not follow through high and up toward the ceiling. Instead throw the racquet *through* the ball and follow with a level continuation.

Now add the *ball* to the above instructional format and swing away. Remember, if you become bogged down in details it is advisable to start afresh. Revert back to the basic three components of the forehand: the pendulum swing, to which is added the readying wrist cock, to which is added the step into the ball.

Now that the fundamental forehand stroke has been covered there are a few other related points which should be mentioned. These are many of the questions and concepts most frequently brought up by the beginner.

How does one "get down" on the ball in order to stroke it at knee height or lower? The only sensible answer is that it depends upon the individual's physical makeup. There are two ways to get down to contact the ball close to the floor: bending at the *waist* and bending at the *knees.* A short, compact player

Fig. 4-20—REAR VIEW OF THE FOREHAND STROKE

Fig. 4-21—FRONT VIEW OF THE FOREHAND STROKE

possessing the anatomical topography of a fire hydrant generally bends more at the knees, since he is built fairly close to the ground in the first place. The tall, lanky ectomorph will usually do more bending at the waist in order to get his giraffe figure down far enough to stroke the ball at knee level. For the majority of the racquetball populace, including most of the professionals, bending is done *both* at the knees and at the waist as in figure 4-21.

As one executes the forehand stroke what happens to the free arm, the one not wielding the racquet? Much like the follow-through and the weight transfer, the action of the free arm will be a natural movement not requiring much thought. Look at the sequence photographs of the forehand. As the swing begins the left arm either hangs loosely, fairly straight and relaxed, or it aids in setting the racquet face in the ready set position. With either method, as the swing is made note that the free arm follows the movement of the body to which it is attached.

Keep your *eye on the ball*. The eyeballs are the clue to one's concentration. What "they" really mean when they tell you to keep your eyes glued to the ball is that you should be concentrating. Watch a karate master muster his mind's forces to literally explode upon throwing a punch or breaking a board, and you will be witnessing total centralization of awareness. Similarly, note the intense concentration and eye contact on the ball in pictures of the pros-in-action. In real life, Steve Strandemo, for one, appears to be glassy-eyed as he intently focuses his large brown irises and dilated pupils on the rubber sphere.

For the tennis convertees in the reading crowd, you will have a few adaptations to make in transferring from your game to racquetball. The racquetball stroke is much more compact, without the roundhouse propeller type swing. The point of contact of racquet on ball is lower in racquetball, obviously since you are placing the sphere low on the front wall as opposed to over a net. But the most significant difference of all is the mandatory wrist snap in the four wall court sport. This is absent in the tennis stroke; because of the much shorter length racquet, the wrist in racquetball must come into play to a very high degree.

How hard should one swing at the ball? People who observe "The Destroyer," Steve Serot, in action are awed by the speed at which the ball caroms off his racquet. Some say Serot has only two pitches on the racquetball court: the fast ball and the faster ball. And, as Charlie Brumfield grudgingly points out, the opponent is obligated to pick up the latter of these shots on sonar in order to make a respectable return. " *His* racquet appears to resemble the exact model I use," witnesses to Serot's overwhelming power often muse. "So he must swing awfully hard to hit those bombshells," they rationalize. To the contrary, Serot does not swing that much harder than this author, who has been justifiably accused of hitting the ball so slowly that the label is fully legible as the sphere floats in due course to the front wall. Serot's devastating power is the result of exquisite timing, weight

momentum transfer, and wrist snap. Again, how hard to strike the ball? Clout the thing with about *80 percent effort. Do not tap* the ball gently on normal set-ups. You lose control if you guide rather than hit the ball. *Do not blast* it as hard as you can, for you are sacrificing accuracy for speed, and will end up with a sore arm to boot. Although it is a seemingly small point, it is truly of major importance: on almost all shots swing with approximately 80 percent full torque.

Remember, the *only* difference between the fore-hand kill stroke and the normal backhand stroke is that on the kill you must contact the ball lower—at ankle to mid-calf level.

Before leaving the forehand stroke there is one more item to cover; it is the question asked almost unanimously by the court greenhorn. Should the forehand swing be an underhanded or sidearmed one? This author strongly opts for the *sidearm stroke*. That is, the swing whereby the racquet handle maintains an almost parallel relationship to the floor throughout the "downswing" and follow-through.

Davey Bledsoe's forehand is one of the best. He lets fly this kill shot ankle high and right off the front foot. Weight transfer to lead leg is complete as the follow-through continues.

Almost all the top players employ the sidearm motion. To be sure, the game's most talented forehands belong to Bill Schmidtke and Charlie Brumfield, who adhere to this technique. Study the sequence illustrations of the forehand and notice how the racquet remains parallel to the floor throughout the swing. It is this author's contention that the sidearm stroke allows the player to break his wrist more easily than if he swings underhanded. By way of analogy, strive to imitate the sidearm baseball pitcher when you stroke the ball with your forehand. The pitch (or swing) starts with the wrist cocked. The sidearm movement carries across the body to the point of ball release (ball contact with racquet), at which time the wrist snap is put into play and level follow-through is continued. You will notice on the court that if you swing with more of a sidearm motion the ball comes off the racquet face with sidespin, as the photo in figure 4-22 shows. This English causes the ball to "wrap around" or speed up on the side wall-front wall kill shot in the right corner. Or it "digs" into the ground for a more irretrievable rollout on a front wall-side wall kill shot

Fig. 4-22—A *sidearm*, rather than underhand, swing puts sidespin on the ball.

in the right corner. On the other hand, the English resulting from the more underhand swing is often an undesirable "hopping" effect—as the ball hits the front wall and then the floor, it will rebound off the latter with a topspin hop rather than a flat roll. Therefore, make like a sidearm pitcher when you stroke your forehand and achieve more bottom board kills.

This has been a detailed explanation of the model forehand stroke. Adhere closely to the points emphasized in the instruction and experiment with the lesser stressed ideas. Remember, no one taught Brumfield, Muehleisen, Serot, Schmidtke, or this author how to properly scurry around a 20' x 20' x 40' rectangular sauna in our underwear swatting at a lopsided rubber sphere with a sawed-off tennis racquet. We taught ourselves the strokes without previous models or instruction. It had to start somewhere, as this book's dedication insinuates.

FOREHAND DRILLS

Words and pictures are of little use. Any athletic in-structor, despite his genius and his pupil's natural prowess, could expound indefinitely with little transmission from teacher to student. Do not expect to read this book, stick it under your pillow like an uprooted tooth and expect to gain knowledge via osmosis. The reader has hopefully acquired through previous explanation a general grasp for the model forehand grip and stroke. The next ingredient to add to the potential pot of success is *practice*. After this has been done the last requisite may be thrown in—actual game competition.

How to practice alone? All you need is a racquet, ball, court, and proper mental approach. Do not anticipate instant success but expect that gains will be made. When Charlie Brumfield lived in with this author in Michigan during the summer of 1971, he practically existed on the courts. Racquetball was his opium as he played 2 hours a day and practiced 2 hours a day, every day for 3 months. Brumfield used to go into the court alone and practice the exercises listed below, counting *100 shots* from *each* position for *every* drill. It is little wonder the bearded San Diegan turned out to be a national champion. If the reader is understandably less fanatical than Brumfield, playing mainly for fun and exercise, he probably will not desire to practice 2 hours per day. The point is that the amount of practice is directly related to the rate of skill improvement, which in turn is often directly related to the sum enjoyment extracted from playing the game.

Exercise 1: *Drop and Hit.* This drill is simple and self-explanatory but the wise beginner will not forego its execution just because it seems elementary. Standing about 3 feet from the right sidewall (for right-handers) and just behind the second service line, drop the ball and stroke it from *knee height*, not waist high —knee high. Strive to have your shots hit the front wall about 3 to 5 feet above the floor. Do not kill the ball—attempt only to make solid contact with sufficient control that the ball rebounds off the front wall and right back to you. (A drill for mastering kill shots will be given later.) How many times should you perform the drop and hit exercise from this position? Brumfield counted 100, your count will depend upon your time availability and the degree of your desire to improve. Twenty-five hits is a good number to start off with. See figure 4-23.

Now that you have soundly swatted 25 shots from position one, retreat a few steps backwards from the front wall (still stationed approximately 3 feet from the sidewall) to about the middle of the court. This is position two where you will hit 25 more shots. Then

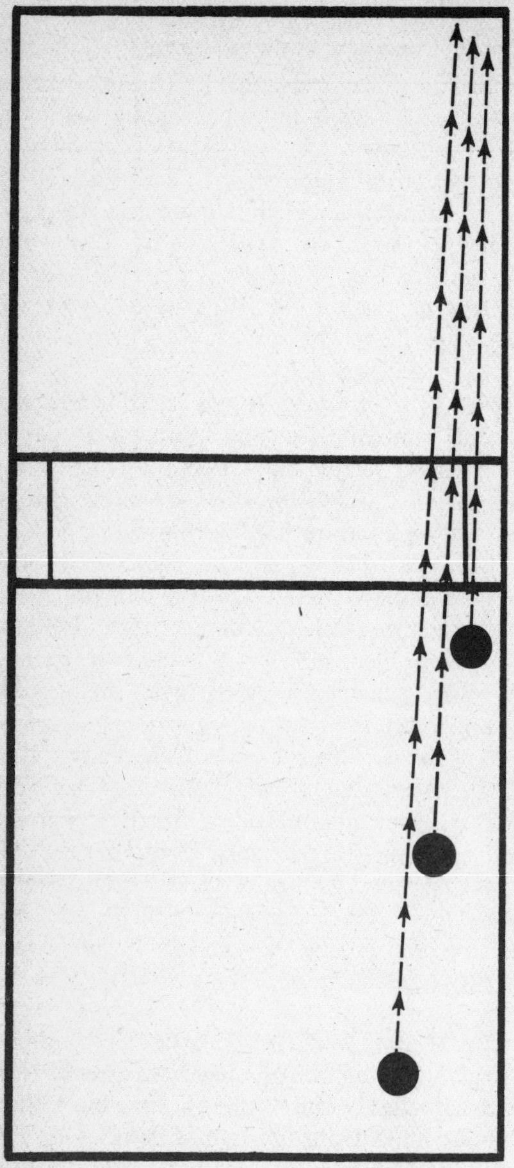

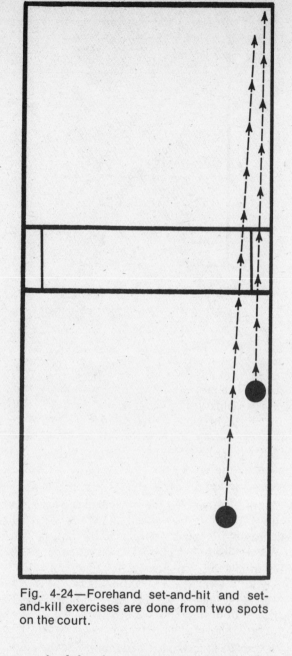

Fig. 4-23—Forehand drop-and-hit and drop-and-kill exercises are each performed from three progressively deeper spots on the court.

Fig. 4-24—Forehand set-and-hit and set-and-kill exercises are done from two spots on the court.

back up to within 5 feet of the back wall and clout another 25 from position three.

Exercise 2: *Set-up and Hit.* This drill is to be performed from two positions on the court and is a logical succession to Exercise One. From position one give yourself a soft easy set-up to your forehand off the front wall. Maneuver yourself into position to properly strike the ball and make contact with the racquet *knee high.* As with Exercise One do not attempt to kill the ball yet; the purpose of this assignment is to perfect the stroke and not bottom board the shot. The racquetball should again strike 3 to 5 feet high on the front wall and rebound to within

easy reach of the player. Do this 25 times and move back a few feet to position two. (Figure 4-24.)

After a few attempts at this second routine the greenhorn racqueteer will no doubt realize this is one of those "easier said than done" activities. The ball just does not seem to want to rebound off the racquet and subsequently off the front wall in the manner in which the author of the shot intended. Persevere— the ball cannot roll too far away, due to the confining four walls, so chase it down and try again. Keep in mind in performing Exercises One and Two that the goal is to imitate—not copy exactly—the model forehand stroke in making solid contact and touch control. Achieve these aims, perhaps, by slightly

CEILING

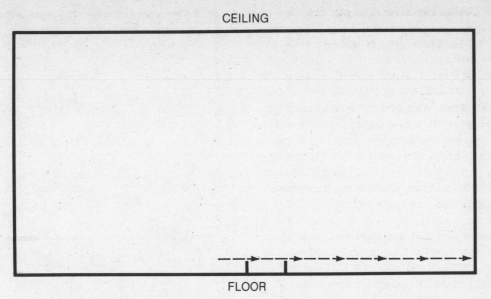

FLOOR

Fig. 4-25—(Side view) The kill shot strikes low on the front wall and rolls off with equally low rebound.

deviating from the model stroke described on previous pages. If a particular adaptation or alteration of the swing yields a walloping improvement, *experiment* further. Maybe you have found you generate more stroke power when contacting the ball a little posterior to the off-the-front-heel contact point demanded by the text. How about a little change in stance as you approach the oncoming ball? In other words, do not feel compelled to adhere rigidly to this book's picture-perfect recommendations. Ruminate and innovate.

If one thinks about it for a moment, it comes to mind that the only difference between the preceding drop and hit exercise and Exercise Two is that the latter requires a small amount of footwork. All the other parts of drills One and Two are identical. After executing 25 shots from each of the two positions you are adequately prepared to progress to Exercise Three.

Exercise 3: *Drop and Kill.* Now we are ready to *kill* the ball. You will be aiming to hit the sphere as low as possible on the front wall. The kill shot is to racquetball what the homerun is to baseball and the hole-in-one is to golf. The flat kill is the premeditated basis of the professional's game plan, but to the flailing novice it is more of a hopeful prayer. Therefore everybody and his doubles partner practices the kill, which is as it should be. The reader has already been informed of the mechanics involved in adapting his forehand stroke to the forehand kill shot. Re-read this carefully. Now practice the next two exercises until they become executive realities.

From position one (as in Exercises One and Two), simply drop, swing and kill the ball. Try to strike the front wall within inches of the floor. (Figure 4-25.) Catch the rebound as it trickles from the forehand corner and repeat at least 25 more times. Backpeddle to position two for 25 more and then to the third court position and drop and kill. The only difference between this drop and kill routine and Exercise One is the height of contact of the ball. In this roll-off drill try to hit the ball at about ankle or *sock height* (3-12 inches). You may even hear your racquet frame scrape on the hardwood floor as it carries from the backswing, to approximately ankle high contact, to the carry-through.

Top pro money winner Steve Strandemo hit thousands of these drop and kill series as he matured from fledgling hacker to feared howitzer. This loosey-goosey Minnesotan utilizes this exercise during the few days preceding important tournaments in order to ensure that his eye concentration, low point of contact, and perpetual motion swing are finely tuned.

Exercise 4: *Set-up and Kill.* This is similar to Exercise Two except the idea here is to take the soft rebound off the front wall, set-up, and bury the ball into the forehand corner for a roll-off. Once again proper footwork is mandatory as you perform this routine from positions one and two. (Figure 4-24.)

It is always advisable to try to acquire some *feedback,* especially as the drills become increasingly more difficult in later chapters. Some of the most helpful information can arise from an observer of your practice sessions. For example, it is astonishing the number of beginning players who sincerely believe they are striking the ball knee high when in truth their height of contact is at waist level, which is too high. Do not be afraid to question your critical cornerman. You may want his opinion as to whether you are snapping your wrist satisfactorily, or whether your weight transfer from back to front foot appears to resemble normal human coordination. Your helpful observer need not be a top "A" player, though the constructive criticism offered by a proficient individual is generally more highly revered.

If dedicating infinite hours to engaging in the above four exercises and the soon to follow drills sounds like great fun then the reader is advised he possesses the mentality of an advanced vegetable or that of a latent national champion; it is difficult to tell which. For the record, it *does* require a very different type of mind to go into the court daily and swat hundreds, even thousands, of the same shots over and over again. The factor limiting solo practice is not a physical one. Rather it is the mental fatigue which discourages most aspiring players from making like Charlie Brumfield and transforming a 20'x 20'x 40' sweat box into one's Walden Pond. *Boredom* is the killer—there are ways to stave it off.

You may want to vary your exercises to break the tedium. That is, work mainly on the forehand one day and the backhand the next. Or, practice nothing but defensive shots during one session, leaving the offensive kills for the next four wall get-together. Another means of sidestepping the repetitive doldrums is to figure percentages as you practice. Estimate what your forehand proficiency is from position one for the kill shot exercise. Compare this percentage of successful roll-out to the percentages at positions two and three. Or, how does your forehand kill percentage off the back wall compare to the same shot with the backhand? Or, see how many ceiling balls or down-the-line passes (in later chapters) you can clout in a row. Find the mean, median, mode and standard deviation; you can go crazy with figures.

For the less mathematically inclined, use your imagination to make racquetball practice a less dull routine. This author used to set up empty (pop) cans near the front wall and attempt to accurately kill the ball below a chalk line marked low on the front wall

Fig. 4-26—Racquetball version of "kick the can" makes practicing more entertaining.

and between the cans, much as a hockey player shoots the puck between the two poles of the scoring net. As an alternative to this ruse, you may want to stand a solitary can up in either corner and endeavor to knock it off base with kill shots. (Figure 4-26.) *Blast* the hunk of aluminum! One top player painted a brightly colored stripe on the ball to see if it was spinning off his racquet to his best advantage on ceiling shots. The possibilities are endless but do not kid yourself—practice, in order to make perfect, is long and monotonous. (Also see figure 4-20.)

These have been four very elementary drills (and hints on how to make them more enjoyable) in enhancing the beginning player's forehand strokes. If you have just returned from the court after performing these racquetball rituals and are satisfied with the results, you may proceed to the mirror image of the racquetball forehand—the backhand. Be content but not smug in having mastered the forehand, for the very same stroke which you have been patiently persuing will be utilized in upcoming chapters on the forehand pass shots and backwall play.

chapter five
BACKHAND

CHAPTER 5 SUMMARY

I. Backhand grip
   A. Rebuttal of the one-grip system
   B. Start with forehand grip
     1. Rotate handle ⅛-turn in hand. (Top of racquet toward front wall)
     2. Racquet face should be parallel with front wall
     3. Juncture of thumb and index finger should be on edge of handle
   C. Use of 'off' hand to facilitate grip change and set position

II. Backhand Stroke
   A. Two main differences from forehand
     1. Grip change
     2. Point of contact—slightly more anterior with backhand
   B. Assume athletic position facing left side wall
   C. Three-step procedure—without, then with ball
     1. Pendulum swing—imitation of left-handed golfer
       a. Backswing
       b. Body weight transfer in conjunction with hip rotation
       c. Uncoil hips
       d. Racquet handle passes nearly parallel with floor
       e. Follow-through—dictated by rest of stroke
       f. Strive for fluid movement
     2. Wrist snap
       a. Wrist cocked at top of backswing
       b. Wrist broken at bottom of downswing at potential ball contact point
       c. Listen for swish sound
       d. Point of contact near lead toe
       e. Backhand wrist snap is essentially forehand wrist snap in reverse motion.
     3. The step forward
       a. Ensures proper body momentum and weight transfer
       b. Toe will point direction of shot
   D. Combine the three steps for fluid backhand
   E. If backhand stroke becomes ungrooved, revert to left-handed golf analogy and three-step procedure
   F. Reminder points from forehand chapter
     1. Get into set position quickly
     2. Point of contact in relation to floor: knee high for passes, lower for kills
     3. Kill and pass strokes basically the same
     4. Point of contact in relation to body— about 2 feet away
     5. Body momentum important
     6. Eye on ball (mental concentration)
     7. Hit with approximately 80 percent effort

III. Backhand drills—identical to forehand
   A. Drop and hit
   B. Set-up and hit
   C. Drop and kill
   D. Set-up and kill
   E. Three-quarter court random set-ups
   F. Work on weaknesses. Practice what you know to discover what you don't know

Fig. 5-1—Close the racquet face for the backhand by turning the top of the racquet head slightly toward the front wall.

THE BACKHAND GRIP

The backhand grip seems to present more of a dilemma to the rookie racquetballer than any other aspect of stroke work. We shall *not* allow this here, as will be explained below. First a note on the one-grip system. Many beginning players use the same grip for their backhand as for their forehand. This is wrong, wrong, *wrong*. Of the top ten players in the country today, nine-and-a-half of them switch grips when going from a forehand to a backhand stroke or vice versa. Nine-and-a-half? Yes, the one-half exception is Steve Serot. This strong armed lefty retains the same grip when he is in front court and is forced to rush his shot. At all other times he switches his grasp on the racquet, as the other court superstars do. Therefore the possibility of employing a one-grip system should no longer exist in the mind of the reader. The major failing of this no-switch scheme is that if one uses a forehand grip to stroke backhand balls the resulting shots will "float" off the strings. That is, the racquet will strike the ball at a slight angle and it will come off with unintended backspin, less force and at a greater height than predicted. Use two grips: one for the forehand and one for the backhand.

Before continuing further it is mandatory that the reader page back and quickly review the explanation and illustrations of the forehand grip. This is because the backhand grip is the same as the forehand, with only a slight twist. Assume a normal forehand grip on the racquet now in your hand. Make the shift to the backhand by rotating the handle within your hand approximately *one-eighth* of a full turn. Assuming you are standing facing the left side wall ready to hit a backhand to the front wall, this means that the handle should turn within your gun hand such that the top of the racquet tilts *toward,* not away from, the front wall. The change in position of the top of the racquet is about 1 inch. Closing the face of the racquet, as such, eliminates the unwanted backhand floater. Look at figure 5-1.

If you have rotated more than one-eighth of a turn then the face of the racquet is overly closed and the ball when hit will undoubtedly be smothered downwards into the floor. On the other hand, if you have rotated the racquet in the wrong direction when shifting grips (that is, tilted the top of the racquet frame away from the front wall) then the racquet face has become overly open and a terrible slice will invariably result. Try it.

With the proper amount of turn (one-eighth of a full turn) in the correct direction (top of racquet toward front wall) one is assured of making solid,

Fig. 5-2—With the proper rotation, the racquet face lies *parallel* with the front wall at point of ball contact. (Steve Serot)

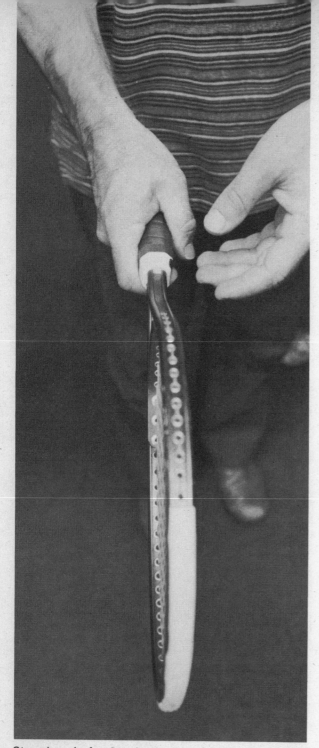 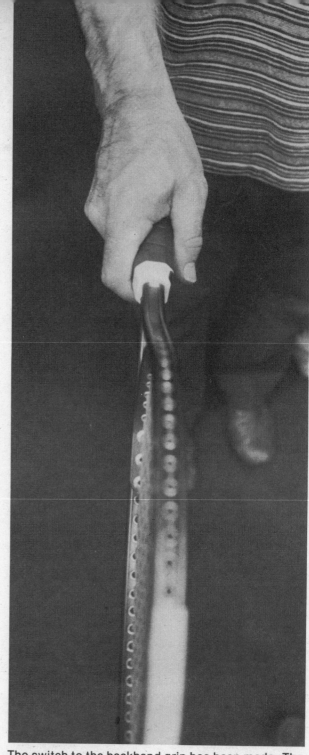

Strandemo's forehand grip. Note the trigger finger and the V-juncture of thumb and index finger on uppermost flat surface of handle.

The switch to the backhand grip has been made. The major difference here is where the V-juncture falls on racquet handle.

flat contact with the ball (since the strung face will be parallel with the front wall), which is what the grip is all about. (See figure 5-2.)

Still confused? Another way to explain grip change technique is to utilize the shape of the racquet handle and the anatomical joining of the thumb to the index finger as guidelines. First examine the handle of your racquet. If it is comparable to most, the handle is octagonal, having eight sides. Now inspect your hand where the thumb and index finger meet—they form a "V" in most people, as pointed out in Chapter 4. Assume the forehand grip, making sure the "V" is precisely positioned over the middle of the top-most flat surface. A quick glance back at the illustrations in

Racquetball's backhand resembles the left-handed golf stroke. Hips twist and right shoulder turns and dips.

conjunction with the forehand grip will provide clearer explanation.

Now switch to the backhand grip by changing the position of the "V." Do this by rotating the racquet an eighth of a turn within your hand so the racquet face is more closed, as instructed in the preceding paragraphs. Now examine the "V." If the correct amount of rotation has been performed then the thumb-finger "V" is no longer on the middle of the flat surface; it is right over the *edge* where the top surface and its adjoining flat plane meet. In other words our guiding "V" is over the "bump" where the two flat planes adjoin. Study the accompanying photos of the backhand grip and try it out.

You may presently be pondering the mechanics behind the actual turning of the racquet within your palm. Unfortunately the handle does not twist upon mental command. Some players facilitate the grip transformation from forehand to backhand through utilization of their *"off" hand* (the left hand for a right-handed person). These individuals do this by lightly grasping the bottom portion of their racquet

with their "off" hand and making the necessary twist of the handle to the backhand grip, as demonstrated in figure 5-1. This is not mandatory. Other players make the shift without using the additional hand. If you try this you should feel additional pressure on the thumb as you make the alteration. Try the grip change to the backhand with and without the "off" hand. Check the "V" to see if it has been done correctly. Now do it both ways with your eyes closed and check again. Practice until you get the feel of the racquet with its handle surfaces and the transition is second nature.

You are now armed and ready to hit the ball with the backhand stroke.

BACKHAND STROKE

Ever since the first primate descended from his lofty environment in the trees, took a stick in hand and started clubbing assorted articles for various purposes, man has been compelled by an inner urge to swat objects. Throughout history the swatting has been done with the forehand stroke. Who ever heard

Fig. 5-3—THE BACKHAND STROKE

Start with wrist cocked, pelvis turned and weight mostly on rear foot...

of a Neanderthal man clubbing the evening meal with a *backhand* stroke? Or of a lumberjack backhanding a redwood? This innate nature to always revert to the forehand swing is unfortunate, for the racquetball player must be able to swing *both* ways to be competitive.

Assuming the reader, descendant of that original tree-swinging ape, has satisfactorily mastered the grip change, we are primed to consider the backhand stroke. Furthermore if one is able to hit a sufficient forehand then the backhand should not be difficult to acquire, for there are only *two main differences* between the two strokes. You are already cognizant of the first difference, the grip change, and the second difference requires only a slight adaptation in the point of contact between racquet and ball. This will be expanded upon in a moment.

The player's body must be initially positioned correctly for the ensuing backhand stroke to flow smoothly and with power. Recall that when hitting a forehand, the body faced the right side wall. That is, the hitter's feet lay approximately parallel with the front

wall and his left side pointed toward the front wall. The same basic position (this is essentially the set or ready position) holds for the *backhand*, except one should face the *left* side wall when about to administer a backhand smite. The player's *right* side thus will be pointed at the front wall and his feet will be about parallel with that same wall. (This explanation again assumes the reader is right-handed. Reverse the "rights" and "lefts" if you are a southpaw.)

A good *athletic position* should be observed in this ready set stance: feet approximately shoulder width apart and knees bent a bit. Perhaps also a slight bend at the waist. Do not stand there posed as though rigor mortis is setting in—jibe the predescribed athletic position with whatever feels comfortable for your particular anatomy. With a proper backhand *grip* on the racquet handle, you are now fortified and ready to perform the same *three basic steps* which made up the forehand stroke. Do not use a ball yet in these practice swings.

One—The Pendulum Swing. If you can imitate a *left-handed golf swing,* you can almost be assured of an

as the downswing begins, step into the ball and uncoil the hips...

make contact with a wrist snap...

and follow through with weight now on lead foot.

ideal pendulum swing and therefore a powerful backhand stroke. In fact, at first put *both* hands on the racquet and pretend you are swinging a golf club instead of a racquetball racquet. Then try the following motion with the normal one hand grip on the handle.

Bring the racquet into a backswing set or cocked position near the left ear. (I employ the term "near" loosely because some players prefer a shorter backswing than others. If you have absolutely no feel for how far back to bring the racquet on the backswing, first look at the sequence photos in figure 5-3 and then experiment from there with whatever feels best.) In this set position of the backswing, the elbow joint will naturally be crooked at around 90 degrees and the gun hand's wrist will be laid back slightly in a "cocked" position. This is much easier to picture than explain so examine the close-up illustration in figure 5-4 at this time.

The *body weight* at the onset of the pendulum downswing rests mostly on the rear (left) footsie, as in the golf stroke. This rear displacement of weight is the product of the *lower torso twist*. That is, the hips are rotated around to the left (toward the back wall)

Fig. 5-4—The backswing ready position.

and the right shoulder is tucked just a tad. It should feel as though you are giving the front wall the "cold shoulder." Again, note this rotation in the picture sequence.

From the above ready and rotated position, the pendulum downswing commences. The coiled hips *uncoil* forcefully as the racquet sweeps downward. Simultaneously, the body weight transfers to the front foot. The arm straightens as the racquet flows by the lead foot which causes the racquet handle to pass *nearly parallel* with the floor. Let me emphasize that: THE HANDLE PASSES NEARLY PARAL-LEL WITH THE FLOOR. That is, the handle should not dip a lot so that it points at the floor; neither should it be slanted up at the ceiling. See figure 5-5.

The acceptable pendulum swing *follow-through* is dictated by the acceptable pendulum downswing. The follow-through should be fairly compact and low (knee to waist high) and level. Note that this is one contradiction to the golf stroke analogy, where the follow-through terminates higher.

The average beginner is apt to read the foregoing exposition on the pendulum swing and translate the

Fig. 5-5—Racquet should be approximately *parallel* (not underhanded to the floor at instant of ball contact.

words into a jerky body language. No doubt, each written sentence will become a separate movement to be followed by a pause before the next sentence—movement—starts. The resulting swing is like looking at a pendulum in a strobe light. Or, like viewing a movie that has been slowed down so each frame is separately distinguishable. Bad. The purpose of the pendulum analogy is not to induce jerkiness, but rather to emphasize a *fluid movement*. Therefore, speed read those instructional sentences until they blend into one continuous thought. Turn up the speed of that movie projector until the separate

frames merge into one continuous picture. This will smooth out those body jerks and pauses.

Two—The Wrist Snap. Now you have the fluidic carnal pendulum going. Back and forth, back and forth. Like clockwork. The *effortless power* generated by this body movement is delightfully remarkable. It is a human form of perpetual motion—but the best is yet to come. Now, when we add the *wrist* snap, even more power is engendered. The ball (when we add it to this scheme) will really smoke off those silicone-coated, monofilament, braided nylon strings. For the

Fig. 5-6—Close-up of WRIST SNAP at point of contact. (Above and facing page.)

moment, though, be content to swish just the air. Take the SWISH literally, for when the wrist is broken at the *bottom* of the downswing the racquet will move so fast through the court atmosphere that a sound like Superman flying past a phone booth will be audible.

As with the forehand, the wrist snap (swish) occurs precisely upon *contacting* the ball. For the backhand, this contact position is *near the lead toe* and comfortably away from the body. Do not yield to the common error of swishing too far posterior. Too, do not jam yourself with the stroke by swinging too close to your body. For the proper way to execute the wrist snap, study the close-up photographs in figure 5-6.

Speaking specifically of the wrist, it would be beneficial to re-read at this time the explanation of the wrist cock and snap for the forehand. Done? Now, picture the described motion in your mind, the same way you envision a piece of chocolate cake when you are hungry. Then translate this mental image into physical reality by doing it with your racquet. More specifically, we want to execute the *backhand* wrist motion. Run the picture of the *forehand* wrist movement *backwards* in your mind's eye. (It is just like running a home movie backwards.) Then do it backwards with your racquet. Congrats, you have just

performed the backhand wrist snap. In other words, the forehand wrist snap is an extension to a flexion of the wrist, while the backhand wrist snap is a flexion to an extension.

Add the wrist to the backhand downswing at the potential point of ball contact. Feel the power? Hear Superman whizzing passst the phone booth? We are now ready to add easy Step Three to the pendulum swing and wrist snap.

Three—The Step Forward. This step forward ensures *anterior body momentum* in agreement with the uncoiling of the hips and weight transfer from rear to front foot. For most people, the length of the step into the ball with the backhand will not be as long as with the forehand daddy-sized stride. Nevertheless, this forward step is very important. As your right foot advances with the downswing, your toe will point to where you are aiming the ball. Study the sequence photos again.

Okay. Combine Steps One, Two and Three to get *one fluid motion.* The pendulum, wrist and step should merge into a physical continuum. Did you ever visit Tijuana, Mexico, and look at the way they make tacos at those grubby street vendor wagons? Deft fingers apply catmeatcheeselettucetomatoeshotsauce in one incredible continuous sweep from bowl to taco shell to bowl to taco shell. Such harmonious

perpetuity in shelling a 3-second taco should be no more difficult for the racquetball backhand.

The left-handed golf swing analogy is important in teaching the model racquetball backhand. From the corresponding backswing, wrist cock and hip rotation to the corresponding downswing, wrist crack and hip de-rotation—all are amazingly similar with both sports' strokes. Do not be surprised if your golf game helps your court play, and vice versa.

Terrible backhand form...sometimes the game's lightning action necessitates getting the ball back any way you can. Strandemo probably won the rally with this flat-footed flail because Schmidtke is blocked out of position.

If, during the course of your stellar racquetball career, your mentally and physically grooved backhand inexplicably gets off track, do not despair. Just revert back to our left-handed golfer: get the image in your head and then convert the mental picture to body movement. And, in such times of backhand strife, remember that the three building blocks are the pendulum swing, to which is added the wrist snap, to which is added the forward step. Swat just the air a few times utilizing this procedure, then add the ball to it all and swing away.

The backhand stroke has been described in somewhat less detail than the forehand because an elaborate elucidation again in this chapter would have been redundant. The two strokes—backhand and forehand—are practically mirror images. (Except the grip change and the slightly different point of contact.) Therefore it will benefit your backhand to glance back over the highlights of the forehand chapter.

You may recall from the forehand chapter, for example: 1) The stroke starts with a set position—quickly. 2) The point of contact in relation to the floor is usually *knee high* for passes, slightly lower for kills. 3) The stroke is basically the same whether you are striving for a pass shot or kill shot. 4) The point of contact in relation to the body is about 2 feet away—comfort alters this precise measurement. 5) Body momentum is of monumental significance in generating sufficient power for the racquet-to-sphere energy transfer. 6) You can't hit what you can't see—keep the eyeballs (mental concentration) on the racquetball. 7) Do not daintily tap the ball nor smack it flailingly—hit the thing with about 80 percent effort.

Look for evidence of these seven points in the backhand sequence illustrations. Incorporate the text and the sequence photos with your own ability to become *one* with the backhand stroke. Sad to say, becoming one with anything from nature to buffalo chips to the backhand demands practice. Read on.

BACKHAND DRILLS

The importance of solitaire drilling in the court has been stressed. Now re-read the introduction to the forehand drills in the previous chapter. The major component of the aspiring hacker's training routine is *solo practice.* For when one drills alone in the court he can concentrate on one specific shot or strategy without the interruption of the other shots and strategies inherent to a game situation. The solitaire player also hits about *four times* as many shots in a given amount of time as he would were he playing against an opponent.

Getting down to specifics, the drills for the backhand are *identical* to those for the forehand stroke,

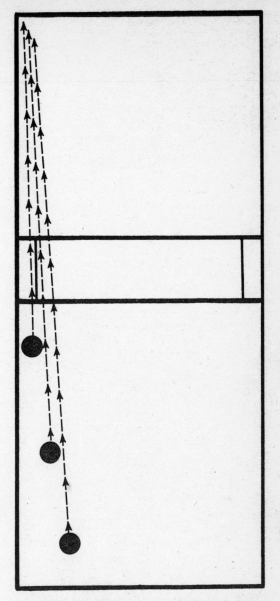

Fig. 5-7—Backhand drop-and-hit and drop-and-kill exercises are, as with the forehand, performed from three court positions.

except the player will be performing the exercises from the opposite side of the court. That is, the right-handed person will execute backhand exercises one through four on the left side of the court, and vice versa for the portsider. Review the four forehand routines presented in Chapter 4. Now, using the model backhand stroke presented in this chapter, lock yourself into a racquetball court for an hour or so and carry out the drop and hit, set-up and hit, drop and kill, and set-up and kill exercises. Refer to figures 5-7 and 5-8 for the two or three positions for each of the four workouts. Again, these are identical to forehand exercises one through four.

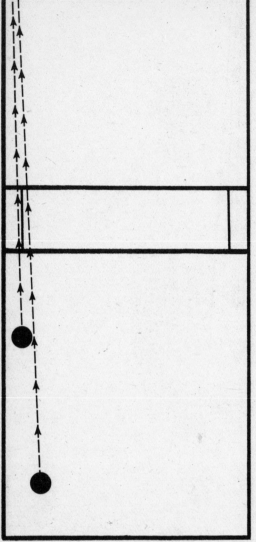

Fig. 5-8—Backhand set-and-hit and set-and-kill drills from two stations.

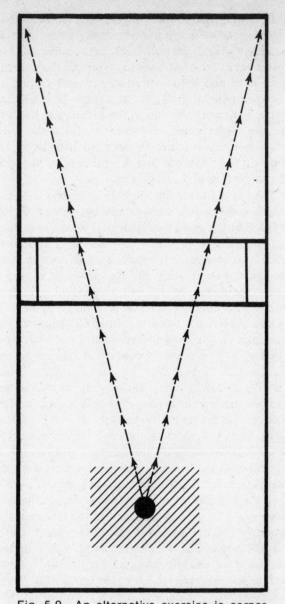

Fig. 5-9—An alternative exercise is corner killing with either stroke from three-quarter court.

To augment these four drills, you may find it beneficial and mentally stimulating to stand at three-quarter court and midway from either sidewall and give yourself a set-up off the front wall. If the resulting rebound comes to the right side, stroke the ball with your practiced forehand swing. Vice versa for a backhand set-up. See figure 5-9. When performing these exercises work to improve your *weaknesses* rather than spending the majority of time on your strengths. If your forehand is humming accurately and your backhand basically stinks, spend greater time practicing the latter. So what if you stink in practice; you will stink less in competition if you work on your personal court deficiencies.

A final encouraging word on the concept of non-competitive practice: There is one significant fringe benefit. Although you practice what you know and already can do, you will discover and conquer things you did not know and could not do.

chapter six
PASS SHOTS

CHAPTER 6 SUMMARY

I. **Pass shots**
   A. **Definition**
   B. **Four types of passes**
      1. **Backhand down-the-line**
      2. **Forehand down-the-line**
      3. **Forehand cross-court**
      4. **Backhand cross-court**

II. **Down-the-line passes**
   A. **Backhand utilized more frequently than forehand**
   B. **Use model stroke**
   C. **Point of contact knee to navel high**
   D. **Contact front wall 2-4 feet, 1-3 feet high from sidewall**
   E. **Use top or back spin**

III. **Cross-court passes**
   A. **Forehand utilized more frequently than backhand—is bread-and-butter shot**
   B. **Point of contact knee to waist high**
   C. **Contact front wall 2-4 feet high, 1 foot left of center**
   D. **Pool table analogy**

IV. **Pass drills**
   A. **Drop and hit**
   B. **Set-up and hit**
   C. **Perpetual drives**
   D. **Practice with partner**

V. **Common errors**
   A. **Hitting too hard—use 80 percent effort**
   B. **Hitting too high—aim low on front wall**
   C. **Not enough angle on cross-courts**
   D. **Contacting too high—strive for knee level**

PASS SHOTS

The pass is exactly what its name implies: it is a shot which is hit *past*, as opposed to at, the opponent. It is sometimes a defensive, and sometimes an offensive play. The pass may be used *defensively* to move one's rival out of center court position. An example of this is hitting a cross-court pass off a drive serve which has come to your forehand. You drive the serve past the opponent's backhand and he is sent scurrying. In this instance, the opposition is forced to retreat deep into the backhand back court, though you realize he will be able to make a play on the ball, and you subsequently occupy the now vacant center court. The pass can be a potent *offensive* weapon also. Many times you will catch your opponent in the act of "poaching," or anticipating, one of your kill shots. Frequently it is possible to outwit his strategic anticipation by blasting the ball by him as he is leaning in total commitment toward the front wall. Both as a defensive bread-and-butter shot and as an offensive

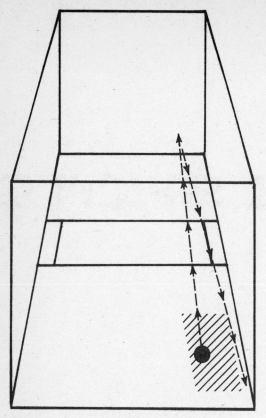

Fig. 6-1—Forehand down-the-line pass.

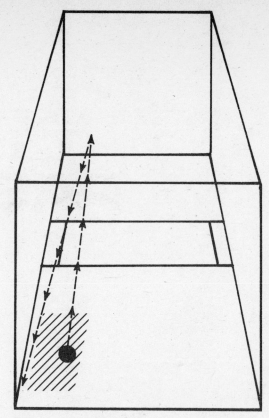

Fig. 6-2—Backhand down-the-line pass.

threat, the pass is a mandatory component of any serious racquetballer's game.

There are two types of passes, or drives, which can be initiated from the backhand side of the court, and another two from the forehand side. That is, there are four different possible drives: the backhand down-the-line, forehand down-the-line, the backhand cross-court and forehand cross-court.

DOWN-THE-LINE PASSES

The basic forehand and backhand down-the-liners are diagrammed in figures 6-1 and 6-2. Synonymous with the R.A.W. ball (run along the wall ball), the down-the-line pass is almost always utilized on the left or *backhand* side of the court. (As usual, it is assumed two right-handed players are involved.) Although beginning players should not entirely discount the feasibility of the pass hit along and parallel to the forehand sidewall, such a drive must be caressed with utmost precision or a set-up to the opponent's lethal forehand will ensue. In concurrence with this, rarely does one witness a professional player intentionally hitting the forehand down-the-line, although more than one pro has been observed walking casually

away after aiming for a low kill shot in the forehand corner only to have the ball rise, hit the front wall 3 feet high and run along the right wall for a winner.

A much more effective down-the-line pass is hit along and parallel to the backhand sidewall, and the reader is urged to devote a majority of his pass practice time to this particular shot. This, the backhand R.A.W. ball, is most often struck from fairly deep in the backhand back court. The stroke is the model one outlined in the chapter on the backhand. The height of contact of racquet on ball is *knee to navel high,* and the ball should contact the front wall 1-3 feet from the left sidewall. That is, it should travel in parallel and close to the left sidewall in its forward movement, rebound off the front wall 2-4 feet up from the floor and slide back along the same sidewall to backcourt. Note in the illustrations (figure 6-3) the point of racquet contact and the other important stroke mechanics of the backhand R.A.W. ball. Try it yourself.

Now that you have attempted a few down-the-line passes with the backhand, you have no doubt walked away disgruntled by the fact that your shots rebound off the front wall alright, but they unfortunately do not parallel the left sidewall for perfect "wallpaper"

Fig. 6-3
THE BACKHAND PASS.
The mechanics of the
pass stroke are essentially
those of the regular backhand stroke.

Fig. 6-4

Slice the ball with *backspin* to make it run along the wall.

OR *topspin* the ball...

to make it run along the wall.

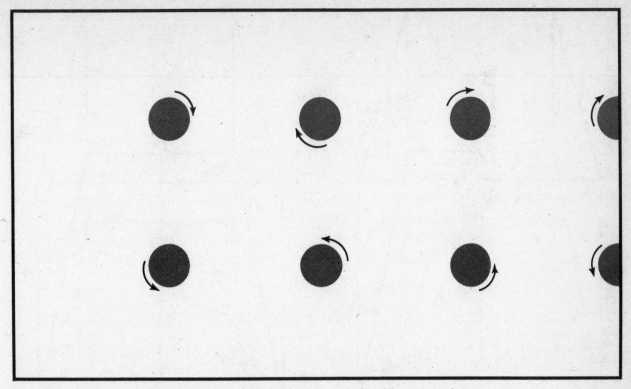

Fig. 6-5—(Side view) The top racquetball has been struck with a topspin or "closed" racquet face. The bottom ball has bottom spin due to being sliced or being hit with an "open" face.

shots. Instead, your shots carom off the front plaster only to strike the left sidewall at about mid-court. Your balls thus ricochet into the middle of the court for potential set-ups for happily salivating opponents. There is a simple secret—though difficult to master—to making the ball slide along rather than popping out off the side wall. The key is that the ball must be hit with *spin*, either with top spin (similar to the way a tennis player comes over the ball with his racquet) or with backspin (much as a squash player chops down on the ball in order to straighten its path along a sidewall). These two types of English may be better comprehended by referring to figures 6-4 and 6-5. Most seasoned racquetball players employ the backspin method, although the inexperienced individual is encouraged to experiment with both. Now attempt a few more down-the-line passes utilizing the paralleling effect of top or bottom spin.

Even with the use of spins, it is difficult to slam wallpaper drives down the backhand lane. The first player who masters the backhand R.A.W. ball will be the next to join Muehleisen, Serot, and Brumfield in the legion of racquetball super-heroes. And whoever learns to consistently execute this elusive drive shot with exactness will have done so because of spin.

Practice the exercises listed at the termination of this chapter, until at least with moderate consistency and accuracy, you are able to hit picture-perfect backhand R.A.W. balls. That is, strive for a drive struck knee high from about three-quarter court which rebounds approximately 3 feet high off the front wall and then skims along the left sidewall until it dies at the backwall.

CROSS-COURT PASSES

The basic forehand and backhand cross-courts are diagrammed in figures 6-6 and 6-7. The cross-court drive is often termed a V-ball in the racquetball vernacular because of the "V" letter design the ball's flight path makes from point of contact to point of termination. The V-ball may be struck with either the backhand or forehand. Obviously when two right-handed players are in court combat, the more effective shot is the *forehand cross-court,* since it is hit to the opponent's weaker backhand. Too, the more easily executed shot of the two is the forehand V-ball because the author of the shot is employing his stronger forhand to stroke the sphere. For these two reasons the forehand cross-court drive can be justifiably termed the "bread and butter" shot of our

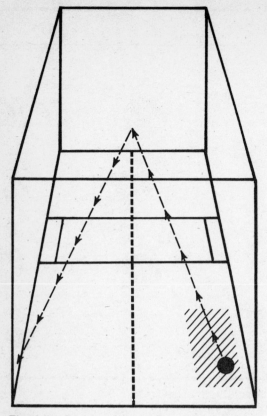

Fig. 6-6—Forehand cross-court drive (dotted line represents midpoint between the two side walls).

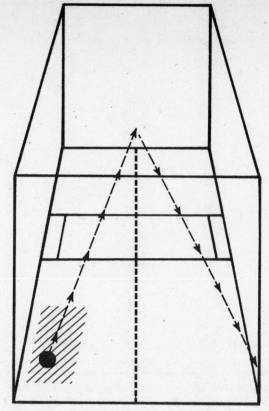

Fig. 6-7—Backhand cross-court drive.

court sport. The forehand cross-court is an easily performed shot with a wide margin for error and, most importantly, it may be used to return *almost any ball* that comes to the player's forehand (excluding a well-placed ceiling ball). Think of it, especially the beginning to intermediate aspirer: a shot to use on practically any forehand set-up on the right side of the court . . . bread-and-butter.

Although it may be initiated from closer to the front wall, the forehand V is more often hit from a more posterior vicinity on the court. The set-up for this bread-and-butter drive may result from a ceiling ball that comes up short, or a too-high kill or a pass which rebounds off either the side or back walls. Whatever the presentation, be prepared on any ball coming to your forehand to set and tee off with a slashing drive.

As with the down-the-line shot, the cross-court should be contacted with the racquet *knee to waist high*. Note: because of the high percentage nature of this shot, these limitations may be exceeded in many cases. However, it is generally advantageous to back up a step or two on the ball and stroke it at knee level. Propel the ball with your normal forehand mo-

tion, striking it such that it caroms off the front wall *2-4 feet high* and zooms past the opponent's outreached racquet en route to the backhand rear court. A few attempts at this shot should yield rapid gratification as it is perhaps the easiest shot to develop in the fetal learning stages of the game. (See figure 6-8.)

Now that we have tackled the forehand V, at least superficially, it is time to delve more deeply into this multi-purpose shot by presenting some useful hints. There are three "dimensions" involved in hitting the cross-court drive: how hard, how wide and how high. How hard will be dealt with momentarily. In considering the other two dimensions, how wide and how high, it is helpful to visualize the floor of the racquetball court as an oversized *pool table* surface. As you peruse the following explanation refer to figure 6-9. Now, how wide? Suppose the racquetball were a pool ball and you wished to propel it from the right rear corner to the left rear corner on a "bank" shot off the front wall. For this to occur the ball must bank off the front wall exactly in the middle, or equidistant from either sidewall. According to any pool hustler or geometry text, the resulting rebound will carry precisely into the opposite rear corner. There-

Fig. 6-8—THE FOREHAND PASS. Stroke the ball exactly as you would a kill (see forehand sequence photos in Chapter 4), only knee to waist high.

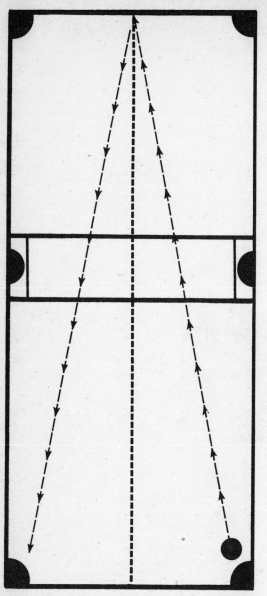

Fig. 6-9—Pool table analogy for forehand cross-court pass. Better to err a bit toward the left front wall pocket rather than right one.

Also it is much "safer" to err too far to the *left* than right, in considering the ball's point of contact on the front wall. That is, a ball hit at too wide an angle (let us say 2 feet instead of 1 foot left of center on the front wall) will nevertheless present a difficult return—the drive frequently "handcuffs" the opponent after ricocheting off the sidewall. To the contrary, an error a tad to the right—striking, for example, just a foot to the right of center on the front wall—sends the rebound directly at the opponent's racquet. This latter example is a suicide shot.

Now for the "how high?". It has already been mentioned that the ball should rebound off the front wall 2-4 feet high for the most effective cross-court pass. Superficially this is all well and good, but it has been this author's experience that with 90 percent of all racquetball players—from hackers to hotshots, their passes tend to *rise* as the ball jets off the strings. Therefore, the ball gains elevation after coming off the racquet face and strikes the front wall at least a foot higher than intended. Players with better controlled passes have compensated for this inherent miscalculation by aiming *1 foot lower* on the front wall than the actual desired height of contact. A *reverse* analogy here may be borrowed from the sport of archery. The avid bowman aims above the bullseye to allow for a natural fall in trajectory as the arrow whizzes to the target. The racquetballer should aim at a point *1 to 3 feet high* on a cross-court drive in order that the ball will slightly elevate during its course of flight to strike the front wall at the desired 2-4 feet off the floor. See figure 6-10 as a visual aid in understanding this concept.

If you have satisfactorily performed the forehand V-ball, move to the backhand side of the court and strive for the mirror image shot, as demonstrated in figure 6-11. As before, contact the ball knee to navel high, aim for 1-3 feet high on the front wall (the ball should actually rebound off 2-4 feet high) and aim at a point on the front wall midway or slightly to the *right* of center. Note: since you are now bidding to power the ball past your rival's forehand, it is helpful to aim for a *wider angle* pass. This is because the reach of the forehand to the side exceeds that of the backhand, as pictured in figure 6-12.

We have now covered the four types of passes: the forehand and backhand down-the-line drives, and the forehand and backhand cross-courts. Before presenting a practice routine for these, let us round out the chapter with a few additional highlights which encompass all four passes.

It was previously promised that the answer to "how hard?" would be considered. In this regard, passes are a bit of a paradox, since if you touch them

fore, the answer to "how wide?" is to hit the middle of the front wall.

That last sentence is made with slight reservation. Actually the sophisticated racqueteer will endeavor to hit about *1 foot to the left of center* on a forehand V-ball. (The exactness of this off-center target will vary a bit with the position of the opposing player and the spot on the court from whence the ball contact originates.) The left of center striking area on the front wall dictates a wider angled shot. This more obtuse angle ensures the ball will carry well beyond the hyperextended backhand reach of the groveling opponent.

The forehand "bread and butter" cross-court pass elicits an instant point or weak return. Keeley vs. Strandemo.

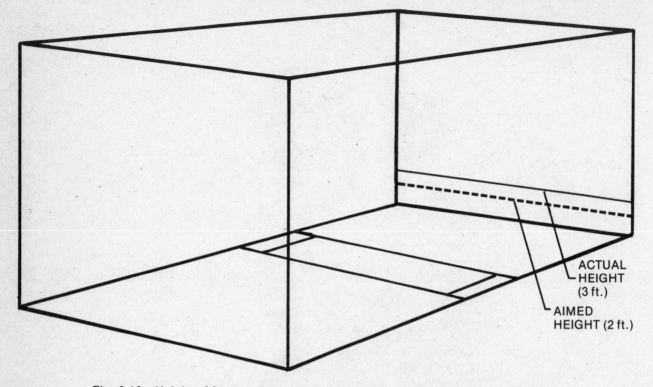

ACTUAL
HEIGHT
(3 ft.)

AIMED
HEIGHT (2 ft.)

Fig. 6-10—Height of front wall contact for most passes (about 3 feet). Aim lower than you think you should.

too lightly, they will not have enough force to carry past a well prepared opponent. On the other hand, if you blast them too hard they will surely rebound off the back wall for just as ill an error. It was noted earlier, and it will be emphasized later, strike almost all shots (including passes) with *80 percent power*. This ample force will impart sufficient momentum to the ball without sacrificing the crucial control.

By way of summary, keep in mind the purpose of the pass. It can be used for defensive as well as for offensive play. Therefore, do not worry if your intended rally-ending drive does not immediately win a point or side-out. If instead the pass forces a weak return, then an alternate goal has been accomplished. Put away that flimsy return by your adversary for the point or side-out. The passer must be a patient player as opposed to the every shot, hit-or-miss, flailing killer.

As has been demonstrated above, the two most effective passes (with two righties in court combat) are the R.A.W. ball from the backhand side and the bread-and-butter V-ball from the forehand side. The former is more difficult to control and usually re-

quires the use of spin, while the latter is an excellent shot to be utilized off most any forehand set-up.

On cross-courts, aim lower and wider than you think you should; on down-the-liners just aim lower.

When should one attempt a pass shot? This is a difficult question to answer simply, and the best solution lies in individual experience. This is not meant to side-step the issue; you will learn through playing and analyzing your strong and weak points when and from where certain drives work best for *you*. If Brumfield tried to employ Serot's drive shot strategy or vice versa, their games would go haywire and it would be a cakewalk to the National Championship for this author. As a guideline to "when?", it is not advisable to squander the opportunity of killing an easy plum ball in favor of a less offensive shot. That is, play aggressively and kill the set-ups in front court. Neither is it recommended to attempt a drive when off balance while stationed very deep in the backhand back court. In this particular instance a more defensive shot, such as a ceiling ball, might be wiser.

Hit a pass when given a set-up at midcourt that you

Fig. 6-11—Contact the backhand cross-court pass ahead of the lead foot.

Fig. 6-12—A wider angled cross-court pass to your opponent's forehand is necessary because of the arm's natural extension to that side.

are unsure you could accurately kill. Hit a pass when your opponent is leaning toward the front wall in expectation of a kill. Hit a pass if your ambition is to erode your opponent's energy reserve through the use of a punishing running game. Hit a pass as a change-up in order to alter the momentum or pace of the game. Some of the "whens" of pass shooting are shown in figures 6-13a and 6-13b.

Finally, there will be times when your pass shots, instead of rising off the racquet as per norm, actually will go as low or lower than you aim for perfect rollouts. Luck shot. In other instances, your intended kill shots will somehow ascend and evolve into picturesque passes. Luck shot. In such cases, play it like the pros: straighten that crack between your lips, elevate your nose rather than eyebrows, ignore the gallery's thundering adulations and strut sanctimoniously for the service box.

PASS PRACTICE DRILLS

Despite the immediately preceding paragraph, it is

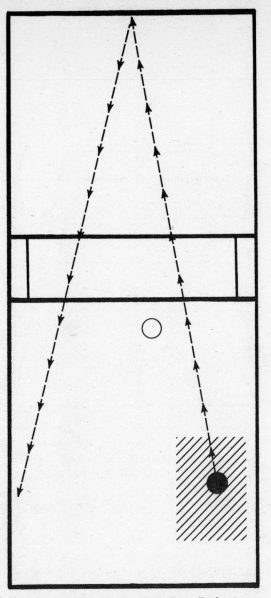

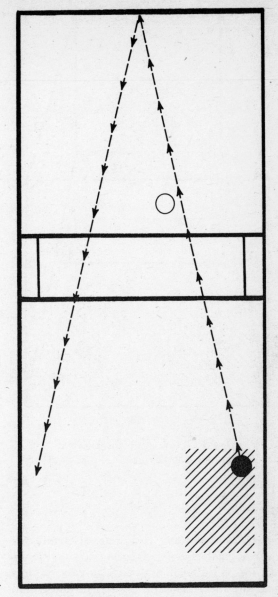

Fig. 6-13a—The two main "whens" of cross-court pass shooting: 1) When you are presented with a set-up in three-quarter court with your opponent in center court position and...

Fig. 6-13b—2) When your opponent "poaches" for an anticipated kill shot.

preferable to have your shots go where you direct them, rather than have a poorly struck bumper-ball accidentally develop into a lucky winner. The answer, as before, is *practice*. The drudgery is not quite so arduous for the pass shots as with other shot exercises, provided you are swinging a satisfactory forehand and backhand. In fact, the four drives are basically just these two strokes—given purpose and direction.

The down-the-line exercises are relatively easy to practice alone.

Exercise 1: *Drop and Hit*. Standing at three-quarter court about 3 feet from the sidewall (left side if you are practicing backhand R.A.W. balls and vice versa), drop the ball and hit a pass down the alley. Contact the ball, knee to waist high with top or backspin such that the rebound closely hugs the sidewall prior to dying in the rear corner. Repeat the motion the desired number of times from this position, then slightly anterior or posterior, as in figure 6-14. Satisfied? Now drop and hit down-the-liners on the other side of the court with the opposite stroke.

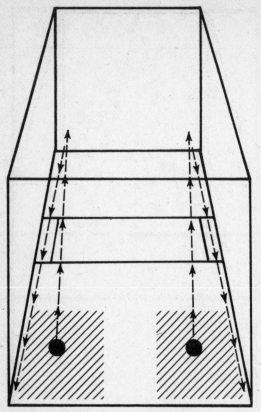

Fig. 6-14—Down-the-line pass drills. Drop and hit and set-up and hit from both forehand and backhand sides.

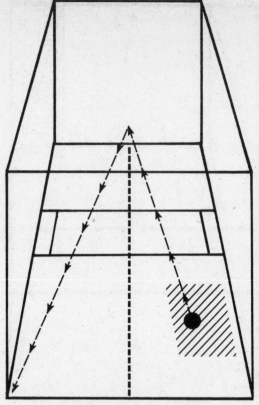

Fig. 6-15—Forehand cross-court pass exercises, for the drop and hit and set-up and hit. (Note the midpoint dotted line in this and the next three diagrams.)

Exercise 2: *Set-up and Hit.* Refer to figure 6-14; while reading the following repeat Exercise One, only strike the ball after it has taken an easy set-up rebound off the front wall. This is obviously more similar to a game situation. Catch the drive you have hit and repeat. When satisfied, go to the opposite side of the court, give yourself another series of set-ups and hit down-the-line passes off of them.

Exercise 3: *Perpetual Drive Drill.* This somewhat advanced routine is much more difficult than the previous two, but it is more fun. The object is to carry on a down-the-line drive rally with yourself. The better you control the elusive orb, the longer your rallies will last, and this volley count is a good measuring stick of progress. From the backhand side, hit continual R.A.W. balls to yourself, then do the same on the forehand side. The perpetual drive drill especially enhances racquet control.

The cross-court drive drills are next. These shots normally will be developed much more rapidly by the beginner than the down-the-line exercise sequence.

Exercise 1: *Drop and Hit.* Contact the ball about kneecap high and aim lower on the front wall than you would imagine necessary. The ball's path of travel is displayed in figure 6-15. Experiment with various angles, for example with wider or less acute V-balls. Hit with 80 percent effort for the optimal combo of accuracy and speed. Practice this exercise with forehand and backhand. (Figures 6-15a, 6-15b and 6-15c.)

Exercise 2: *Set-up and Hit.* This is fairly self-explanatory, but for help see figure 6-15. The most common mistake here is contacting the ball too high. Knee high is the key. Hit the cross-court drive off a variety of set-ups: soft lobs off the front wall, harder rebounds, short ceiling balls and back wall set-ups all should be utilized as practice set-ups for the V-ball. Perform from both sides of the court with forehand and backhand. (Again, see figures 6-15a, 6-15b and 6-15c.)

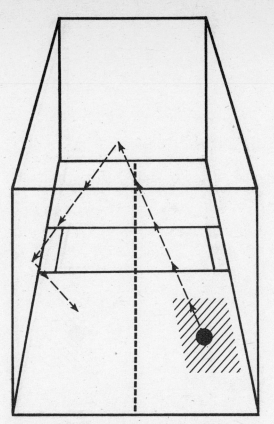

Fig. 6-15a—Same drills, only a wider angle drive is hit. Ball contacts left side wall at short line.

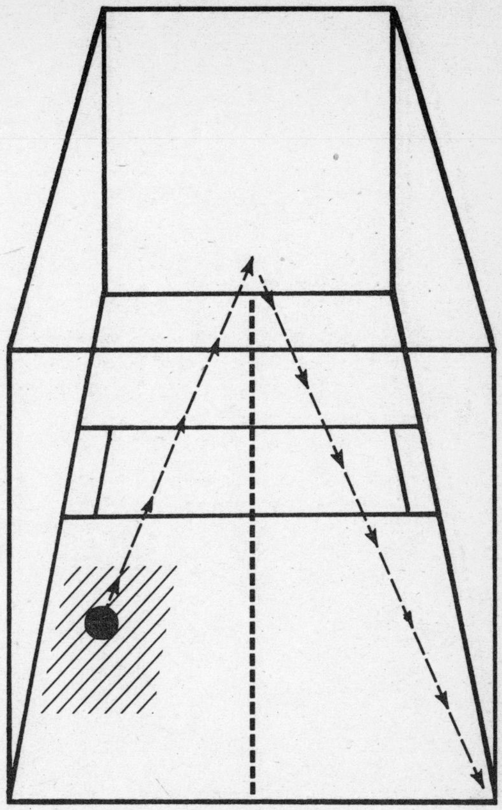

Fig. 6-15b—Backhand cross-court pass exercises.

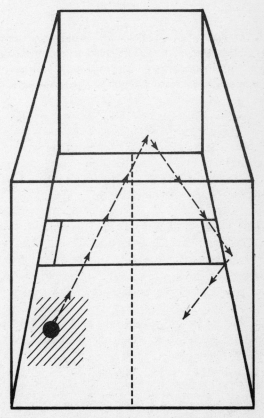

Alternate exercise: One of the superior methods of developing your drive game, after performing the above solitary routines, is to dig up a *partner* of similar ability who possesses a comparable mental capacity for entering a racquetball court specifically to bat back and forth a few hundred R.A.W. and V-balls. You and your partner in this exercise act as mutual ball returners in taking turns hitting the ball. Thus a practice drive rally is perpetuated. Strive for control rather than trying to bang the ball past your practice peer. This continual drive exercise works well for both the down-the-line and the cross-court pass shots. These pick-a-partner drills are diagramed in figure 6-16a and 6-16b.

In a nutshell of admitted redundancy, what are the most common errors in pass making? There are four of them which are almost universally miscalculated by court dwellers, even in the lofty ranks of the professionals. The first is hitting the ball *too hard*. Be an intelligent controller instead of a brainless blaster. The second is hitting the ball *too high* on the front

Fig. 6-15c—Wider angle backhand pass drills.

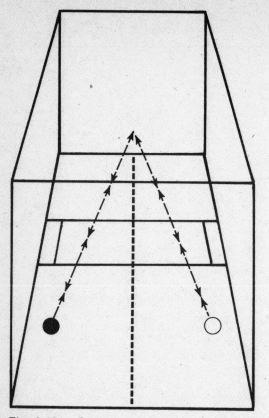

Fig. 6-16a—Perpetual cross-court drive drill with two players.

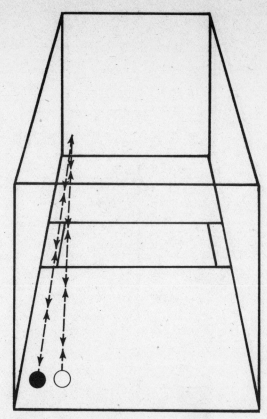

Fig. 6-16b—Perpetual down-the-line drive drill with two players.

wall. Remember, most balls will usually rise above the intended target area. The third common mistake occurs on cross-court passes, and it is not getting enough *angle* on those V-balls. Better to err with too much as opposed to too little slant. Finally, it is mandatory that the player contact all potential drives at a height no greater than above the waist, preferably hitting at *knee level*.

chapter seven
DEFENSIVE SHOTS

CHAPTER 7 SUMMARY

I. Three defensive shots
    A. Z-ball
    B. Around-the-wall ball
    C. Ceiling ball—most important one
    D. Discount use of lob as defensive shot

II. When to hit a defensive shot
    A. Rule of thumb—when it is unacceptable to
       hit offensive shot
       1. When out of position
       2. When off balance
       3. When in deep rear court
    B. Use defensive shot to recover center court
       position and to limit opponent's shot
       selection

III. Z-ball
     A. History
     B. Is an exotic shot—difficult to hit
     C. Important features
        1. Must be anterior in court and next to side
           wall to hit
        2. Always driven cross-court
        3. Always hits front wall first
     D. Bullseye—3 feet down and 3 feet in on front
        wall

IV. Around-the-wall ball
    A. History
    B. When to use—when in deep court, especially
       off of soft service and ceiling ball
    C. Hit it cross-court and strike side wall first
    D. Bullseye—3 feet down and 3 feet in on
       side wall
    E. Ball must not strike ceiling

V. Ceiling ball
    A. The major defensive shot
    B. Neutralizing shot—only return off it is
       another ceiling ball
    C. Bullseye—1 to 5 feet on ceiling from
       front wall
    D. Avoid contact with side wall
    E. Forehand ceiling ball
       1. Baseball pitcher analogy
       2. Tennis serve analogy
       3. Two swings—three-quarter overhead
          (recommended) and full overhead
    F. Backhand ceiling ball
       1. Golfer analogy
       2. Baseball hitter analogy
       3. Rotation and de-rotation of hips
       4. Regular backhand shot analogy—waist
          high contact
    G. Backhand more significant than forehand
       ceiling balls
    H. Common errors
       1. Healthy stride
       2. Forehand—snap wrist; backhand—
          body into ball
       3. Contact at proper height
       4. Avoid side wall contact

5. Most important—1- to 5-foot
striking bullseye
I. Front-wall-first ceiling ball—nonpercentage

VI. Defensive shot drills—use lively ball
A. Z-ball drills
1. Drop and hit
2. Set and hit
B. Around-the-wall drills
1. Drop and hit
2. Set and hit
3. Ceiling set and hit
4. Perpetual around-the-wall balls
(with partner)

C. Ceiling ball drills—spend most practice
time on these, majority on backhand
1. Drop and hit
2. Set and hit
3. Perpetual ceiling drill (solo)
4. Perpetual ceiling drill
(with partner)
5. Perpetual cross-court ceiling drill
(with partner)

VII. Center court-control important
A. Occupy center court position following
defensive shot
B. Defensive shots can be offensive shots

DEFENSIVE SHOTS

It is convenient, for the purpose of descriptive categorization and simplified learning experience, that there are *three* separate defensive shots. They are the Z-ball, around-the-wall ball and ceiling ball. Of these three, by far the strongest and most frequently employed among the better quality players is the *ceiling ball*. Therefore, after brief introductory remarks and superficial coverage of the other two defensive weapons, the ceiling game will be described in particular detail.

First, a fleeting word on the lob. It will be explained in Chapter 10 why the lob serve is not often utilized by tournament players in this day of the final (?) evolutionary age of livelier, less controllable racquetballs. For the same reasons, to an even greater degree, the lob should *not* be a part of a player's defensive repertoire. The only time this lofty, arching shot should be used is in a desperation situation where a reflex upward flip of the wrist is all one can muster to return a rival's well-placed ball. The only veteran in the game today who still employs the lob is one-time national champ Bud Muehleisen. Even with his precise control and highly developed hand-to-eye coordination, "the Mule" has found the lob to be less effective than other defensive choices. So if Muehleisen, as the best lobber in the game, cannot employ the shot successfully then it is illogical for us players of lesser capacity to even consider its use at all. Better to practice your Z's, A.W.B.'s, and C.B.'s.

When should one hit a defensive shot? This question will be dealt with as each specific shot is taken up. However a general rule of thumb to apply here is:

The time to go defensive is when it is unacceptable to smite a more offensive shot. This is not double-talk; re-read the last statement. For example, if during the course of play you are presented with an easy set-up somewhere in the area of the service box, the acceptable play would be offensively oriented. Do not squander offensive opportunities by hitting a defensive shot. By way of further example, if the ball rebounds off the back wall for a routine "plum," your choice of logical shots includes only a pass or kill. Do not go to the ceiling or for a Z or around-the-wall ball off a back wall set-up.

These have been examples of when *not* to use one of our three defensive thrusts. The time *to* hit one of these is usually when you are out of position (or your opponent is in excellent strategic position), off balance, in deep back court (figure 7-1) or so psyched out for whatever reason that it seems to make sense to play it safe. A portrayal is called for to explain this latter circumstance. As a greenhorn oozing with inexperience, this author entered his first tournaments psychologically hindered by any rival who strutted confidently onto the court in aseptic whites or otherwise color-coordinated gym garb. It did not matter that the well-manicured moron could not hit the front wall; he presented the image of a well-versed racqueteer who could clean this naive gym rat's clock. I overcame the deplorable situation by pounding the first 20 or so shots, wherever they came to me, to the ceiling. With this respite, my nervousness abated, I discovered my court foe was truly human and/or inferior, and I proceeded to clean his clock.

Continuing with the proper times to stroke defensive shots, an excellent instance in which to apply the

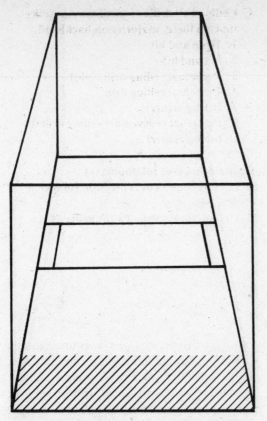

Fig. 7-1.—Shaded area depicts location from which most defensive shots originate. (Deep court.)

oric. Charlie Brumfield and this author were the first players of national prominence to employ the Z in tournaments. As the Brum and I unholstered this shot in the 1970-71 seasons against unsuspecting opponents, they (having never encountered the many-angled Z perviously) were tied into anatomical pretzel-shaped knots in center court while awaiting the ball's precipitous descent from the court's upper atmosphere. In eyeball popping muddlement, our competition waited for the rubber blob to come down . . . and waited . . . and when the racquetball finally did descend and rebound off the final side wall at a bizarre 90 degree angle, even the most grizzled court veterans were unprepared for the crazy "walking" effect of the spinning sphere parallel to the rear wall. The reader can well imagine the chagrin of nationally ranked racquetmen standing dumbfounded in center court as the ball came down and collided with their bodies instead of their racquets.

All good things must end. Imitation bred propagation of the Z-ball, and its recognition and use became widespread within a year. The Z has lost its surprise attack effectiveness because wiser players now simply step back in preparation for the abnormal bounce off the final side wall.

The name tacked on this particular shot is descriptive, although in its earlier stages the Z-ball was more nebulously referred to as "that weird shot they're hitting out in Southern California." Actually, Brumfield and I initially termed it "the Mouradian" shot, in honor of one of the all-time great paddleball whizzes, Al Mouradian. Later we even called it the around-the-wall ball, for lack of anything better, before the true around-the-wall ball of this modern era was innovated and named. Nowadays the Z is termed "the Z" by almost everyone (except Al Mouradian) because of the unique multiple zigzag pattern the ball makes after zipping off the racquet strings. This pattern is shown in figures 7-2a and 7-2b.

Today the Z can best be classified as an exotic shot. It is a nicety but not an expediency to have in one's bag of tricks. A perfectly struck Z is undeniably satisfying to hit. It gives back a solid, zinging vibration through the racquet handle. And the result is gratifying to witness as the returning player vainly attempts to scrape the ball away from the plaster of the rear wall. But a well hit Z-ball requires a simultaneous combination of racquet control, power and accuracy. A little luck is a helpful ingredient, too. Although it is utilized only a few times per game in singles play (it is extremely effective and more frequently used in doubles), its how-to-do execution shall be covered here.

A cardinal rule to apply in hitting the Z is that the nearer one is to the *front* wall and the closer one is to

around-the-wall or ceiling ball is when returning the serve. Too, the best way to return a good ceiling ball is with another ceiling ball. The Z-ball is sometimes employed as a change-up to return a shoulder high ball in the mid-court area. In other words, the opportunities to display your defensive prowess are endless, and experience will dictate when these opportunities actually do arise during a game.

In perusing the following shot descriptions, keep in mind that the fundamental concept surrounding defensive play is twofold: 1) Avoid giving your opponent either court position or a set-up. 2) Hit the shot in order to gain that precious extra second to recover center court yourself, as well as handcuffing the other player's offensive attack. Be patient and remain alert to capitalize on his first mental or racquet error. Let us now examine the main trio of defensive choices.

Z-BALL

When the Z-ball made its premiere appearance in the racquetball court in the early 1970s, its impact was astounding and its subsequent rise in use was mete-

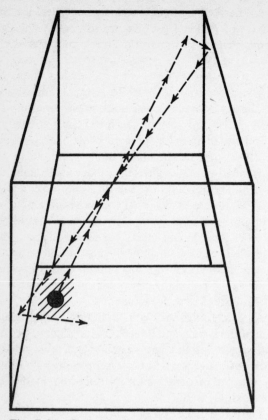

Fig. 7-2a—Path of the backhand Z-ball.

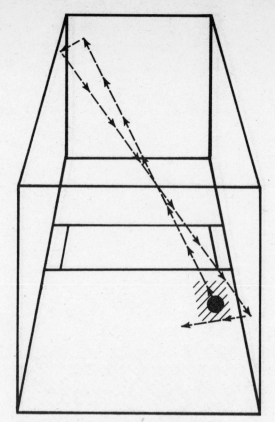

Fig. 7-2b—Path of the forehand Z-ball.

the right *side wall* (assuming the ball is to be hit with the forehand stroke), the easier it is to attain a satisfactory Z-ball. To prove this point to yourself, after reading the mechanics of the Z, enter a court and try to hit the shot from anywhere near the back wall. Then attempt the same from anywhere along the center of the court midway between the side walls. Unless you are Superman, you will have no luck from either of these positions; the player must be both close to the service box and near the side wall to execute the Z-ball, as in figures 7-2a and 7-2b. Also bear in mind that this three-wall defensive shot is always hit *cross-court* and must always contact the *front wall first*.

To hit the Z-ball with the *forehand* stroke, stand just behind the second short line and about 3 feet from the right side wall. Drop the ball well in front of your body and contact it waist high with a good deal of gusto. All you have to do is hit the bullseye on the front wall in order to reap an adequate Z. This bullseye is a spot approximately *3 feet down from the ceiling and 3 feet in from the left side wall*. Recall you are driving the ball hard and cross-court such that it strikes the front wall first. To stray from this general 3 feet down and 3 feet in target area (see figure 7-2c)

is disastrous and will provide your opponent with a ball that, although it will probably rebound off numerous walls and/or ceiling before finally plopping onto the hardwood floor, will almost always end up as a plumball set-up somewhere in midcourt or off the back wall.

Once again, the forehand Z-ball is designed to strike the front wall high in the left corner with sufficient angle and force. The ball caroms off the front wall and cuts quickly into the left side wall, laces high and diagonally cross-court in the air to the right side wall and rebounds off this at an angle nearly parallel to the back wall. (The ball should never hit the ceiling.) The ultimate goal of the Z-ball executioner is to place the ball a foot or so out from the rear wall as it carries out its paralleling, or walking, effect. The Z-ball is more easily explained than executed, and is more easily diagramed than explained. Again see figures 7-2a and 7-2b.

If the reader has deciphered the text and diagrams and found the description vague or unbelievable, enter a court alone and actually practice a few Z's. Do not at first become discouraged, for power and accuracy beyond the capacity of most beginners are requisites. Also try a few with the *backhand* from the

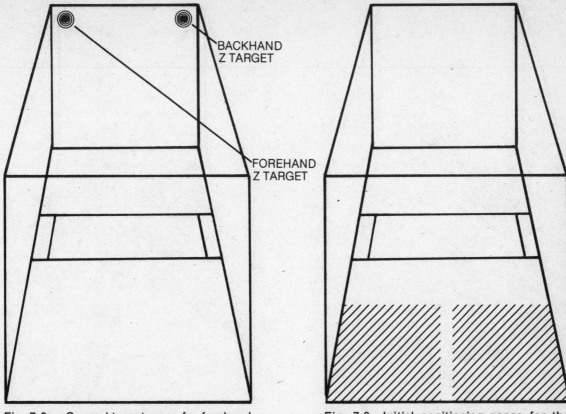

Fig. 7-2c—General target areas for forehand and backhand Z-balls. The precise bullseyes are 3 feet down from ceiling and 3 feet in from side wall.

Fig. 7-3—Initial positioning zones for the forehand (right) and backhand (left) around-the-wall balls. All A.W.B. shots are sent cross-court into opposite side wall.

left side of the court. (Figure 7-2a.) Next throw this zigzagging ploy at your partner in your next practice session. You both may be stunned by the results. It should be mentioned that the effectiveness of the Z drops drastically as the caliber of play advances into tournament level. Also, the Z-ball is illegal on the serve (three-wall serve), the rules stating that the served ball must strike the floor prior to hitting a second side wall in the air.

AROUND-THE-WALL BALL

Let us preview an explanation of the around-the-wall ball by comparing it to its close cousin, the Z-ball. The around-the-wall ball (A.W.B.) is not quite as effective as the Z but is much easier to hit, there is greater margin for error on its "bullseye" and it can be smitten from virtually anywhere posterior to the service box on the racquetball court. By further comparison to the Z, the A.W.B. is also always driven high and *cross-court*, but, unlike the Z, this shot is designed to strike the *side wall* instead of front wall first. Both shots have a place in singles and even

more application in doubles play. We therefore have the around-the-wall ball—a practical defensive shot which is quickly mastered and has a broad range of application.

Historically speaking, the around-the-wall ball came into tournament existence soon after the inauguration of the Z-ball, in the early 1970s. As in the case with the introduction of the Z, first time witnesses to this newer shot were astonished at the multiplicity of walls and angles involved before the ball finally returned to the floor. Would-be returners of the around-the-waller were flabbergasted by the aerial acrobatics and were discouraged every time they tried to home in for solid racquet return of the zigzagging, high flying sphere. Then, as with the Z, the court folk gradually caught on and it was back to the drawing boards for a fresh shot to buffalo the general playing public. Nonetheless, even today, the around-the-wall ball remains a fairly effective defensive ruse which compels the receiver to retreat from center court position, at the same time allowing the other player to fill that vacated premise. It is especially potent against

Fig. 7-4 —The backhand around-the-wall ball . . .   is a nifty change-of-pace shot . . .

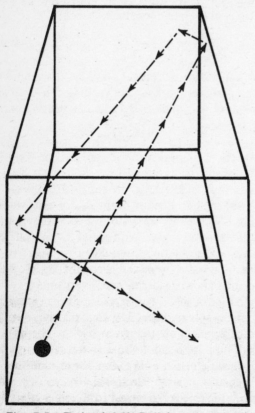

Fig. 7-5—Path of A.W.Ball from backhand side.

beginning and intermediate racqueteers, and is well worth adding to one's arsenal of shots.

The strategic time to employ this shot was alluded to in this chapter's earlier generalized briefing on ''when to use all the defensive shots.'' The around-the-wall ball is more specifically applicable in four situations: as a return for any ''soft'' service (e.g. garbage or soft reverse Z serve), as an alternate return off of a ceiling ball (especially a ceiling ball hit high to one's backhand), as a means of safely punching back up another A.W.B. which has been hit to you, and as a change-up tactic, to send back other shots from deep court.

How to hit the A.W.B.? The around-the-wall ball is usually struck from *deep court* (three-quarter court or posterior) as in figure 7-3. Let us assume for the sake of instructional simplification that we are going to learn the backhand version of this shot. This is also the more frequently employed stroke. Since the ball must be sent cross-court, as pointed out above, it follows that the backhand around-the-wall ball can be initiated from anywhere on the backhand side of deep court. This ''firing range'' is also pinpointed in figure 7-3. Thus stationed on the racquetball court,

that puts a little offense into your defensive repertoire . . .

as long as you hit somewhere near the side wall bullseye (**X**).

bounce the ball in front of your body and strike it with moderate power at about waist height. As usual, the point of contact is off the front (right) foot for right-handers. The racquet swing commences with a normal backhand ready position and arcs around in the same manner as a baseball player swinging a bat left-handed. This can be seen in the picture sequence in figure 7-4. The grip, stroke, step into the ball, weight transfer, eye contact with ball and other factors are the same as represented by the model stroke. All these should be familiar to the reader and should be natural motions in his regular stroke.

The bullseye to aim for for the backhand A.W.B. is a spot on the side wall (not front wall first) about *3 feet down from the ceiling and 3 feet in from the front wall*, as in figure 7-4. Unlike the precise target area demanded by the Z-ball, the around-the-waller allows one to shoot for a target area within a couple of feet either way of this 3 x 3 imaginary spot on the wall and still get away with a satisfactory shot. At no time should the ball strike the ceiling, a common error. (As an experiment in what *not* to do, hit a few around-the-wall balls including the ceiling in the combination of wall ricochets; it soon becomes ap-

parent why it is safer to miscalculate a little low rather than a little high into the ceiling.)

And presto . . . you hath struck your first around-the-waller. You have guided the ball properly up into those court heavens unknown and unseen by myopic four-wall spelunkers such as this author, so your task is completed. The ball will do the rest, in a manner most disconcerting to the average potential returner. The correctly placed backhand A.W.B. travels cross-court to strike the side wall high in the front right corner. Due to a side spin the sphere quickly "wraps around the corner" and steams off the front wall at many mph in a diagonal direction toward the left side wall. It contacts the left side wall at mid court about two-thirds of the way up and then angles downward toward the floor. Herein lies the effectiveness of the around-the-wall ball: Due to the snowballing sidespin from the front and two side walls, the rubber sphere plunges like a crazed boomerang directly at the receiver's head. He has one of two choices, neither of which is especially gratifying. He may tackle the ball directly out of the air, in which case he must compensate for the ball's top-like English and is thus forced to contact the ball about shoulder high—no offensive shot can be hit off this rapidly revolving blob of rub-

Fig. 7-6—The ceiling area between the front wall-ceiling juncture and the line on the ceiling (about 5 feet from the front wall) marks the proper striking area for the ceiling ball.

Fig. 7-7—A ceiling ball usually forces a ceiling return; thus a ceiling rally ensues.

Fig. 7-8—The forehand ceiling stroke closely resembles a baseball pitcher's throwing motion. See illustrations 7-9.

ber at shoulder height. The receiver's other choice is to allow the ball to bounce on the floor (a well-placed A.W.B. will hit the hardwood at about three-quarter court), in which case the ball's maddening antics are only perpetuated by its continuance to the right side wall in back court and subsequent "dying" with sudden descent off the rear wall plaster. Your rival therefore is damned if he does and damned if he does not, having to pick from the lesser of the two evils. (The catch is you must have hit the around-the-waller bullseye in the first place.) Figure 7-5 plots the above described flight course.

The around-the-wall ball does not react as erratically as the Z-ball, but it is easy to hit and is a compliment to anyone's defensive repertoire. The difficulty in the execution of this shot is paradoxical—it is tough to hit it deep enough to carry over the head of the opponent without having the ball rebound too far

off the back wall for a set-up. The A.W.B. is racquetball's wanderlust shot, exploring every corner during its trajectory. It is also the game's single most underused defensive play. But, is it the shot of the future which—as occurred with the rapid evolution of the ceiling ball—will knock the status quo court strategies topsy-turvey and send the game's bona fide technicians back into secluded practice sessions in search of a sure means of handling this multi-purpose shot? The answer is definitely not: however, the around-the-wall ball does precipitate set-up situations, does force countless panicked errors and can be worth extra points every time the reader steps into the concrete chicken coop to do racquet battle for a Gatorade wager.

The forehand around-the-wall ball is used infrequently because in the end it comes off the right side wall to the opponent's powerful forehand.

132

one shot is struck with less precision, accuracy and grace (even by some of the top players) than the ceiling ball. If the reader is a relative newcomer to this racquet sport, his visceral reaction to that last brash statement may have been something like, "absolutely ludicrous. Henry Hero, our local YMCA champ for the past 6 years, has been slammin' those ceiling balls lickety-split for as long as I can remember. After all, he's an old handball player too." Begging to differ, but back in the ancient era of wooden racquets, sweat-pungent non-gallery courts and diminutive trophies or T-shirts for tourney prizes, the lob or drive shots were employed in lieu of the yet undiscovered ceiling ball. The main reason the ceiling ploy remained obscured so long is because the deader balls of old would not allow the involvement of the "fifth wall." Only with the advent of the more highly pressurized racquetball did the game speed up enough to make the ceiling ball a mandatory component of any aspiring hacker's barrage of shots.

Admittedly, the ceiling ball is not all that easy to hit, but neither is it impossible to learn provided one can secure a fairly lively ball and enough court time to ensure solo practice for 15-minute sessions two or three times per week for a couple of weeks. All this work is to be for a primarily *neutralizing* shot. Yes, what the ceiling ball does is to put an effectual damper on any offensive shot. Can one repel a ceiling ball with a drive? A kill? No, and no. Not only is it impractical to offensively attack a well-placed ceiling shot, *the only way to properly return a decent ceiling ball is with another ceiling ball.* (Although as an infrequent exception in non-professional play the around-the-wall ball is a sometimes feasible return.) This concept will be repeated often throughout this text until it is drilled into the reader's ball-pocked skull. In a nutshell, although the ceiling shot is not the easiest, it is the strongest and safest defensive weapon in racquetball.

The ceiling shot is performed by striking the ball hard and directly up to the ceiling near its juncture with the front wall. The bullseye here is any spot on the ceiling which is *1 to 5 feet* from the front wall, as in figure 7-6. Any closer to the juncture or any further out than 5 feet results in a ball that comes up "short" in the court for potential cannon fodder. Ceiling balls are almost always directed toward the opponent's *backhand* side, whether you are using the forehand or backhand to make the shot.

After zooming off the racquet strings, the ball strikes the ceiling, front wall and then cannons quickly to the floor where it rebounds high into the air. This flight pattern is diagramed in figure 7-14b. The sphere does not come down until near the back

CEILING BALL

The "B" class to "A" class player division is bridged only after a satisfactory ceiling game has been acquired. If the reader is content to dwell within the crowded shadows of court mediocrity, then he may skip the following recitation and continue with the next chapter. But if he is of more tenacious character, willing to practice and desiring to some day enter tournament competition or at least beat the boss from work at noon hour, then this subject matter is geared toward him. For the ceiling ball adds an entirely new dimension to one's game.

If the Z-ball is "exotic" and A.W.B. a "compliment" to one's store of shots, the ceiling ball is the *essential* meat of any intelligent player's defensive strategy. No one shot has changed racquetball more, no one shot will affect the future game more and no

Fig. 7-9—FOREHAND CEILING BALL (Above and facing page). Pretend you are throwing a baseball with a *three-quarter* overhead motion.

wall and therein exists the innate safeguard: It cannot be returned by the opposing player from any other than a position in deep court and at a contact height of at least shoulder high. Note this typical return position of the racquetman in figure 7-7. The ceiling ball should not touch the side wall during its entire course of travel, except for a harmless side wall brush very near the back wall. If it does, it will invariably pop brusquely out toward the center of the court for a fatal set-up. (Exception to this rule: the rare wallpaper shot may touch the side wall as it skims up and down the line toward rear court. Now let us concentrate on the aggravating duplicity of the ceiling game,

for the forehand and backhand ceiling strokes differ sharply.

The *forehand ceiling ball* is executed most often with the overhand stroke. The grip is the same trigger finger grasp which has been employed for previous shots. The point of racquetball contact is ordinarily head high and approximately a foot ahead of the head, off the front toe. Enough for diffuse verbosity; an analogy here will replace a muddled explanation. The forehand ceiling stroke is practically identical to the throwing motion of the *baseball pitcher.* If you are an ex-Little League rawhide flinger, then this should be elementary. There are paralleling wrist

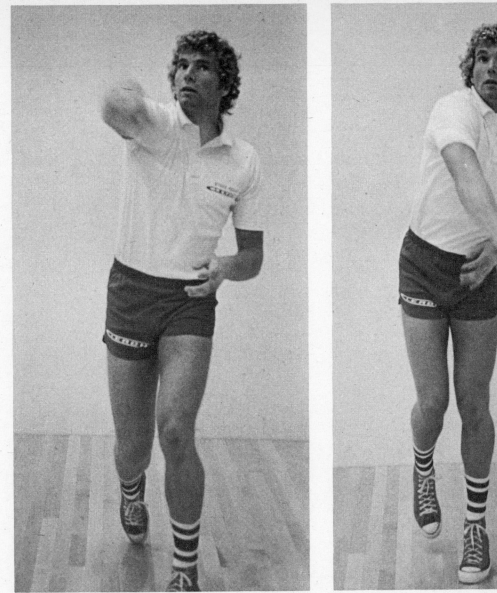

cocks, forward sweeping motions with the action arm, wrist breaks or snaps, forward steps into both athletic movements with corresponding weight transfers from rear to front foot, and similar follow-throughs. Review each of the subskills in that last long-winded sentence, because to leave out any of them during the stroke is to drastically reduce the power necessary to propel the ball over so great a distance. Without further elucidation, now refer to the photo sequence in figure 7-9, and attempt to emulate the demonstrator in these pictures.

The ceiling progress may be painstaking for many individuals who boast no tennis or baseball background. In fact, many readers will no doubt become discouraged and dejected to the point of giving up. If your practice strokes become a maelstrom of tangled appendages, uncoordinated spasms and emotional turmoil, then just relax for a few moments . . . recess time . . . relaxed? Now take on a fresh positive attitude and get on with the basics: Everyone has thrown something to somewhere or at someone sometime, so fall back on this inherent heaving instinct. Pretend you are flinging a baseball across home plate (which in this case is glued 1 to 5 feet from the front wall on the ceiling) with the benefit of an added pro-

Fig. 7-10—A *full-overhead* swing (above and facing page) may be used to return high bouncing shots. Compare this sequence to 7-9. There is little difference in the strokes, except the angle of the racquet at the point of contact.

pulsion device called the racquetball racquet. It is not that hard.

By the way, if the imitation of the baseball pitcher does not fit your anatomical fancy then pretend you are serving up a ball in tennis. The athletic movement of the tennis serve is here again fundamentally the same as the forehand ceiling stroke.

You say there are various ways of tossing a baseball? Agreed. Basically there is the full overhand pitch (similar to Joe Namath throwing a football), the three-quarter overhand pitch (which most of us

utilize in throwing objects) and the old playground sidearm. The first two of these motions are demonstrated with a racquet in figures 7-9 and 7-10. Most ceiling game greenhorns discover through trial and error that the most readily acquired method for ceiling play is the *three-quarter overhead* swing—this imparts a three-quarter slice to the ball (which makes sense).

Of course, the reader may choose and feel more comfortable with the full overhand swing, though this is generally not the case. In this instance, the natural English given the ball is a backspin or "feather

touch" which has the fringe benefit of causing the rubber sphere to bounce higher and farther into deep court. This too will be dealt with later. As an interesting sidelight, the *full overhead* is required when the ball must be hit with an extended arm reaching high over the head. This is because it affords a longer reach than the three-quarter swing. Finally, reserve the *sidearm* swing for passes and kill shots at ankle to knee height, but not intentionally for ceiling balls. Start with the three-quarter swing for forehand ceiling balls and later add the full overhead if desired. Leave the sidearms on the playground.

A how-to-do-it, literary portrayal of *backhand ceiling ball* is a hopeless task and will not be attempted here. Instead, the reader is offered a brief text sketch of the stroke mechanics, two or three analogies borrowed from extraneous sports and a comprehensive sequence of demonstrative photographs.

Begin by looking at figure 7-12. Examine these pictures as you have with others throughout this instructional manual—with microscopic intent and purpose. In addition, you will have to envision a left-handed golfer blasting a golf ball, and later a southpaw base-

Fig. 7-11.1—THREE-QUARTER
swing at point of contact.

baller hitting fly balls to outfielders. Got them conjured up? Continue.

Stand a few feet from and facing the left side wall near the back wall as in figures 7-14a and 7-14b. Drop the ball (or imaginary ball) off from the front foot and swing in a fashion similar to a *golfer* coming around on a ball that has been teed up *waist high*. To start the swing, the knees should be slightly bent and the racquet brought to a ready position near the left ear. Now rotate the hips to the left (toward the back wall) and dip the right shoulder down into a semi-tucked position. As the hips and shoulder move posteriorly, the body weight should naturally shift almost completely onto the back (left) foot. Done? If so, the human spring is coiled and ripe to explode in a twisting, forward striking motion.

This forward rotating movement into the ball is simply a matter of disassembling the wind-up gyrations described above. Reverse those movements quickly and smoothly: Twist the hips around to the right (toward the front wall) and shrug the right shoulder out of the tuck by stroking at the ball. The all-important weight transfer to the lead (right) foot is accomplished by this disassemblement, or "de-rotation," of the hips and right shoulder along with the step into the ball. Your body is now disassembled, de-rotated and about to hit the ball.

The swinging (right) arm has been kept rather stiff and extended throughout the stroke, although at the last instant upon blasting the ball the wrist may be snapped. The ball is contacted about waist high for now, but this elevation may range from waist to

Fig. 7-11.2—
FULL-OVERHEAD swing
at point of contact.

above-head high in actual play, depending on where the ball presents itself. Upon contact, the face of the racquet should be slanted backwards (open faced) in order to direct the sphere in an upward angle. If indeed this open faced position is observed, a back-spin or reverse three-quarter spin will be imparted to the ball. You have now completed your backhand ceiling stroke, presumably without personal affliction or injury during rotation or de-rotation. Try the shot or "shadow" it without a ball a few more times. If you are an absolute novice to the ceiling game, do not fret about inaccurate placement of the first few balls. Concentrate more on form and power.

The secret to either the racquetballer's backhand ceiling stroke or the golfer's waist high tee stroke lies within the popping of the *hips*. Study figure 7-12 and note the pelvic rotation and shoulder dipping as the player's weight shifts back to the rear planted foot. Farther along in the sequence observe the energy materialize as the swing of the racquet (with the pelvis *leading* the coordinated movement) and the lead foot stride transfer the body weight forward, and therefore communicate maximum momentum to the ball. It is coil and uncoil; wind and unwind.

Another analogy for the backhand ceiling stroke may crystalize the reader's present cerebral mix-up. Forget the golfer. Now hallucinate a *left-handed baseball hitter*. The motion of this hitter's right arm movement in swatting at a baseball is remarkably similar to that of stroking the backhand ceiling ball. Both swings commence with a ready position near the left ear in preparation for the forward eruption. The

Fig. 7-12—BACKHAND CEILING BALL . . .   the hips and shoulder rotate in preparation . . .

hips twist forcefully around with a corresponding front foot stride toward the pitcher's mound (front wall). Collision occurs about waist height, depending upon the height of the pitch (ball presentation). This contact is marked by a breaking of the wrist as the ball is smacked upward and outward. The baseball follow-through is fairly level, whereas the racquetball follow-through is carried smoothly forward and up toward the ceiling. Watch the ball right on to the racquet strings. When stroking the racquetball do not concern yourself with the positioning of the left arm. This non-swinging appendage should flow with the natural body rhythm. Got it? Scrutinize the picture sequences once again and particularly note the similarities between racquet and baseball bat kinetics.

There is a third analogy which may prove even more helpful to the reader than the previous two. The stroke for the backhand ceiling ball is the same as that for the *backhand kill shot and/or drive*, with one discrepancy. In going to the ceiling, the point of contact is obviously higher (about the waist) and the angle of projected direction for the ball obviously loftier. Everything else is the same and it may be ad-

vantageous to re-read Chapter 5 on the regular backhand model stroke.

The *backhand* stroke to the ceiling is much more significant than the forehand because among "A" class or better players 90 percent of ceiling shots in singles play are carried out with the backhand. It is logical that the reader should aim his backhand ceilings to his opponent's weaker side, his backhand. The smart rival will no doubt do the same right back, and in such a manner a backhand ceiling rally is spawned.

The forehand and backhand ceiling strokes have been covered. We come again to our regular feature, the "most common errors of the universal player" critique. Concerning the ceiling game, there is a series of oft-repeated blunders. One frequent error is not taking a *healthy stride* into the ball, thus leaving a good deal of the body weight planted on the back foot. This is a grim no-no, for a languid step forward precipitates futile weight transfer (or momentum), which in turn yields feeble power. Take a giant-sized rather than a baby-paced step. Other typical maladies afflicting the novice are not *snapping the wrist* on the forehand ceiling ball stroke and not getting the *body*

and then uncoil forcefully . . .

as the ball is hit waist to chest high, if possible (see sequence 7-13) . . .

and guided to the ceiling bullseye.

behind the ball (via emulating a golfer or baseball hitter) on the backhand. Concentrate specifically on these areas when drilling in solitaire. Another problem is contacting the ball *too high* on the backhand stroke. You should back up on any approaching ball—if you are able—in order to facilitate contacting it waist to chest high. (Of course, you cannot retreat through the ball wall, so in many instances the backhand ceiling shot necessitates hitting above the head.) Yet another serious issue characterizing poor ceiling play pertains to that pesky *side wall*. Do not allow the ball to pop off the side wall when going to or coming from the ceiling, unless it is on the cross-court ceiling ball which is angled into the rear corner side wall near its juncture with the back wall. The fetal ceiling shooter is advised to aim a little closer to the center of the court when sending a ball at the ceiling, rather than risk side wall interference.

The most disastrous error in this area is to *miscalculate the striking point* on the ceiling. Remember, our designated target tolerance for ceilings balls is 1 to 5 feet from the front wall. Nothing in the sport is more disheartening than to pulverize a ball with ex-

Fig. 7-13—Sometimes on high bouncers you must take the ceiling shot *above the head* . . .

get set as usual with pelvis and shoulders rotated for action . . .

as the ball comes within striking range, start to uncoil . . .

quisite timing and fluid grace, only to grossly miscalculate the bullseye and hit 10 or 12 feet from the front wall. In this instance the stupid sphere drops listlessly to the floor in the service box area for the opponent's rapid consumption. You can perform a multitude of things incorrectly on the ceiling and still salvage an acceptable shot; however, if you perform everything right *but* the placement spot on the ceiling then it is grab-your-buttocks-and-pray time. There are a few more rather sophisticated ceiling miscalculations mispracticed every day in ignorance by many of the even higher caliber court habitués. These subjects, such as advantageous and disadvantageous English, angling the ball into the corners properly and the question of power, are rightfully the subject of another, more advanced, text.

There is another item which must be covered superficially, if only to discount its reliability. The type of ceiling game which has heretofore been described has been the "ceiling-first" ceiling ball. There is also a variation termed the *"front-wall-first" ceiling shot.*

Here the ball traverses the court, incipiently striking the front wall, ricocheting upward into the ceiling, shooting rapidly to the floor usually within the service box area and then terminating with a lackadaisical arcing bounce toward rear court. The awkward angle of incidence required in hitting the front-wall-first ceiling shot dictates that it must be struck from a much more anterior position on the court than with normal ceiling shots. Note this striking range in figure 7-15. As can be seen, it is even possible to hit this corollary ceiling ball from within the service box, but it is unfeasible to make the play in very deep court. Examine figure 7-15 again and apply a little deductive cogitation in rationalizing why this shot is contradictory to the percentage-conscious racqueteer's way of thinking. We have been educated by this book to execute the most offensive shot possible under normal circumstances; a ball taken in midcourt should not normally be hit defensively; the front-wall-first ceiling ruse is a defensive play; therefore a more offensive drive or kill shot should supercede the

make contact way up there with a stiff wrist . . .

and follow through toward the floor (instead of toward the ceiling, as in sequence 7-12).

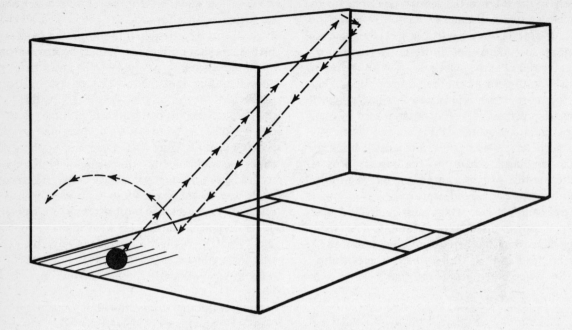

Fig. 7-14a—Initial positioning zone and flight pattern of the back-hand ceiling ball. Hit the ceiling first within 5 feet of front wall. (See 7-14b.)

Fig. 7-14b

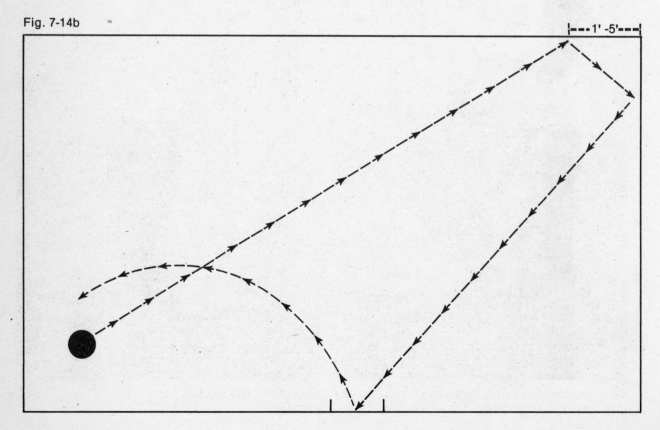

Charlie Brumfield's ceiling ball game is one of the best, though it is not apparent from this tournament photo. If possible, *step into* your ceiling shots.

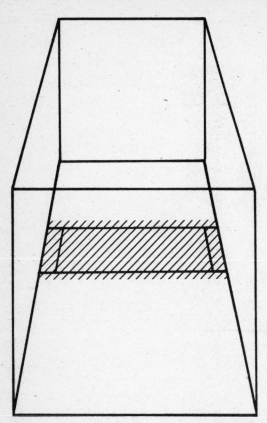

Fig. 7-15—Initial positioning zone for infrequently used front-wall-first ceiling shot.

front-wall-first ceiling shot's use. Skirting the fancy lingo, the front-wall-first ceiling ball stinks, in that it often does not carry deep enough into back court to prevent a set-up, thus catering to a kill-happy rival. Out of logic, hit the ceiling first.

DEFENSIVE SHOT DRILLS

Out of respect to your gun arm's musculature, your first act in preparing the *drill* on defensive shots should be to secure a fairly lively ball. Employing a mush ball to try to hit the Z, A.W.B. or ceiling balls is like attempting to polish pig iron, and the most valiant efforts will go unrewarded.

Z-BALL DRILLS

Exercise 1: *Drop and hit.* This is self-explanatory and its execution has been previously described in this chapter. The starting position for the backhand is just posterior to the service box near the left side wall; for the forehand it is at a similar station near the right side wall. Aim upwards and cross-court at the front wall bullseye, 3 feet down from the ceiling and 3 feet in from the side wall. Hit 20 or so balls with either stroke and calculate the percentage of successful Z's. Note again figures 7-2a and 7-2b.

Exercise 2: *Set and hit.* This resembles Exercise One but is more practical and more difficult. Instead of dropping and hitting as above, give yourself a soft set-up off the front wall which rebounds back to you about waist high in the general area indicated in figures 7-2a and 7-2b.

AROUND-THE-WALL DRILLS

Exercise 1: *Drop and hit.* Ready for immediate results and ego elevation? Try this relatively easy solitaire routine. The incipient positioning is indicated in figure 7-5, a very flexible area in general deep court on the backhand or forehand sides. From the backhand half, drop and hit cross-court twenty or so around-the-wallers. Then from this *same* position (on the backhand side) strike a few forehand cross-court A.W.B.'s into the upper front *right* corner. The right side wall bullseye for both strokes is three feet down from the ceiling and on the side wall three feet in from the front wall.

Now move to the forehand half of rear court and hit mirror shots with forehand and backhand into the *left* side wall. How do your percentages stack up for each particular shot? Recall that the forehand around-the-waller is rarely used and drill accordingly.

Exercise 2: *Set and hit.* This is a sterner trial of your around-the-wall capabilities. The striker's original positions are the same as above, as in figure 7-5. And the bullseyes are identical except they must be hit off of soft set-ups off the front wall.

Exercise 3: *Ceiling set and hit.* This is similar to Exercise Two, except your set-up here is a ceiling ball. First, hit ceiling set-ups to your backhand and clobber backhand around-the-wall balls. Then provide forehand ceilings to the forehand. If your percentage of successful A.W.B. shots approaches 80 percent then you are prepared to endeavor this ploy in actual game play.

Exercise 4: *Perpetual A.W.B.'s (with partner).* Now for the fun. Find a friend and dig your ground grabbers into the hardwood positions indicated in figure 7-16. The man on the deep forehand side starts things off by bouncing and hitting a cross-court A.W.B. into the left side wall. This ball should eventually end up in perfect position for the player on the deep back-

Some say Serot doesn't know what a defensive shot is—even when pinned against the back wall he shoots the ball.

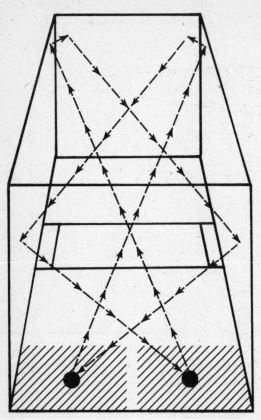

Fig. 7-16—A diagram worthy of a Chinese puzzle maker: The perpetual around-the-wall ball drill with two players. Easier done than diagramed.

Exercise 1: *Drop and hit.* The beginning positions for the forehand and backhand are in the respective rear court corners, as plotted in figure 7-17. Simply drop and hit a ceiling shot, and then catch the rebound. Repeat again and again with both strokes until your kinetics and accuracy are satisfactory. Review the highlights for the ceiling strokes to ensure you are adhering fairly stringently to the important model movements. The reader is once more invited to experiment with slight deviations from the text in quest of personal improvement.

(Note: Dropping and hitting the *forehand* ceiling shot presents a mildly sticky situation in that the point of contact for the "baseball throw" stroke is at least head high. Therefore you may desire to toss up (rather than bounce) and swat the ball to the ceiling in the same manner as a tennis player serving up a tennis serve.)

Exercise 2: *Set and hit.* Give yourself a soft set-up off the front wall on the backhand side of deep court (Figure 7-17) and smite a perfectly divine ceiling ball. Hips pop, ball is contacted waist to shoulder high in aiming at the ceiling bullseye, and your shot carries to the backwall. Right? All backhands (for right-handers) should be directed up and down the left side wall. After the big bounce into the backhand corner, catch the ball and repeat over and over.

When satisfied, perform the same routine on the forehand side, hitting the ceiling-bound sphere up and down the right line. Now vary the forehand exercise by hitting the set-ups cross-court into the backhand corner. See figure 7-18.

Exercise 3: *Perpetual ceiling drill* (*solo*). This is the single most beneficial defensive shot drill which one is able to practice *alone*. Start first on the backhand side indicated in figure 7-17 and hit a ceiling ball. If properly struck, it should come back to the backhand corner where you are to return it back up to the ceiling with another backhand. Continue this self-imposed up and down the line ceiling volley until you flub up. Calculate percentages, maximum records and averages if you wish. If the reader's tally for *each* rally is around ten in a row, he has probably achieved a ceiling touch comparable to that of the better professionals. This arbitrary figure of ten provides the enthusiast with something to shoot for. It requires that each ceiling shot closely hug the left side wall and carry deep enough into back court, and that continuous backhand returns are obligatory. In other words, each shot must be a "good" ceiling ball for your count to be meaningful.

Practice the same routine with an endless barrage

hand side to return with a cross-court around-the-waller into the right side wall. Another A.W.B. is sent flying from the right sider, and so on back and forth. Either player may employ his backhand or forehand; the only requirement is that all returns must be A.W.B.'s.

Now switch sides to gain overall court experience. Make a game of it and see which of you commits ten errors first. Or, keep track of the total around-the-wallers in each rally, striving to outdo the prior record number.

Besides the foregoing foursome of A.W.B. routines, the reader is encouraged to innovate his own drills, either solo or using a partner. The possibilities are endless.

CEILING BALL DRILLS

Remember, this is the most relevant of all defensive shots and hence deserves proportionally greater practice time. Fortunately, the ceiling ball is ideally suited for solitaire practice.

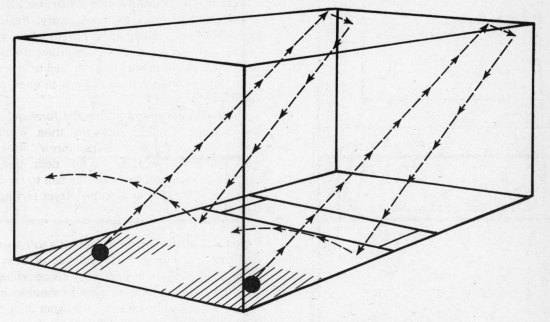

Fig. 7-17—The forehand and backhand down-the-line ceiling balls.

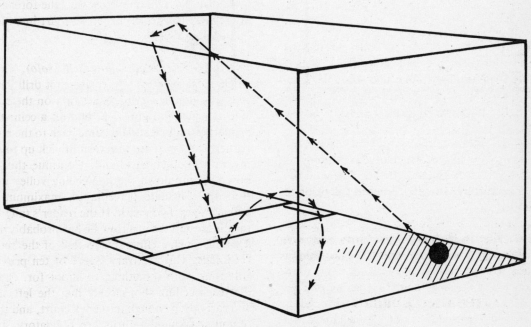

Fig. 7-18—Forehand cross-court ceiling shot.

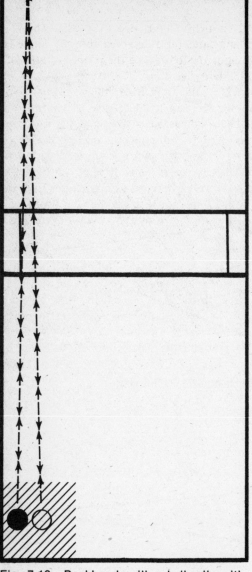

Fig. 7-19—Backhand ceiling ball rally with two players: The single best defensive shot exercise.

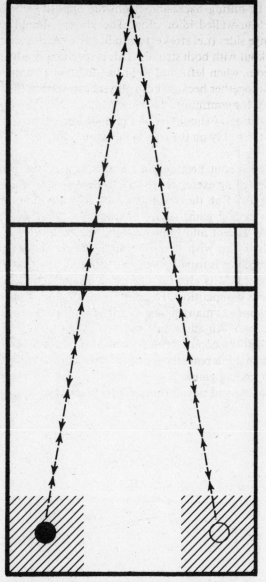

Fig. 7-20—Perpetual cross-court ceiling ball routine with two players. (Especially beneficial for a righty and lefty.)

of ceiling shots up and down the *forehand* alley, as in figure 7-17.

Exercise 4: *Perpetual ceiling drill (with partner).* Time again to pick a partner with a shared fanatic compulsion toward perfunctory practice. This exercise is very much the same as the foregoing one except *two* players here must alternate returning ceiling balls to each other up and down the backhand and forehand lines. To make the routine more enthralling, do as with the perpetual around-the-wall drill and perform mathematical gymnastics with each rally total. If you have to, make it a contest and bet a

nickel on each series of shots. If Exercise Three is the most beneficial defensive drill in solitaire, this partnership exercise arrangement makes for the most profitable defensive workout with another player. The starting positions are diagrammed in figure 7-19.

Exercise 5: *Perpetual cross-court ceiling drill (with partner).* If the reader is not already body-weary from the prior ceiling practice, this one should send him scurrying for the I.V. Gatorade. Here the two players alternately hit ceiling balls cross-court to each other. Obviously one man will be stroking almost all forehands from the forehand corner, and the other will be hitting backhands from the opposite side of the four-walled idiot coop. The players should exchange sides (i.e. strokes) periodically so each gains a workout with both strokes. This is specifically advantageous when left- and right-handed court rompers joust together because both players can station themselves for continuous *backhand* rallies. (In this case, the southpaw should be on the right side of the court and the righty on the left, as in figure 7-20.)

Talk about beating your brains against the wall; these ceiling exercises are sure to deplete your energy reserves. But they will also dramatically improve your ceiling game and, consequently, your overall game. Invent and improve upon the battery of five drills if you wish. Keep in mind that the backhand ceiling shot is usually the more difficult stroke to acquire, but it is also the one more often employed in serious competition. Therefore, spend about four or five times as many hours on this as compared to the forehand. An additional word to the wise: The ceiling ball is a copious component of doubles play and as such it is a realistic use of practice time to enhance your ceiling game. If at all possible, choose to play the backhand side during doubles practice in order to facilitate the sophistication of this more pertinent stroke.

Had enough? Climb out of those sweaty jock straps and tutus for a deserved shower. There is always tomorrow to practice the proper *returns* off of the three defensive shots.

The Z . . . the A.W.B. . . the ceiling ball. Now, a final word on racquetball defense. After one pounds a satisfactory defensive shot in a game, it is imperative for him to subsequently occupy *center court position*. Usually his ball is countered with yet another defensive shot, the control of center court exchanges, another defensive shot ensues and so on with his cat-and-mouse continuum until one of two actions transpires: Either a poorly hit defensive shot results in a set-up for the other player, or a well struck defensive shot forces an ace or weak return.

Which unearths further subtle reasoning. As the old football adage suggests, the best offense is a good defense. Rehearse your around-the-wall, Z and ceiling balls until they border upon offensive shots. A proficient racquetballer deals a blend of offensive gambits as well as defensive counters, such that it becomes increasingly difficult to differentiate which is which.

BACK WALL PLAY

CHAPTER 8 SUMMARY

I. **Back wall play**
  A. Footwork is the key
  B. Player's directional movement same as ball's
  C. Two styles of playing ball off back wall
    1. Stop-and-step
    2. Jog-and-hit (stop-and-three-step)
  D. Sideways shuffle when pursuing ball to back court

II. **Back wall drills**
  A. Shadow play—start 3 feet behind service box
  B. Toss and hit
  C. Hard set and hit—start 3 feet behind service box
  D. Soft set and hit—start 3 feet behind service box

III. **Three common back wall errors**
  A. Point of contact off lead foot—retreat close to back wall prior to stepping into ball
  B. Healthy step into ball to generate momentum
  C. Watch the ball

IV. **Back wall variations**
  A. Front wall to back wall to floor—return with offensive shot
  B. Front wall to back wall to floor to front wall—return with "dump"

V. **Shot selection off back wall—usually offensive**
  A. Drive shot
  B. Kill shot

BACK WALL PLAY

A unique situation, which is especially indigenous to our four-walled court sport, occurs when the racquetball rebounds off the back wall. This is the only time during the course of a rally that the ball travels *with* the racquet's swing toward the front wall. Such a situation begets *power*. In scientific jargon, the summation of the ball's force vector plus the racquet's force vector yields a more powerful—and, as will be seen, an easier—shot than is possible in any other instance. Even to the non-physicist racquetman, back wall play should become a strong point in his game.

Assuming one's swing is in tip-top form, the secret here is the *footwork*. The addition of proper footwork to a satisfactory stroke nets a skillful back wall play. The strokes utilized in playing the ball off the back court wall are the same ones as described in Chapters 4 and 5. You should have these model swings down pat before putting into practice this chapter's instruction. By way of brief review, estimate where the ball will be when you are going to strike it, position yourself appropriately next to this estimated point of contact (body parallel to the side wall you are facing), prepare with the backswing in a ready position while you are stationing yourself, as the ball rebounds past you from posterior and into the hitting zone—let 'er rip. This description assumes you have ample time to get back, set and wait for the rebounding sphere. However, in some cases you will find yourself frantically pursuing a drive hit past you toward the back court. Then the above steps will apply; you just have to modify them by performing more than one step at a time at an increased rate such that the result is a smooth execution of back wall play. Though it may sound difficult, it is nothing a little practice cannot overcome.

Many players are able to solidly contact the ball off the back wall, but here their expertise terminates. What kind of shot should be used off the back wall? The shot selection is unlimited. Provided you make good racquet contact, you can try any shot that you could equally well attempt from the same position on the court were you taking the ball straight off the front wall. (An exception to this would be on a "soft" rebound that drops very close to the back wall.) Choose from a kill, drive, ceiling ball or any of the variety of shots outlined in previous chapters. The *smart* shot selection is limited, as will soon be touched upon.

Footwork: This is a major nemesis of all court-dwelling bipeds. When it is stated back wall play requires special footwork, what actually is meant is that the player's body must be moving correctly. In other words, the feet-containing-tennies must at all times (on back wall play) locomote the racquet-wielding carcass in the same direction as that of the sphere. So, as the ball courses from front court toward the back wall, the player's movement should be in the same direction as the ball's. And as the racquetball strikes the back wall and reverses direction, now carrying toward the front wall, the player's direction change and movement must be likewise. Now, with player and ball advancing in harmony toward front court, the human half of this united movement makes the forehand or backhand stroke. In a summarizing statement, one must closely follow the ball with his body as well as his eyes.

Now that the reader has assimilated the basic groundwork for back wall play—realizing that footwork and momentum are the keys to its success—we are primed to issue an important addition to our explanation. There are *two* ways to play the ball on a rebound off the back wall. The first is the stop-and-step method and the second the jog-and-hit method. Both of these are acceptable, both are used by the game's elite pros, and both are consistent with our written rule of momentum: The player's physical motion must be direction-congruent with that of the rubber orb.

The *stop-and-step method* is fairly self-descriptive. Coordinate the following explanation with figure 8-1. The player trails the ball back to the back wall, then stops and plants himself in set-up preparatory position as the sphere strikes the rear wall. As the ball rebounds off the plaster and subsequently arches for-

ward and floorward, the player *steps into* it (as per a normal stroke) and contacts it in the proper position. This "proper position" for ball contact is once again just off the "biggie" toe of the lead foot for the backhand, or just off the heel of the lead foot for the forehand. If the shot is intended to be a kill, the ball should be struck at an elevation of no higher than the knees. If it is to be a drive, then the height of racquet-ball collision should be knee to waist high. Also note figure 8-3.

The crucial factor here is *where* the player stops and plants his ground grabbers to await the rebound off the back wall. You can obviously either overestimate, underestimate or accurately estimate the setting-up distance from the back wall. This precise stopping and setting up point must be close enough to the rear wall such that *after* stepping into the ball, racquet contact is made just off the lead foot. To be sure, this sometimes necessitates planting the back foot on the floor right at the wall-floor juncture. The most frequent error, of which at least 90 percent of all greenhorns are victim to, is to set up *too far* from the rear wall. That is, you will probably tippytoe back and plant your treads too anterior in the court. In this instance you no doubt will step past the ball with the healthy front foot stride into the swing, causing the racquet to contact the ball much too posterior to the lead foot. With surprisingly little practice (relative to other court techniques) the stop-and-step method should come quickly. Just track the ball to the back wall, set up camp in the ideal place in rear court and then confidently issue the controlled wallop.

The alternative approach to back wall play is the *jog-and-hit method*. This style differs from the stop-and-step in that instead of planting yourself and then taking one step into the ball, this newly presented technique requires you to take more than one step—usually three—into the ball as you prepare to make the stroke. This three-step shuffle is termed the "jog" in our nomenclature and this movement could also be descriptively named the stop-and-three-step method. (Figure 8-2.)

The advantage of the jog-and-hit (stop-and-three-step) approach is that more forward momentum is garnered as the player multi-steps into and then swings at the ball. Try both routines; the differences in momentum, and power imparted to the ball, will become apparent. Also the three steps (as opposed to one) allow for position adjustment as the jog is executed. If you misjudge the ball's rebound off the back wall, it is possible to compensate for the distance miscalculation by lengthening or shortening the length of the steps.

In summation, the jog-and-hit involves retreating

Fig. 8-1—THE STOP-AND-STEP METHOD: Plant yourself in the proper position . . .

as the ball rebounds off the back wall, step into it . . .

the stroke begins
as the ball drops . . .

contact it at ankle to
knee high and off the
lead foot.

Fig. 8-2—THE JOG-AND-HIT METHOD: Plant your-self near the back wall . . .

as the ball rebounds off the back wall, "jog step" with the front foot, then the rear foot . . .

at approximately equal speed with the ball to the back wall, stopping and reversing direction, three-stepping forward and swinging as the last step with the lead foot is tread. For the forehand, the three-step begins with the left foot, followed by a right and then a final left step into the ball with the simultaneous swing. The rights and lefts are interchanged for *backhands* off the back wall. See figure 8-4.

Which method is superior? Neither. Brumfield and Strandemo invariably utilize the stop-and-step motion, while Serot and this author unconsciously fall into the jog-and-hit routine whenever presented with a back wall shot. However, there are some occasions when one style is more suitable than the other. On a

ball which rebounds very gently off the back wall (for example on a well-hit lob serve that has glanced off the side wall, hit the floor and then barely come off the rear wall) the stop-and-step approach is advantageous. This is because a soft rebound off the back wall does not carry far enough out into the court to allow the player the distance-consuming three steps. On the other hand, it is far more feasible to employ the jog-and-hit method on a ball which ricochets fairly hard off the back wall. By way of example, a down-the-line drive which rebounds quickly and high off the rear court wall provides enough distance to require more than just one step into the ball. Indeed, in such a case an ad-libbed five-step jog routine

then step with the normal lead foot into the ball . . .   and make the sock-high stroke off the lead foot.

might have to be suddenly employed to make the play.

Give both approaches to back wall returns fair trials. Study sequences in figures 8-3 and 8-4, taken at different angles from figures 8-1 and 8-2, for further comparison. Choose the means which feels more comfortable and which permits your footsies to remain more tangle-free.

Speaking of two left feet—the *retreat* after an opponent's ball into back court is a neat piece of footwork in itself. This backward pursuit should be somewhat graceful, must cover a good deal of hardwood real estate and, of course, preferably should not involve tripping. An uncoordinated weekend hacker frantically chasing down a passed ball often makes for haphazard and hilarious locomotion. Somehow the shoelaces or the floor cracks always get underfoot, causing the stumblebum retreat to be neither graceful, distance-covering nor performed in an entirely upright position. The correct way to pursue such a ball is not with a back-pedal (see figure 8-5) nor with the turn-around-and-sprint (see figure 8-6). These two means do not permit the player to *visually* follow the ball throughout its total flight course. Proper posterior retreat is depicted in figure 8-7.

The *sideways shuffle* is the best method. This movement is analogous to the lateral movement of a basketball player. As the rubber sphere whizzes past

Fig. 8-3—BACKHAND BACK WALL PLAY (here and facing page). This is the stop-and-step method. Also try the jog-and-hit.

Fig. 8-4—FOREHAND BACK WALL PLAY (above and facing page). This is the jog-and-hit method. Also try the stop-and-step.

you at mid-court, you must immediately turn 90 degrees to face the side wall. (Face the right side wall for a forehand coming off the back wall and left side wall for a backhand.) Your eyeballs are still glued to the ball and your racquet is already drawn back in a ready position. Simultaneously, you must side-pedal in a backwards direction and then smoothly complete the shuffling motion with either the stop-and-step or jog-and-hit technique. The sideways shuffle is demonstrated in figure 8-7 (for the backhand). Utilization of this sideways means of retreat (avoiding excess crossing of the legs) enhances graceful movement as well as enabling the player to observe the ball as it rebounds off the rear wall onto his racquet strings. You should control the ball; do not allow the ball to control you.

BACK WALL DRILLS

It was mentioned earlier that stroke plus footwork yields proficient back wall play. Since the reader is presumed adept in the art of forehand and backhand strokes, it remains only to add and practice the magic footwork. Most newcomers to the game find it diffi-

cult to believe their progress after drilling on the following four exercises only a few times.

Exercise 1: *Shadow play.* Like a shadow boxer, the devoted racqueteer does not require an opponent to practice against. Begin facing the front wall about 3 feet behind the second short line in the center of the court. Now *pretend* Charlie Brumfield has just lobbed the ball over your head into the rear forehand corner. Turn sideways so you are facing the right side wall, draw back your court weapon into the forehand ready position and retreat posteriorly with a sideways shuffle of the footsies. Pursue and watch that imaginary ball as though it were really a Brumfield lob. Stop *within 3 feet* of the back wall and step forward (or three-step forward, depending on which method you are practicing) into the phantom sphere. Now swing with confidence, for this is one time you cannot miss. Repeat this exercise until satisfied. Obviously, here we are emphasizing the critical footwork factor. Do not forego this drill simply because a crowd of gawkers gathers to stare with uniform raised eyebrows at the kid with the flappy feet in a make-believe world. If they knew you were jousting

Fig. 8-5—Improper *back-pedal* retreat to the back wall.

Fig. 8-6—Improper *turn-around* retreat to the back wall.

Fig. 8-7—The *sideways-shuffle* retreat allows movement *plus* eye contact on ball.

Fig. 8-8—EXERCISE 2: TOSS AND HIT.

with Charlie Brumfield, their looks would change from incredulous to admiring.

Exercise 2: *Toss and hit.* Witness any of the pro superstars warming up for a match, and you will no doubt observe ball after ball being rolled off the front wall using this and the following two exercises. In this particular routine, the player commences by standing facing the right side wall about 5 feet from the rear court barrier. With racquet in confident ready position, toss the ball into the back wall about 5 feet up. As it rebounds to the floor and forward, move anteriorly along with it, utilizing either the stop-and-step or jog-and-hit method to perform this movement. As the racquetball descends into the knee level or below hitting range, smite a kill or drive shot.

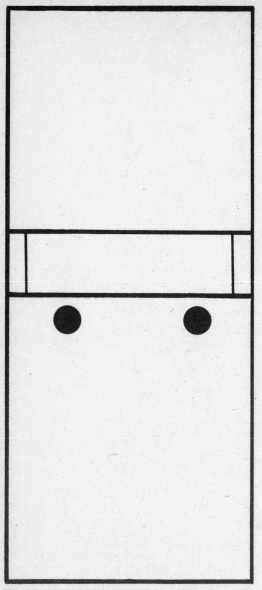

Fig. 8-9—This diagram is included to emphasize the importance of the proper *starting positions* for the forehand (right) and backhand (left) back wall set-up practice drills.

centration of technique in separate areas. Therefore, both kinds must be practiced. That is, back wall set-ups may be in either the form of *hard* or *soft* rebounds. This drill emphasizes the hard, the next exercise the soft.

Start in the position shown in figure 8-9, about 4 feet from the right side wall and *3 feet posterior to the service box.* As in Exercise One, the rationale behind this initial positioning near the second short line is to force the player to develop the compulsory footwork entailed in ideal back wall play. Too many individuals feign accomplishing Exercise One, Three and Four with a starting point within a few feet of the back wall. Wrong, wrong, wrong. These would-be practicers are either hopelessly lazy or just ignorant of what back wall movement in an actual game situation consists of.

Now that the reader has been convinced to initially idle his tennies 3 feet behind the service box, give yourself a set-up off the front wall which rebounds moderately *hard* off the rear wall. In other words, the ball should be driven firmly into the front wall such that after the bounce on the floor there is a big rebound off the posterior plaster. This rebound may carry 4 to 7 feet toward forecourt. Now is your chance to star in the picture-perfect rollout scene without the pressure of observers or an opponent. When the ball whizzes past your body from the front court, you must side-shuffle after it toward the back wall as described previously (racquet is cocked back in ready position), stop and reverse direction in the appropriate position near the rear wall, then step or three-step into the rebounding vulcanized orb and clout it with purpose. You did it? Commendable, for a debut performance without audience.

Exercise 4: *Soft set and hit.* Everything for this exercise—the beginning position, side-shuffling, etc.—is the same as with the previous one, with one important exception. The rebound off the back wall here is to be a *soft*, rapidly dropping one rather than the harder ricochet involved in the earlier drill. Imagine a fresh mud pie rebounding off a concrete wall, and you get the exaggerated idea of the proper soft set-up. To attain this type of rebound, simply lob the ball high and gently into the front wall. Since the bounce off the back wall does not carry out very far, you will discover it helps to retreat from the starting position to a stop (direction-reversing) point within 3 feet of the rear court wall. Then execute the kill or drive shot as before. Exercise Four is more difficult than number Three, so do not expect as immediate gratification.

The preceding four exercises have been for the

Remember, it is imperative that you contact the ball off the lead foot. (Since we are using the forehand at present this would be the left appendage for a right-hander.) Do not be content with even a flat roll-off unless the proper footwork and point of contact during the stroke have been strictly adhered to. Note figure 8-8 (backhand is demonstrated).

Exercise 3: *Hard set and hit.* When speaking of back wall play, it is soon discovered through court encounter that there are basically two types of back wall rebounds which occur, each demanding specific con-

Top-pro Jerry Hilecher rips off a back wall photon against unidentified competitor. Note Hilecher's eye concentration and cocked-wrist ready position as he waits for the ball to drop into sub-knee level hitting position.

Jeff Bowman's forehand back wall form. The stop-and-step method perfectly executed.

forehand stroke. Only after all four have been repeated to self-satisfaction should the same exact drills with the *backhand* be executed. As in all the solo practice routines presented in earlier chapters of this book, you will no doubt make frustrating small mistakes at first; here again, a critical observer (a friend or fellow player) can upgrade dramatically the productivity of your practice sessions.

COMMON BACK WALL ERRORS

There are three common errors which nag the inexperienced hacker who is undertaking back wall play for the first time. Be highly self-critical to the point of introspective masochism in evaluating your own technique—closely examine *your* back wall play and see if you are not falling into one of these every-day traps. The first two pitfalls deal with the point of

contact of racquet and ball, while the last is hinted at in the most often uttered adage since Homo sapiens first jumped down from the trees and began toying with spherical objects.

Recall from the opening chapters dealing with strokes that the proper point of contact for the forehand is out and away from the lead foot's heel, while clobbering time with the backhand ideally transpires in an area off the lead foot's toes. Most court neophytes do not fall back (side-shuffle) far enough on back wall play. They take a few begrudging steps in the direction of rear court, set up and swing—off balance. This is because their point of contact is invariably *too far posterior*. (Figure 8-10.) Predictably, the ball slices off the racquet strings and glances into the side wall. Be sure you are retreating to a point close enough to the back wall so that when you step into the swing you do not stride past the ball. Some-

Fig. 8-10—Beginners typically contact back wall balls way back here . . .

—instead of way up here.

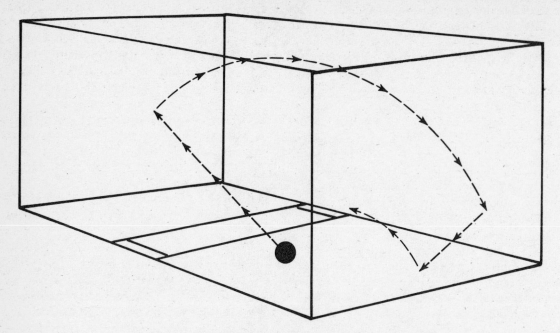

Fig. 8-11—Flight pattern of front wall to back wall shot.

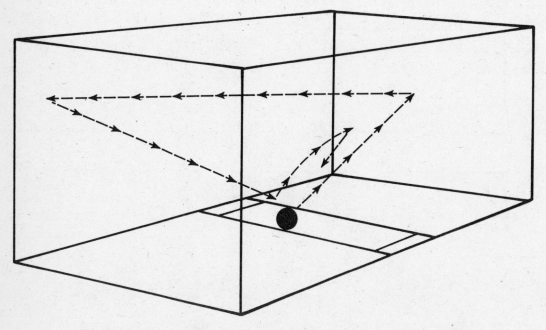

Fig. 8-12—A very lively ball may be struck so hard it hits the front wall *twice* before taking a second bounce to the floor.

times, as emphasized previously, it is necessary to begin your stop-and-step or jog-and-hit right *at* the back wall to assure proper point of contact.

The second major error among newcomers to the realm of freak and tweak balls is not stepping into the ball correctly on back wall play. If you have planted your perspiring carcass in the proper plot to await the back wall rebound, then you have allowed yourself enough room to take a *very healthy step* (or three-step) along with your downswing. A complete body weight transfer from rear to front foot during the stroke ensures that you have indeed stationed yourself correctly for the downswing. If you find yourself hitting the ball with the majority of your weight still on the back foot, then either your point of planting is too far anterior or you are not taking that momentum-generating giant step into the ball.

Finally, there is an almost universal tendency to *not* watch the ball during back wall play. Concentrate with total focus on the sphere during its flight, bounce, rebound and string contact—see if your back wall game does not improve vastly by simply observing the oldest of sports maxims: *"Watch the ball."*

BACK WALL VARIATIONS

A variation of the off-the-back-wall shot occurs when a solidly smacked ball hits high and hard on the front wall, arches straight to the rear wall without bouncing in between on the floor, and rebounds off the back court wall far into the front court before finally descending, striking the floor and thus finally coming to within hitting range. (Figure 8-11.) When this happens, some heavy duty scrambling is called for. Shuffle rapidly after the ball into the front court as it caroms past you off the rear wall. Have your racquet bobbing along in constant ready position as you advance anteriorly and as the ball drops into striking distance make an offensive shot.

Once in a great while, a gorilla-man will send a well-clouted ball into the court heavens where it performs the following aerial gymnastics: Front wall to back wall to floor to front wall. That is, the ogre's bash strikes the front wall a second time before you even have an opportunity to poke at the speeding sphere (figure 8-12). Although the ball has hit the front wall *twice,* it is perfectly legal to wait and play it on its second rebound off the front court wall, as

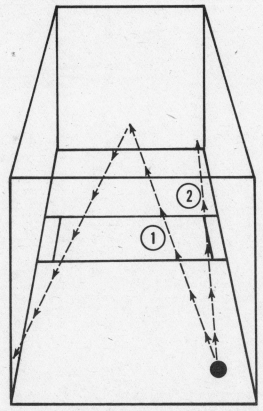

Fig. 8-13—Two normal options for a forehand back wall set-up: 1) cross-court drive or 2) right corner kill.

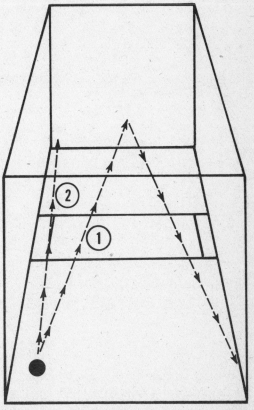

Fig. 8-14—The backhand back wall options are the same as for the forehand. In addition, a backhand down-the-line pass may be attempted.

long is you hit it prior to its second bounce on the floor. In this rare instance of the "double-front-wall ball," it is usually most strategic to "dump" the ball into either corner with a light caress.

SHOT SELECTION OFF BACK WALL

We have only nebulously hinted at what kind of shot to make when returning a ball off the back wall. Among better players this repertoire of shots is limited to *two*, under normal circumstances. The first is a *kill* and the second a *drive,* either down-the-line or cross-court. Note figures 8-13 and 8-14. Therefore, when the reader labors tenaciously through the four back wall exercises presented, it will be advantageous to get into the habit of employing one of these two offensive shots. It was pointed out in this chapter's introductory comments that a unique situation unfolds when one takes a rebound off the back wall in that the ball is traveling *with* the direction of one's racquet swing. Therefore, a threatening thrust, in the form of either a drive or kill, is a very sound stratagem.

chapter nine

OTHER SHOTS

CHAPTER 9 SUMMARY

I. Volley
  A. i.e. Taking the ball out of the air; on the fly
  B. Difficult to execute
  C. What shot to use off of volley—usually offensive
  D. When to take ball on volley—complex
    1. Volley if you expect ball to die at back wall
    2. Do not volley shots above head
    3. Volley soft serves
  E. Stroke mechanics
    1. Use normal forehand or backhand
    2. Knee to waist contact height
    3. Do not tap or push ball
  F. Exercise—set-up and volley

II. Half-volley
  A. i.e. Taking the ball on the short-hop
  B. Stroke in same manner as the volley
  C. Practice is difficult and not mandatory

III. Drop shot
  A. Exclusive execution by forehand
  B. The stroke
    1. Stride forward with left foot
    2. Catch ball on short hop
    3. Stiff wrist with racquet rolling motion
    4. Push ball into near corner
  C. Is difficult play whose mastery is not mandatory

IV. Overheads—two types

  A. Overhead kill
    1. Hit cross-court generally
    2. Hit side wall first generally
  B. Overhead drives
    1. May be hit cross-court or up and down line—former allows greater margin of error
    2. Bullseyes: apparent—1 foot high on front wall; actual—about 3 feet high
  C. Stroke—the overhand forehand; forehand only
    1. Similar to ceiling ball overhand swing
    2. Full overhand or three-quarter overhand
  D. Degree of difficulty of control of overheads— easiest to hardest
    1. Ceiling ball
    2. Drive
    3. Kill
  E. Overheads rarely employed by pros; more common among beginners and intermediates
  F. Practice—off ceiling balls, solo and with partner

V. Ball-into-back-wall ball
  A. Employed only in emergency when no other shot is possible
  B. Often is an addiction which must be bucked
  C. Return of the B.I.B.W. ball
    1. Rush ball and volley it in mid-air
    2. Kill into near corner
  D. Do not practice B.I.B.W. ball. Its return may be practiced.

OTHER SHOTS

The fundamental shots of racquetball have been laid out in a methodical manner for voluntary consumption by the reader. These have been the basic sustenance, the bread-and-butter ploys, utilized 90 percent of the time in frolicking within the confines of a cement sweatbox. And strange but true, the more adeptly one employs these essentials the less freely he sweats and strains. It is mildly confusing, but one thing is for sure—true racquetball adequacy is not merely acquired by digesting and spewing out the basics. It is that extra 10 percent of infrequently employed shots which distinguishes the court technicians from the run-of-the-millers.

Though not exactly commonplace, these *"other shots"* nonetheless surface every time a racquetball game is played. Involved in this 10 percent category are the volley, half-volley, overhead and dump shot. As each of these is pursued in the text, a brief practice schedule will be provided. The ball-into-back-wall ball will also be touched upon in this chapter.

VOLLEY

The volley is perplexingly paradoxical in that while it is true your opponent has little time to set up for the volley, it is also a fact that you have little time yourself to clout the volley in the first place. Time is surely gained but at the expense of accuracy, and time is surely lost but in the quest of center court maintenance.

By definition, the volley is any ball which is taken in mid-air before it has a chance to bounce on the floor. This is synonymous with taking the ball "on the fly" or "cutting the ball off." (Do not confuse this use of the term as a verb with the noun "volley," denoting a rally or exchange of shots during the course of play.) Because there is no floor bounce of the ball, there is less time to set up and issue the stroke. This means that killing the ball on the fly is one of the most difficult executions in racquetball. This is a disadvantage, though not prohibitive. The advantage of volleying the ball is that one can often catch his rival off guard lolling in back court. And by cutting the ball off—for example intercepting a cross-court drive and pounding it into an available corner—you keep tight reins on center court position. All in all, this author contends the volley is paramount in the general control of racquetball play.

What shot to whack off of a volley? Any shot listed in previous chapters is possible and acceptable, depending upon the presentation of the ball. As a basic guideline, an *offensive play* should usually be made when cutting the ball out of the air. This indicates either a kill or drive. Of course, it is absurd to just randomly hit the ball out of the air; try for a specific shot.

When to hit the ball on the fly is a much more subjective query, and the various professionals react to a potential volley in different ways. By way of illustration, Steve Serot invariably prefers fly killing a ball, whereas Charlie Brumfield waits for a bounce and rebound off the back wall. This "when" issue is a complex question of strategy which is left to a more advanced text. In general, however, you should take the ball out of the air if, after its bounce, you expect it to "die" with little rebound off the back wall. On a more strongly hit shot (e.g. a down-the-line drive) which will carry easily to the rear wall, the player may choose either to cut the ball down in mid-flight or to allow its passage untouched for a back wall set-up. A broad rule of thumb is *not* to volley shots which are above your head. A prime time *to* rush right up and cut off the sphere is on the service return of a lob or garbage serve. In volleying a garbage serve, the usual return shot is a devastating, surprise cross-court drive which sends the server spinning on his tennie treads before his undergarments have time to twist with the rest of him.

The *mechanics*, or stroke execution, of the volley is open to wide-ranging variation—more so than most other shots made within the four-walled realm. Some players contact the ball at waist height, while others wait patiently for it to drop to knee level or lower. Many experienced individuals espouse the use of a stiff wrist when stroking this particular shot, contrary to the normal flaccid wrist technique recommended by many others for full power. This author suggests that the reader use his *typical forehand or backhand stroke,* with personal adaptations based upon his volley experience. Contact the ball from *knee to waist height*, where ever it feels most comfortable. These individual adaptations will arise mainly from practice—solo workouts. The following drill is admittedly an advanced exercise by which the court fledgling will experience considerable problems. In fact, usually the volley is the final shot to be skillfully developed by the maturing player. Examine figures 9-1 and 9-2 and note in particular the demonstrators' similar and contrasting tendencies in taking the ball on the fly.

Exercise: *Set-up and volley.* From position one for the forehand, as indicated in figure 9-3a, give yourself a soft set off the front wall. Be prepared to mobilize your footsies and do a little anterior or posterior locomotion. The ball should rebound back far enough

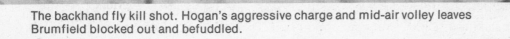

The backhand fly kill shot. Hogan's aggressive charge and mid-air volley leaves Brumfield blocked out and befuddled.

Fig. 9-1—Volleying a shot involves charging the ball . . .   hitting it on the fly . . .

that it does not bounce, but rather is contacted in mid-air. Attempt to place the ball low and into the right hand corner for a roll off. Repeat at least 20 times and then perform the same stroke from position two, farther back in the court.

Hints: Do *not* push or tap the ball into the corner. Hit it with firm conviction, utilizing your normal swing. Since the set-up off the front wall is highly unlikely to come directly to the most opportune point of racquet contact, move your feet to gain proper positioning. You must literally be on your toes at all times in order to successfully execute the volley.

With the forehand drill completed, move to the opposite side of the court and perform the exercise from the two assigned stations with the backhand, as in figure 9-3b. (See also photo sequence figure 9-4.)

The reader may compose his own drills by altering this one in regard to the type of shot made off the volley. That is, you may wish to practice driving the ball cross-court from the forehand side or hitting it

on the fly up and down the line with the backhand. The dirty, rackafracking ball just will not go where you aim it? Again, this volley shot is anything but easy. If you become discouraged after extensively practicing with terminal results of too-high kills and too-low drives, console yourself in the revelation that every player has at one time or other temporarily stalled at this same frustrating barricade.

Frequent mistakes made when volleying are: attempting to fly hit at shots over your head when you should let them go to the back wall, and volleying without aiming for a specific shot.

THE HALF-VOLLEY

If the volley is one of the most nagging shots in racquetball to master, then its half-sister, the half-volley, presents the epitome of perplexity. The half-volley is simply a volley with an added troublesome short-hop. The reader has no doubt witnessed a ten-

and finishing as per a normal stroke.

nis player start to rush the net from the court base-line, only to hesitate half-way through his move. By the time the ball comes zooming back over the net at our misplaced subject, he may be found groveling and/or praying for any kind of return. He has fallen into a two-sided dilemma, unable to reach ahead far enough to catch the ball before it hits the ground and yet much too committed by forward momentum to reverse direction a step or two in order to stroke the ball after it takes a normal bounce. The skillful tennis player reacts to this situation by taking the ball on the *short-hop*, or half-volley. In other words, he makes the best of a poor maneuver by contacting the ball just after it skips off the ground.

The same reflex reaction situation occurs less frequently in racquetball, but when it does a successful half-volley roll off return makes for a picturesque mix of poise, grace and hand-to-eye coordination. With such punctilious prerequisites for execution, if the reader happens to profess any propensity toward

spasticity he is hereby advised to skip the ensuing explanation.

The best counsel to be offered on striking the half-volley is to swing at the ball just *as though you were hitting the ball on the volley*. That is, basically ignore the short hop and perform your normal stroke right through the ball. If you start pondering the timing, the quick bounce and so on, you will only become unglued and your fluid swing will suffer. This is a potential case of "blinkus of the thinkus," a temporary mental lapse related to the "paralysis via analysis" syndrome mentioned previously in the book.

A "spasticity test" by which a racquetball instructor may essentially evaluate the pupil's hand-to-eye coordination has traditionally been to instruct the student to try to hit a half-volley shot. The pupil's response to this command has traditionally been to gaze upon his racquet teacher with a pug dog expression, as though saying "go eat some dirt." A passing grade is awarded if the student half-volleyer's stroke does not bear resemblance to a palsied victim attempting to scratch his back. Very few rubber pushers pass this stern test.

The photographs of the half-volley stroke (figures 9-5 and 9-6) were grantedly not selected at random, for not even our demonstrator can handle the spasticity test every time. Acceptable pictures were chosen to properly demonstrate the method behind the half-volley stroke. Note the manner in which the player swings, as though he were ignoring the quick

Fig. 9-2—A fly shot may also be killed from waist high (Steve Serot).

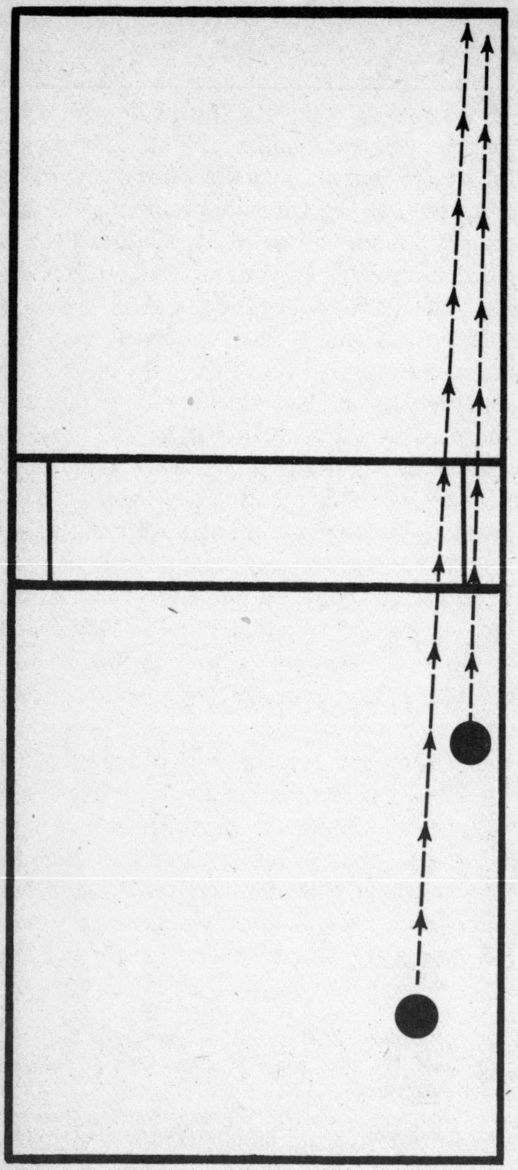

Fig. 9-3a—Drills for forehand volley shots from two positions.

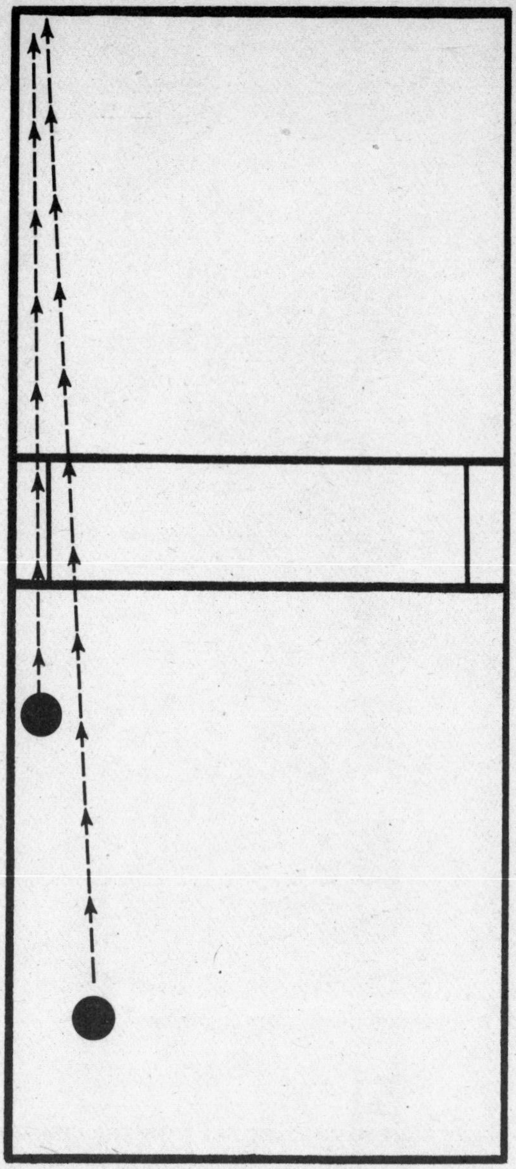

Fig. 9-3b—Backhand volley exercise from two positions.

bounce on the floor and hitting as though it were a volley shot. Racquet to ball contact should be about *ankle high*, and this author favors a smooth, continuous follow-through (through the ball) rather than a stiff-wristed "blocking" style of stroke.

As far as practicing, the majority of professional court combatants never solo drill on the half-volley. Better to devote time and energy to a less ignominious exercise. Concentrate your practice on the *full* volley, as expounded upon earlier, because this play is difficult enough as is and arises much more frequently than the half-volley.

DROP SHOT

By way of inauspicious introduction, this author has strived to develop control of the drop shot for years and has yet to successfully execute a single one in tournament play. I inevitably get duds instead of dumps. The only ranked players in the history of racquetball to fruitfully include the drop, or dump shot, within their stroke inventory are Bud Muehleisen and Charles Brumfield.

The drop shot is a half-hearted half-volley. In other words, it is an offensive "push" of the ball via a gentle guiding racquet motion. It is executed exclu-

Fig. 9-4—THE BACKHAND
VOLLEY SHOT.

Fig. 9-5—The forehand half-volley is just a volley shot plus a short hop.

Fig. 9-6—The backhand half-volley "spasticity test."

sively by the *forehand* in order to cover an opponent's kill shot attempt which has almost rolled off the front wall (but is barely retrievable). As figure 9-7 demonstrates, the player stands in readiness near the front short line with his body and racquet geared toward quickly covering an anticipated kill shot. The rival's ball rolls off the front wall inches high and caroms back low and rapidly. One must react reflexively by instantly dropping his racquet low and at the oncoming ball. The wrist is cocked back in an extended position, as in closeup figure 9-8. As the sphere scoots at him, the dumper must take one giant-sized step forward with his left foot and catch the ball on the *short-hop.*

The racquet motion for the drop shot is more of an away-guide, or reverse caress, in the same fashion as a youngster pushing away a plate full of spinach. The wrist retains the *stiff cock* (does not break) throughout the motion and a slight topspin rolling motion of the racquet *pushes* the ball low into the front wall. This rolling racquet bit may be an underhand, low sidearm or in between, subject to personal preference. Brumfield utilizes the underhand, while Muehleisen tends to sidearm scoop the ball when taking a dump in the front corner.

It must be emphasized that this stroke is a soft, almost dainty, tap which if done correctly will ''drop'' the ball into either front corner with little rebound. The dump is a *kill* shot of sorts. It is to be guided into either corner and may strike the front or side wall insipidly.

The nonchalant dump often springboards the gallery to their feet in fervent adulation for an ostensibly beautiful ploy. Actually, this is but a false display of wizardry and the person-in-the-know realizes it is not a percentage play for most. A speedy, heads-up player will neutralize the dumper's game style through sheer hustle. The dump is most applicable against a lead-footed fellow who lingers constantly in back court, or against the similar individual who moves with the locomotive characteristics of a pregnant snail.

As alluded to in this section's opening comments, this author does not favor the drop shot due to his personal ineptness at it and because of the requirements for its proper execution: massively muscled legs in order to take the necessary daddy-sized step forward to cover the too-high kill, and divine caress for the controlled tap-kill of the ball into the corner. As often as not, the reader will discover *his* dump shot results in either a pushing of the ball into the floor for a skip or a lofting upwards for a 3-foot high pumpkin set-up. As with the half-volley, the reader is

Fig. 9-7—The forehand drop shot starts with a "lunge" . . .

continues with a "push" or dump stroke . . .

and don't worry a lot about the follow-through.

Fig. 9-8—Close-up
of the drop shot.

advised to allocate his practice time to more reliable facets of the game than the drop shot.

OVERHEADS

Overheads here are construed to mean one of two types of shot: The overhead *kill* and the overhead *drive*. Both can be hit cross-court or up and down the line and both will be expanded upon below. As you browse the following, refer if you wish to the picture sequences for the overhead ceiling balls (Chapter 7) and in doing so note their similarities to the photographs provided here.

The overheads are a series of overhand tennis slam-type shots not to be practiced quite as piously as the basic building block shots presented in previous chapters. Master the fundamentals and then concentrate on the superfluous. Among the beginning and intermediate ranks of player ability, the overhead is a fun shot to slam and which habitually forces weak returns due to the high velocity of the ball driven at the opponent. Upon being issued such a blast, a *smart* player will deftly step aside. If he judges the overhead

slam will carry to the rear wall, he will allow it to do so and then smash the back wall set-up for a roll off. The professionals are smart players. Therefore, among these preeminents the overhead is not usually a high percentage shot and is infrequently employed.

Others besides the pros may find the roundhouse overhead slam to be a potent and a reliable weapon on the court. However, the *pros* most often use it when faced by a duffer with the third gear speed of a tree sloth amputee, or they may flaunt it in flamboyant showboating, or use it in rare cases of pure desperation. Only once in a while will one witness a pro let fly a savage overhead kill or drive (when he has ample opportunity for a higher percentage shot, such as an overhead ceiling ball) against another top pro. The only elite players in racquetball to consistently and somewhat successfully utilize the overhead attack are Muehleisen and Brumfield. Potentates in the magic and mastery of court control, this is the same twosome who effectively employ the drop shot on occasion. Steve Strandemo, Bill Schmidtke, Steve Serot and this author are definitely not copious overhead exchangers.

Schmidtke takes a dump in the front right corner. Bledsoe appears disconcerted at the well-executed, stiff-wristed lunge.

Fig. 9-9—The full overhead by Brumfield (St. Louis Nationals in 1973).

Fig. 9-10—THE THREE-QUARTER OVERHEAD (below and facing page) is preferred by most for overhead drives and kills.

Overheads are to be smote with the *forehand stroke* (utilizing the corresponding forehand grip) *only*, except for those yoga devotees with a perversion toward unhinged stretchability. The forehand *ceiling ball* hit from the shoulder or higher could be correctly termed an overhead, but it has been classified here as a defensive shot and was taken up in the ceiling ball portion of Chapter 7. That leaves the overhead kill and overhead drive to contend with. Both are struck in a similar fashion to a pitcher delivering a baseball (as with the forehand ceiling shot). A baseball pitcher throws fully overhand or three-quarter overhand, and the racquetball overheader also has this option. The full overhand (kill or drive stroke) is portrayed in figure 9-9, and the three-quarter in figure 9-10. For a more comprehensive step-by-step representation of both styles of swings, review the instruction offered by the text concerning the forehand ceiling ball.

Overhead kills. Without delving into complex geometrical detail, it is advisable to aim most overhead kill shots *cross-court*. Suffice it to say there is a greater margin for error behind this strategy, as opposed to placing the kills up and down the line. In addition, when going for a cross-court overhead kill the best bet is generally to hit the *side wall* rather than

front wall first. This side wall action causes the ball's energy to dissipate and results in a lesser bounce out of the corner. See figures 9-11a and 9-11b.

On any overhead kill attempt, unless the laws of rebounds come to a standstill, do not expect a perfectly flat roll out because this is a very long range shot taken from about 7 feet off the floor. Shoot cross-court for a large imaginary box, say 3 feet square, which can be envisioned sitting in the front corner. The advantage of the overhead kill is the element of *surprise* sprung upon the unsuspecting slipshodder lagging in back court. As in countering the half-volley, any Henry Hustle with rapid transit tootsies will cover attempted overhead kills angled from above in deep court. Note figure 9-12.

Overhead drives. The overhead drive may be slugged either cross-court or down the line, though *cross-courts* allow for slightly greater tolerance of miscalculation. In either case, aim *low* enough on the front wall that the ball does not pop up high off the floor and, due to natural topspin, rebound off the back wall for a plum. Players generally err on the too-high rather than too-low sighting on the front wall. Therefore it may be helpful to aim overhead drives at a bullseye area about *1 foot* off the floor on the front court plaster. An inherent rise given to most players'

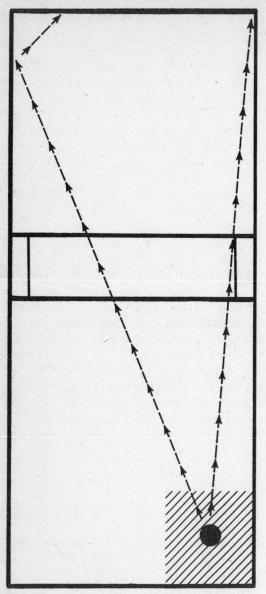

Fig. 9-11a—Overhead kills from right rear court may go down-the-line or, more frequently, cross-court. In the latter instance, the left side wall is usually hit before the front wall.

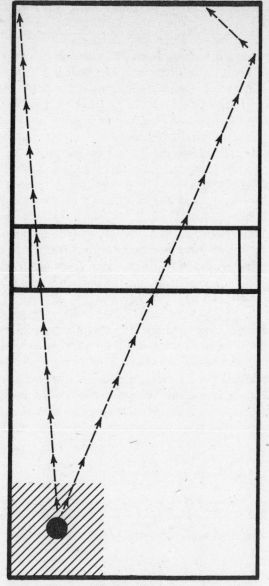

Fig. 9-11b—Overhead kills (forehand) from left rear corner. Again, most go cross-court and initially hit the side wall.

overhead drives will cause the racquetball to hit about *3 feet* up from the floor on the front wall, which in reality is the approximate proper height of contact. (The modifiers "about" and "approximately" are employed freely here since the overhead covers such a large distance of court area.)

Refer to figures 9-13a and 9-13b for the correct placement of overhead drives.

Practice the overheads? Before you unleash such an attack in a game situation, you had better. The best way to practice the *kill* is to give yourself a ceiling ball that returns to at least shoulder height in deep court. Instead of returning the pneumatic sphere to the ceiling, as orthodoxy and logic might dictate, drill the ball cross-court into the opposite corner (3-foot square box) for a kill. Repeat the desired number of times, performing from either side of the court and killing cross-court, but always with the forehand stroke.

To work out in solo on the overhead *drive,* equip yourself with ball and racquet and go through the same motions as with the above kill shot exercise—

Fig. 9-12—The "box theory" for overhead kills. The box in the front corner should be (or imagined to be) about 3 feet square.

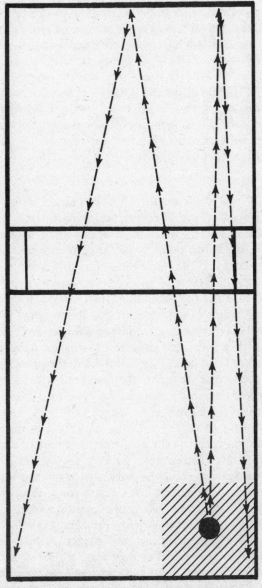

Fig. 9-13a—Overhead *drives* from the right. Almost always drive cross-court to the backhand.

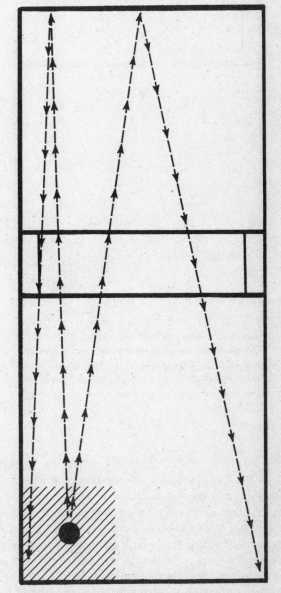

Fig. 9-13b—Overhead *drives* from the left. Use this and diagram 9-13a for drills.

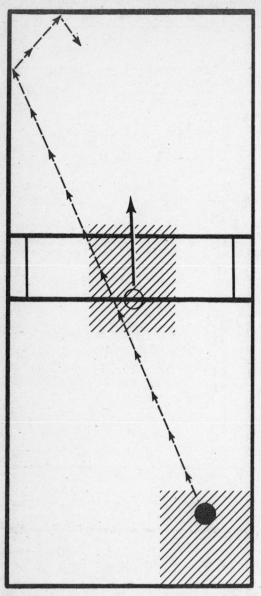

Starting positions for the overhead kills and drives are plotted in figures 9-11 and 9-13. In addition to these solitary drills, the reader may wish to select a peer to relieve the doldrums of working out. If so, player "A" provides the ceiling ball set-up, player "B" slaps down an overhead kill or drive and player "A" attempts to cover and rekill said shot. Then the two exchange parts in the play.

After completing your next overhead drive or kill, take stock of *your position* after the follow-through. You resemble a praying mantis doing limbering up exercises, don't you? That is okay. All is perfectly copacetic with your malposition because the natural follow-through should indeed carry your racquet arm extended across the body. Thus, (refer back to figure 9-10) in the terminal overhead stance the body weight is necessarily practically all shifted to the left foot and the general feeling is one of extreme awkwardness.

Now that you have given your personal anatomy a quick look-see following the overhead, examine and ponder the relative *court positions* of you and your rival. Besides being indelicately off balance, you are probably grossly out of court position, while your opponent is stationed in excellent center court position prepared to scurry after your next shot. Note the relative court positions in figure 9-14.

Fig. 9-14—Relative court positions of offensive and defensive players portray why the overhead kill is considered a low percentage shot.

By the above reasoning, overheads (except the ceiling balls) are low percentage. Furthermore, the kill is the least controllable of the three overheads (kill, drive and ceiling), the drive is next in line in degree of difficulty and the ceiling ball is the easiest to control. Hence if you are ever able to step back and take the ball knee high then do so, instead of going with *any* overhead. If this short retreat is not feasible (e.g. the back wall may hamper one's reversal), then go to the ceiling. Employ an occasional overhead drive as an unexpected change-of-pace weapon, and abandon the overhead kill to more talented personages such as the Mule and the Brum or to the lesser talented hot doggers.

And in conclusion . . . the *backhand* overhead? Discount it before the next heartbeat sends racquetball-shaped hemocytes coursing throughout your blood system. Yes, the backhand overhead stroke from deep backhand back court for a cross-court reverse pinch roll off in the opposite right front corner is a distinct possibility. And yes, it is often employed as an attention (and point) getter by this author in tournament competition. However, do as I say and not as I do. This backhand overhead shot ranks practically zilch on the successful percentage scale, though it may register higher by a more ostentatious reading. Stick to the forehand overheads.

only this time hit flat drives off the ceiling set-ups. From the backhand and forehand deep court (again always employing the forehand stroke), direct these drives either cross-court or up and down the alleys. Remember to aim about a foot high on the front wall (hoping for actual 3-foot high contact), at least until you attain a feel for a more personalized target area. Consider your drive a successful one if the ball does not come off the back wall very hard, or pop off the side wall any more anterior than near the three-quarter court mark.

Who can mistake the identity of the master of overheads? Brumfield unknowingly telegraphs the outcome of this overhead cross-court kill with the "V" for victory finger flash.

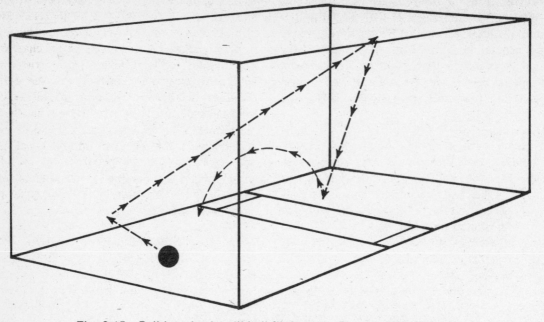

Fig. 9-15—Ball-into-back-wall ball flight path. Result: the proverbial plum.

BALL-INTO-BACK-WALL BALL

And it is on to an even less frequently utilized ruse, and fortunately so, the ball-into-back-wall ball. Ball-into-back-wall ball?

A racquetball which a player blasts in a reverse direction than normal, that is directly into the *back wall,* is hereby appropriately designated the B.I.B.W. ball. The flight course of such a shot is diagramed in figure 9-15, and if for nothing else than the reader's personal edification, its execution is revealed in detail in figures 9-16 and 9-17. Looked them over? Immediately *reject* the B.I.B.W. ball in all but emergency situations; use it only when no other shot is possible.

This forementioned emergency situation usually occurs when a ball is accurately laced past a player and is not destined to carry all the way to the back wall for a rebound. The passed player's only recourse is a ball-into-back-wall ball. Assume the reader is that unfortunate passed player who is stationed in center court when, during the course of a rally, a ball floats out of reach past his backhand. It does not appear as though the stupid sphere will rebound off the back wall; you groan inwardly. You have little choice but to immediately turn in your treads, chase down the fleeing orb, and once you catch up slam it

Fig. 9-16—THE B.I.B.W. BALL (below and facing page) on the return of serve.

forcefully into the back wall approximately five feet of the way up from the floor. The sphere should be struck into the rear court plaster with a slightly upward motion, after which the player should move both his racquet and himself out of the way of the instantaneous ricochet. The save on an otherwise passed shot has been made, for your ball will eventually reach the front wall. (See figures 9-17a and 9-17b.)

Your hurried B.I.B.W. ball will sail high within the upper court strata after rebounding off the rear wall plaster, and will carry clear to the front wall without hitting the floor. The ball hits the front wall, takes a high, lazy bounce, and precipitates an easy set-up near the service box area. The receiver of this luscious plum will immediately shift his salivary glands into overdrive and attempt the routine put-away. Looks bad, but this is better than not even trying for the original passed ball in the first place.

The major reason this section on the B.I.B.W. ball is included in this book is to alert the reader to an erroneous practice which may be observed wherever neophytic duffers take racquet into fist. Frequently the greenhorn player lacks confidence and ability in his backhand play off the back wall. He is able to ef-

fectually handle the forehand back wall shots, but when it comes to that weaker backhand stroke in the left rear court corner, his is a highly retarded execution. Therefore, our player under critical examination, instead of enduring the perpetual chagrin or terminating his feeble backhand stroke with a tangled heap of dislocated appendages, chooses to fall into the ill-fated custom of spinning on his heels every time the ball speeds past his rotten backhand and slambanging the thing with a forehand to the back wall (figure 9-16). This ball-into-back-wall practice soon evolves into an addiction and our misinformed player never does develop his backhand back wall play, though the remaining areas of his game may improve dramatically.

There are two sound pieces of advice to offer this individual. The first is obviously to break out of the B.I.B.W. groove. Begin at least to *try* to scamper toward the back wall and make an orthodox play on the ball. So what if you fail to make the return through correct back wall play? But, this will not happen if the second piece of advice is taken. Page back to the drills for backhand back wall play in Chapter 8 and give them a few go-arounds until the

Fig. 9-17a—Forehand B.I.B.W. ball.

Fig. 9-17b—Backhand B.I.B.W. ball.

ball-into-back-wall ball is merely a bad memory rather than a present malpractice.

That is how to hit the B.I.B.W. ball, when and when not to hit it, where it goes and why not to hit it. Something much more positive can be said about making the *return* of such a shot. As soon as your scrambling rival sends the ball into the back wall on a note of ignorance or desperation, you should be on tippytoes and hustling your carcass toward front court to cover the B.I.B.W. ball. Your travels should almost parallel that of the ball with regard to speed and direction, as you and the sphere converge upon a common meeting point anterior to the service box. Now comes the matter of utmost importance: You must take the ball *on the volley* off the front wall. Do not allow it to strike the floor before contact is made. Furthermore, your fly shot taken from this position near the front wall should be a *kill*. Actually it is an easily executed "poke" to either corner which hits fairly low on the front wall. Many players facilitate this ploy by aiming their kills into the side wall first, but this is not at all expedient. Once one becomes accomplished in the footwork, the ideal fly return of the B.I.B.W. ball is exceedingly hard to blow. (Refer to figure 9-1 for its execution.) In volleying the return, you will leave your disgruntled foe hanging in back court in acute muddlement.

Consider what would have transpired had you watched your rival's ball-into-back-wall ball float toward the front court, make contact and then leapfrog high into the air upon striking the floor. (i.e. Had you not taken the ball on the volley as described above.) Sure, you are presented with a routine set-up near the service box, as was admitted earlier, but in allowing the ball its huge floor rebound you have lost at least two precious seconds of "surprise attack" time. During this lapse your competitor will probably have made a catlike recovery from his reverse plunge in deep court and subsequently daddy long-legged his merry way anteriorly into favorable court position. He now has a decent opportunity to cover your next shot. You have blundered, so do not let it happen again . . . the next time you are hit a ball-into-back-wall ball, you had better react aggressively by stampeding up to administer a fly kill.

Notice the relative court positions of the offensive and defensive players in the diagrams. In figure 9-18 the offensive man has attacked the ball in midair with a volley, and in figure 9-19 he has wrongly let the ball bounce before swatting. In the latter example it can be seen that the defensive man has regrouped and regained a much superior court station.

The ball-into-back-wall ball need not be practiced; in fact, to do so would only encourage a bad habit.

Desperation ball-into-back-wall shot. Even the pros use it as a last resort.

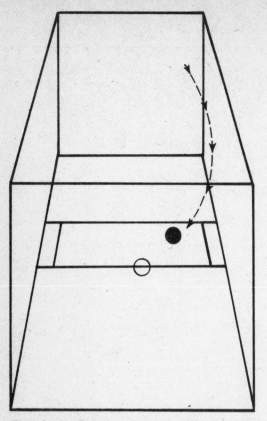

Fig. 9-18—Relative court positions when offensive player rushes ball to take it *on the fly*. It is a shorter kill and the defensive man is screened visually and physically.

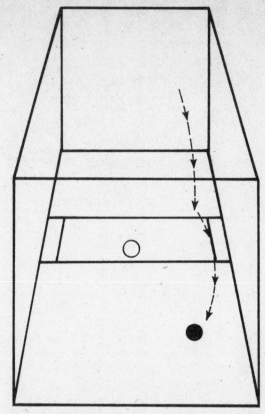

Fig. 9-19—Compare this to 9-18. Here the offensive player has allowed a potential volley shot to *bounce* to the floor. Though this is an easier shot with respect to technique, the defensive man has moved up to cover and is not screened out of play.

To practice the fly *return* off the B.I.B.W. ball, simply work on the drills for the volley, listed earlier in this chapter. As an interesting alternative, with two persons involved, player "A" may hit a ball-into-back-wall ball to player "B," who is initially standing posterior to the second short line. "B" rushes the shot and pokes the ball into the near corner, as "A" attempts to cover the volley. After ten or so of these actions, the players should switch roles.

The "other shots"—volley, half-volley, drop shot, overhead and B.I.B.W. ball—are frosting on the cake. A degree of recommendation has been given for each, and the reader may or may not choose to incorporate any or all of them into his personal game plan.

chapter ten
SERVICE

CHAPTER 10 SUMMARY

I. Importance of the serve

II. Four basic services
    A. Garbage (half-lob)
    B. Drive (low hard)
    C. Z-serve
    D. Lob

III. Purpose of serve
    A. Simply putting ball into play
    B. Striving for weak return

IV. Three basic recommendations
    A. Serve from centralized position
    B. Majority of serves to the backhand
    C. Quality as opposed to variety

V. Garbage serve
    A. Starting position—central service box
    B. Height of contact—navel to chest
    C. Stroke is a "push" or "put"
    D. Front wall bullseye—1 foot left of center and about halfway up front wall
    E. Rear court bullseye—3-foot cubic box theory; ball bounces into top of box
    F. Garbage also possible to forehand, though not as effective
    G. Avoid side wall contact, unless within 3 feet from back wall
    H. Forces ceiling ball return

VI. Drive (low hard) serve
    A. Most effective serve when accurate; is difficult to control
    B. Avoid aiming for "crack"
    C. Starting position—center or just left of central service box
    D. Height of contact—knee level or lower
    E. Strike with gusto—80 percent power
    F. Front wall bullseye—1 foot left of center and about 3 feet high
    G. Rear court bullseye—through a 3-foot cubic box
    H. Stroke is normal drop-and-kill motion
    I. Initiates reaction—kill-pass game style

VII. Z-serve
    A. Easy to execute and highly effective
    B. Four types of Z-serves
       1. Low hard to backhand—a reverse Z
       2. High soft to backhand—a reverse Z
       3. Low hard to forehand—a normal Z
       4. High soft to forehand—a normal Z
    C. Low hard reverse Z to backhand
       1. Starting position—center or left of center
       2. Height of contact—about knee level
       3. Front wall bullseye—3 feet high and 1 foot from right side wall
       4. Stroke is normal drop-and-kill motion
       5. Ball must contact left side wall (1 to 4 feet from back wall) prior to hitting back wall (after floor bounce)

D. High soft reverse Z to backhand
   1. Starting position—left of center
   2. Height of contact—about waist level
   3. Front wall bullseye—5-6 feet high and 1 foot from right side wall
   4. Ball must contact left side wall prior to back wall (after floor bounce)
   5. Approximately 50 percent power on stroke
E. Low hard normal Z to forehand—not recommended
F. High soft normal Z to forehand
   1. Starting position—center service box
   2. Height of contact—waist level
   3. Front wall bullseye—3-6 feet up and 1 foot in from left side wall
   4. Approximately 50 percent power on stroke
   5. Right side wall contact prior to back wall (after floor bounce)

VIII. Lob serve
   A. Starting position—right of center
   B. Height of contact—waist to chest level
   C. Stroke is a lofting "push"

D. Front wall bullseye—(depending upon starting position) three-quarters up and 1 foot left of center
E. Ball must brush side wall—about 6-8 feet in from back wall and 6-8 feet up from floor
F. Always lob serve cross-court
G. Use of lob discouraged

IX. Miscellaneous
   A. Which serves to use
      1. Beginner—experiment with all
      2. Advanced—acquire 2 or 3 bread-and-butter serves
   B. Temper service knowledge with concentration
   C. Do not change serves in mid-swing

X. Service practice drills
   A. Concept of practicing each serve a number of times before progressing to next
   B. Innovate and experiment
   C. Obtain outside criticism
   D. Drill with a helper in court
   E. More practice time should be devoted to serves and serve returns

SERVICE

The most important facet of racquetball is the *serve*, while the second most significant area is the *service return*. (Covered in the next chapter.) These two facts will be repeated frequently throughout this text. One might be able to coast by a few inferior duffers using weak strokes or leaky strategies, but without effective services and returns a player cannot expect to ramrod past even a glue-footed moron wielding a sawed-off squeegee.

Why are the serve and its racquet rebuff so intrinsically pertinent to racquetball? The answer lies partially in the results of a survey conducted by dually capable statistician-racqueteer Paul Lawrence. Lawrence determined that the average (mean) rally in racquetball, including the service and return, is approximately 2.3 shots. There are qualifications to be noted regarding the survey. The figures for Lawrence's statistics arose from observing and recording play in the 1972 national tournament, from the quarter-finals play through the finals. In other words, the 2.3 average rally mark is representative of the game's top performers that year—there were no paid professionals during that era of strict amateurism—and less talented individuals could no doubt make for longer volleys on each point. In addition, it must be stated that the year 1972 antedated the advent of the more highly compressed, bouncier ball now in use in tournaments. The more lethargic ball of 1972 dictated less ceiling balls and more point-ending set-ups for kill shots. This too lowered the average number of shots per side-out.

Nevertheless the ramifications of this 2.3 rally figure are astounding if one dissects it: the serve is made (1.0 shots), its return is accomplished (2.0 shots total) and less than 1.0 shots on the average is completed before the volley is terminated by either a point or side-out. Seemingly there is little more to the game than the serve and its return.

With this as a mathematical basis for the forthcoming, let us get down to the nitty-gritty subject matter: the serves and returns themselves. First, *four serves* will be explained. They are the garbage, drive, Z-serve and lob. In the next chapter the service returns will be presented. They are not so categorically confined as their service counterparts, although the ceiling ball, drive and around-the-wall ball are considered to be the safest returns (in order of effectiveness) off good serves. These serves and returns are the exact ones most utilized by the pros and other superior court dwellers. The pros just use them more consistently and skillfully. Observe any touring pro player and note that although his ball English, or hit force, or initial court positioning may vary slightly, the serve he employs is straight out of the text. Now watch a series of his serves. You should discover an underlying method or strategy worth emulating.

Before going into the four specific serves, it must be understood that the service is rarely a totally offensive shot. Sure, the server is in better than a neutral position, but he should not expect frequent aces, <u>as in</u> handball or tennis. The hopping or blooming serve is just not native to our game. Do not construe this as a de-emphasis of the serve. A well-hit serve will not immediately win a point, but as often as not it will result in a *weak return* at which time the put-away may be executed. On the other hand, a poorly-hit serve will generally lose the service (side-out) in a heck of a hurry. The more patient server who expects set-ups rather than aces is usually the better server.

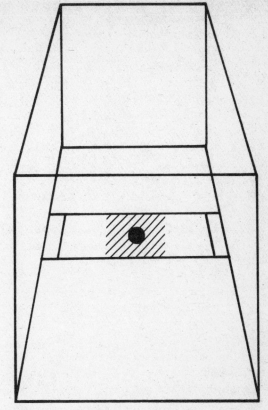

Fig. 10-1—Zone of usual starting station by the server.

THREE BASIC RECOMMENDATIONS

A basic recommendation is that the server assume a position approximately in the *center of the service box* when putting the ball into play. See figure 10-1. Standing too close to either side wall will sacrifice the all-important center court position at a time when that strategic central station is free for the taking. In addition, when the server initiates play from the center of the service box he is able to serve to either his rival's forehand or backhand with equal adeptness and with more chance for masking this choice of sides. Centralize yourself on the court right from the start to force your opponent to work hard to discover a serve return loophole.

More words to the wise from the pen of experience: serve to the rival's *backhand* most of the time. Obviously this is almost everyone's weaker stroke, whatever his level of play. Hence more feeble returns will ensue. Savvy? If not, imagine *yourself* all rough-and-ready to return service against Mort Meek, the braggart from down at the office. Would you rather old Mort served to *your* nuclear forehand or to your sickly backhand, which, as with many of us, probably packs all the potency of catnip, watered down Coors or a bad franchise hamburger?

Besides funneling into his weaker stroke, there is another more subtle reason for sending most serves to the competition's backhand. (This is with the usual righty vs. righty contestants.) That is, when you serve to the returner's backhand side, you are for all practical purposes forcing him to hit up and down the line rather than cross-court to your stronger forehand. If on the contrary, you serve to your opponent's forehand then his most logical choice of return will be a cross-court (bread-and-butter shot) to your weaker backhand. Do not obligate your rival to make an intelligent play; at least give him the opportunity to screw up on the serve return by serving almost continually to his backhand.

Whoever spoke of variety being the spice of life was no accomplished racquetballer. For one, stick to only a few different serves which seem to service you best, as opposed to inventing exotic variations each time you step into the service box. For two, badger the other guy's backhand with the serve. If you want to mix it up a little, then surprise serve one out of every six or seven shots to his forehand rather than one out of two or three.

With these weighty points out of the way, but still in mind, let us embark upon individual explanations of the four fundamental serves: the garbage, drive,

Fig. 10-2—Starting blocks for the garbage serve. (Brumfield in 1973 St. Louis Nationals.)

Z-serve and lob. Note that the names of these services, with the singular exception of the "garbage," are carry overs from shots otherwise utilized in a normal volley. Therefore the reader already has a nodding acquaintance as to their uses and their strong or weak points.

GARBAGE SERVE

The garbage serve is a homely looking thing. When viewed from above in the gallery, it is ostensibly a pansy or "trash" service. Hence its name. But while the garbage is short on looks, it is mighty long on effectiveness.

You are now going to hit some garbages at an imaginary opponent's backhand. Alone in the court, position yourself within the central service box area as indicated in figures 10-1 and 10-2. In brief, the ball should be struck softly—at "change-up" pace—and should be aimed at a level on the front wall which is midway up and a mite to the left of center. If this is performed properly, the ball will rebound gently off the front wall, take a lofty bounce on the floor posterior to the service box, and die in the left rear corner. Remember, this is not a low hard type of serve to be clobbered with a power stroke. Instead, it is a half-

lob of sorts which drifts with deceptive ease toward the receiver. And as it floats lazily posteriorly, it looks easy to return from everywhere except the returner's vantage point.

Now that a general overview has been provided, let us pursue this explanation in greater detail. Starting blocks for the garbage serve are in the service box approximately midway between the side walls. Bounce the ball to the floor such that the rebound peaks at navel to chest height. Racquet contact is made precisely as the ball reaches this zenith, and the stroke is a "push" rather than a normal forceful swing. An analogy may be beneficial here. Pretend you are a shot-putter about to put the cannonball-like shot. The arm motion for this action is a pushing away movement, as opposed to a roundhouse fling. In the same manner, a racquetball garbage serve should be "put" for maximum effectiveness. Compare this analogy and explanation to the close-up illustration in figure 10-3.

Okay. Now you have pushed the ball . . . but where to? Aim for a bullseye on the front wall about *1 foot left of center* and about *half way up from the floor.* (The latter mark has a tolerance of a couple feet up or down on the wall, depending on the force imparted to the served ball. Note figure 10-4.) If you wish, impart three-quarter sidespin to the ball, or topspin, in order to facilitate your change-up serve. Experiment and use whatever feels comfortable—a

Fig. 10-3—The garbage serve is a stiff-wristed "push."

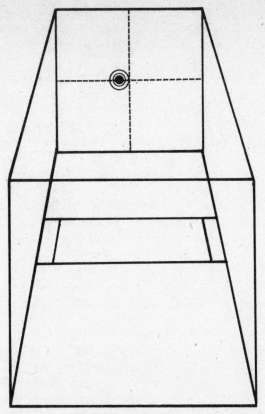

Fig. 10-4—Garbage serve bullseye (to the backhand) is about midway up the front wall and a foot left of center.

about neck high. This is a heck of a hard area from which to power a return with the backhand stroke.) Now examine the sequence photographs of the homely garbage serve in figure 10-6. Also see figures 10-7a and 10-7b.

Thus far we have dealt solely with the garbage serve to the backhand of a right-handed receiver. Unfortunately for us righties, by some fluke of nature approximately 10 percent of the human population came swinging into this world as southpaws. If ever you meet a lefty in court combat, serve up a few well-placed garbages for him to chew on. He will soon wish he were like the rest of us—properly armed right-handers. In addition, the garbage serve may be directed toward the forehand corner of a right-handed player. In this case, what little is lost in effectiveness due to the serve going to the opponent's stronger stroke is compensated for in surprise. The mechanics for the garbage serve to the right corner are the same as for the one to the left side. See figure 10-8.

The foregoing summarizes all the novice requires in order to buttress his service repertoire with the old standby, the garbage serve. But true service sophistication demands deeper study. Let us wrap up this garbage stuff by retracing a couple of significant points, with some new kinks tossed in for the post-novice racquetman.

After the sphere is contacted at its apex at about

good general guide for all facets of this cemented-in sport.

Beside the target spot parameters mentioned above, there is an *alternate* bullseye to aim for on the garbage serve. In lieu of zeroing in on a specific spot on the front wall, you may want to visualize a target area in the rear left corner of the court. This is an invisible box, and the ball must bounce into it after striking the front wall and subsequently bouncing on the floor. I emphasize that the server should strive to bounce the ball into the top (not through) this imaginary 3-foot cubic box in the left backhand corner. If indeed the garbage server is accurate in his placement of the serve into this hypothetical arrangement, he is assured that no opponent will ever hit a strong offensive shot—especially a kill—on that return of service.

In figure 10-5 a real-life cardboard box has been correctly placed to aid the reader in visualizing the "box theory" for the garbage serve in action. Try using this prop yourself in practice, remembering that the ideal garbage serve takes a high bounce on the floor such that it bounces into the box (that is, such that the serve's presentation to the receiver is

Fig. 10-5—Place or imagine a box in the left rear corner for the garbage serve "drop in" target.

Fig. 10-6—THE GARBAGE SERVE. Bounce the ball waist to chest high . . .

contact with a pushing motion . . .

nipple height, and after it ricochets from half-way up on the front wall plaster, it arcs softly as a tossed dandelion toward rear court. The floor bounce occurs at around three-quarter court and—most importantly—the ball must not brush the side wall until arriving deep into the left rear corner. As the ball begins to drop and die in said corner, only then is it permissible for it to contact that left side wall. That is, the garbage serve should slink along the left side wall without making physical contact prior to 3 feet from the back wall.

Not that the garbage serve *must* brush the side wall. It is also acceptable for it to contact the back wall first, but this must be within 3 feet of the left side wall. And whether or not it strikes the side or rear wall initially, it must not hit higher than 3 feet up

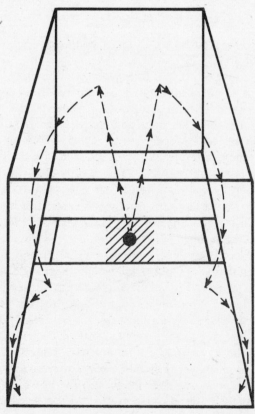

Fig. 10-7a—Course of garbage serves to forehand and backhand sides. Also see 10-7b.

hit the front wall bullseye . . .

back-pedal on a diagonal toward left rear corner.

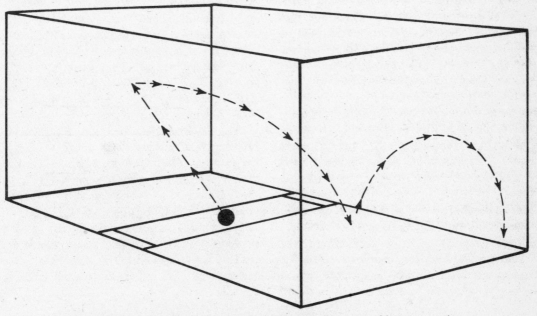

Fig. 10-7b—The deceptive, frustrating garbage serve. Must go to the backhand, though this depicts the forehand serve.

Fig. 10-8—GARBAGE SERVE TO THE RIGHT SIDE (above and facing page).

off the floor. Clear the air of confusion by directing your attention to figure 10-9. As can be seen here, the boundaries call for a garbage serve which does not stray more than 3 feet in any direction from the three-pronged point of the rear wall-floor-side wall crotch. Now perhaps the reader better appreciates the use of an imaginary 3-foot cube as a target area into which to "drop" the garbage serve.

In continuing along the lines of garbage sophistication, the reader may wish to experiment by deviating slightly from the earlier recommended exact center court serving position. Some players find it easier to execute the garbage by taking up a starting stance slightly to the *left* of center; this provides a more acute angle of incidence as the ball is propelled toward the front wall. A lesser number of court dwellers find it beneficial to commence serving to the right of center; a more obtuse angle of incidence is thus involved. However, do not begin more than 3 feet either way of the central serving area, as in figure 10-10.

The reader's initial reaction to his own use of the garbage serve will be undoubtedly negative. You will react with, "the garbage serve? Yep, it's exactly that.

Just some idiosyncrasy I read about in some book by a bug-wit author." This reaction is logical in that most greenhorn hackers innately feel that effort must be expended in order to capture effectiveness. This parallels the weightlifter's "only pain is gain" mandate. The garbage serve entails little effort, minimal touch and no brains. What more can I say than the garbage is the bread-and-butter serve of many of the well-known court superstars.

Why do Brumfield, Serot and others possessing high levels of power, touch and court brains favor the garbage? The answer is straightforward and blunt *strategy*. After the garbage serve's lofty bounce off the hardwood, its presentation to the receiver is nearly shoulder high (figure 10-11). There is nothing the percentage conscious returner can do but sock the orb skyward to the *ceiling*. The garbage serve appears ridiculously simple to kill or pass or take-your-pick, but generally any other return than a ceiling ball is suicidal.

DRIVE SERVE

"Kapow! Whomp! Kapow! Look at Willie Makit

Fig. 10-9—*Boundaries* in left rear corner for garbage serve.

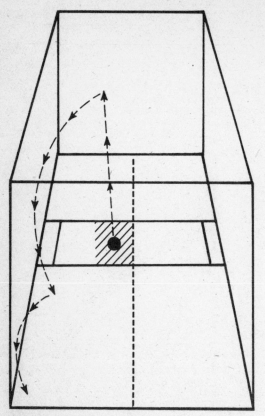

Fig. 10-10—Some players prefer to move a couple feet to the left of center to initiate the garbage to the backhand.

sockin' it to those guys with blazing low hard serves. Kapow! Whomp! No wonder nobody ever touches Willie—who could ever possibly return his blazing fastball service? I know I can't, and sometimes it makes me so frustrated I'd like to forget about the stupid ball and rearrange Willie's face with my racquet.''

Ever been in this movie before, reader? I've heard this line numerous times, and usually the vocalizer of such Batman and Robin sound effects is a once-a-week court dreamer who doesn't know his V-balls from his Z-balls. More than likely, Mr. Makit will rarely drop a game against the court dingbats whom he plays simply because of his dominating, blistering service attack. But if he ever meets up with a Serot, Schmidtke or similar stellar performer, Willie will never make it.

The low drive serve to the backhand is a highly potent means of initiating play, contrary to the cynical introduction above. In fact, I feel it is *the* best serve going, *provided* one funnels it to within the required target area every time. Therein is the kink: it is ex-

Fig. 10-11—The head-high presentation of garbage serve forces a ceiling return.

Brumfield won his first national singles title through the sole use of the garbage serve. His wrist is stiff, ball is contacted at navel to chest height.

Fig. 10-12—Hit the drive serve with *gusto* below knee level.

ceedingly difficult to consistently sight-in on this funnel of accuracy. This brings us to a significant, if paradoxical, point: the low drive service is overrated and overused among the myopically flailing players of bush league category. *But*, the low drive service is underrated and underused by the players of superior stock who possess the control and finesse required to effectively harness this wild and woolly offensive thrust.

Whatever your position in this paradox, if you wish to acquire a certain adeptness for the drive serve then two requisites must be adhered to. First, all low hards must be struck with *gusto*, and second, they must be contacted at *knee level* or lower. If you want to swat flies from the waist, trade in your racquet for a fly swatter and start hanging out at a dog kennel. But if you want to quickly become a cement court whiz, get down on the ball, apply considerable effort on your swing and read on.

Why contact at the knees? If you strike the ball at a higher altitude, say at the navel, the service shot will invariably rebound off the back wall for a set-up. Why the gusto bit? A feeble swing begets a soft, plum ball serve. The receiver could do three whirly-whirlies, shout "I am created in the image of Charlie Brumfield and have come to show you the nature of

Fig. 10-13—DRIVE SERVE TO THE RIGHT SIDE (below and facing page).

the game,'' and still have ample time to roll the ball off the front wall. Glance momentarily at figure 10-12.

Keeping in mind these two important points, peruse the following instructional explanation with an eye for generalities instead of details; the low drive serve is much more difficult than the garbage to execute, and I have found it useful to allow past students to fall into their own natural body rhythms rather than have them try to emulate an exact model movement. To further simplify matters, this text is geared toward hitting the drive serve only to the backhand (left corner). As one becomes more talented in the area of service, especially in the ability to camouflage his movements within the service box, the drive to the right side is an acceptable serve which may elicit aces or near-aces. (Figure 10-13.)

One other matter of concern should receive attention prior to undertaking the drive serve per se. This is the practice of aiming for the ''crack'' at the exact juncture of the side wall and floor. *Don't*. As often as not you will miss the crack by a long shot. The ball will pop up off the floor or off the side wall for a luscious pumpkin set-up to be blasted by an opponent sporting a heavy racquet and toothy grin.

I am put in mind here of my frequent nemesis,

Charlie Brumfield. How many times Chas and I have been on the court together in the closing moments of a seesaw third game. Chas will gain the serve, march into the service box, gaze toward the ceiling as if beckoning some court deity, and unlip a blood-curdling shriek: ''Give me a crack serve! Please give me just one crack serve!'' This is more a psychological ruse than anything else, though on occasions he has somehow hit the exact crack, and I ponder more deeply Charlie's accuracy or the actual existence of a four-walled god. Basically, crack shooting is a nonpercentage gamble which should be used sparingly. The game's eminent players may audibly pray for, but rarely aim for, the crack ace.

Now let us learn to execute the low hard, or drive, serve. Assume a normal central serving position within the service box, as in figure 10-14. As you grow more accustomed to the many factors involved in this type of service, you may wish to move slightly —but not more than 1 to 2 feet—to the *left* of center court to initiate play. It must be noted out of deference to the official rulebook that if one does shade too far to the left, he runs the risk of serving a screen ball. This is a serve in which the server's body blocks, or partially screens, the receiver's view of the oncoming flight of the served ball (figure 10-15). The sub-

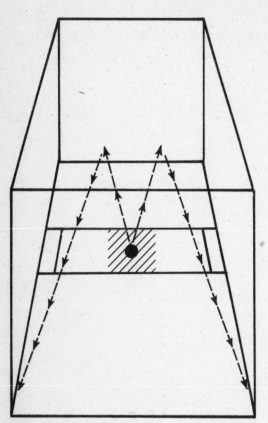

Fig. 10-14—The drive serve: center court starting position with service flights to forehand and backhand sides.

Now, cogitate for just a tick-tock. Isn't this low drive serving motion entirely the same as the *drop-and-kill* exercise for the forehand? This was outlined in Chapter 4 and the reader may wish to page back at this time to review the paralleling motions. Also refer to figure 10-16 for a picture sequence of the drive serve in action. Once in a while at tournaments I will get the "addled brain syndrome" caused by over-thinking or just trying too hard to serve up the perfect drive. When this occurs I simply revert to the singular concept of stroking the ball with my normal drop-and-kill technique. Presto! Instant service.

Aim your kill shot motion, that is your low drive serves, at a bullseye approximately *1 foot left of center* and about *3 feet up off the floor.* (Figure 10-17.) This is not intended to be as precise a target area as it may sound; personal experimentation should once again govern the reader's specific bullseye. The 1 foot left of center mark is for a server who commences serving from exactly center court. If one moves a tad to the left of center, the bullseye moves correspondingly to the left—but be careful, for it is very easy to overcompensate and aim much too far left of center. The mark suggested for *height* of contact on the front wall is also open for mild variance. It is not difficult to deduce that the harder the ball is struck, the lower this mark should be sighted in. Conversely, if a server swings with less than average power, he may find it beneficial to elevate the bullseye to perhaps 4 feet up from the floor.

By way of example on this latter item concerning height of front wall contact, I have tutored many grandmother types to aim almost halfway up the front wall when unleashing their feeble drive serves on unsuspecting gramps, the receiver. Then again, I am somewhat taken aback whenever I find myself on the receiving end of two-time national champion Bill Schmidtke: Schmidtke starts his serve by crouching like a coiled spring just about a foot to the left of center service box—just far enough to the left to partially block the serve with his body, but not far enough that any jello-kneed referee would call an illegal screen on a two-time champ. Wild Bill drops the ball, applies his nuclear forehand at ankle height and the sphere cannonballs off the front wall at an elevation no greater than 1 foot. Needless to say, my fingernails quiver and teeth ache in despair each time the orb comes screaming at my backhand.

Now that *power* has been mentioned, let us take a brief side trip into a subject closely akin to the execution of the drive serve. How much force should one impart to the low drive serve? To answer one question with another, how much power should you apply to a forehand kill? Or a backhand drive, or al-

ject of screen serves is the touchy, subjective basis for many heated arguments among club players. The rules not being crystal clear at the time of this writing, the only logical solution to the problem (where a referee is not present) is for the service returner to have the final say on all such serves. On the other hand, the dilemma of the questionable shade serve is avoided by the server posting his ground grabbers to the right of center. However, for reasons too sophisticated for this presentation, moving to the right of center court is disadvantageous and I have witnessed few top notch racqueteers initiating play from this position.

Resuming with the execution of the low hard serve, bounce the ball in front of your body such that the peak of the rebound is about *knee high* (or lower). As with all serves, this zenith shall be our intended point of string contact. After stepping into this knee high bounce, the point of racquet-rubber rendezvous is off the *lead foot.*

Fig. 10-15—SCREEN SERVE
FROM THE RECEIVER'S
VANTAGE POINT

most any other shot in racquetball? Muster about 80 percent force in all cases. The normal club player tends to utilize more stroke impetus than desirable, again probably because he equates strength with effectiveness. Strive for about 80 percent power.

The flight path of the drive serve is similar to that of the garbage, except obviously the drive travels at a lower elevation en route to the back wall. The angles involved with both serves are comparable. Visualize that three-pronged crotch where the left side wall, floor and back wall assemble to form a dusty juncture (figure 10-18). That's where you are aiming for. The low hard serve should roar (80 percent roar) off the racquet strings and zip along 3 feet or so off the floor toward this target area. You will be pleasantly amazed at how close your drive serves approach this magic juncture after a little practice. See figure 10-19.

Now forget the side wall-floor-back wall bullseye momentarily; recollect the garbage box theory. As with the deceptive garbage, a box theory may be applied with the drive serve. Take up your service stance and simultaneously visualize within your mind's eye a 3-foot cubic box in the left rear corner. (Figure 10-20.) Strive to hit your serve *through* (not drop into, as was the case with the garbage) this imaginary box. When you conjure up this box image, it may help to think of the cardboard container lying on its side with the open end facing the front wall. Now . . . isn't that much easier to hallucinate?

Utilizing the box theory, you realize that thread-the-needle accuracy is not necessary for an acceptable drive serve. Relaxation and a generalized target area foster accuracy. To put the box theory regarding the low hard serve into rhetoric: the served drive may strike anywhere as long as it makes contact not more than 3 feet high on the back wall; if hitting the back wall first, then it must strike not more than 3 feet in from the left side wall and, if hitting the side wall first then it must strike not more than 3 feet anterior

Fig. 10-16—DRIVE SERVE
TO THE LEFT SIDE
(from left to right and below).
(Do not foot fault on
your serves.)

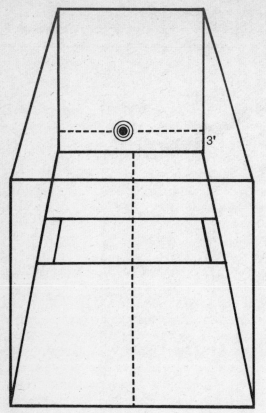

Fig. 10-17—Drive serve bullseye to backhand is about a foot left of center and 3 feet up from floor.

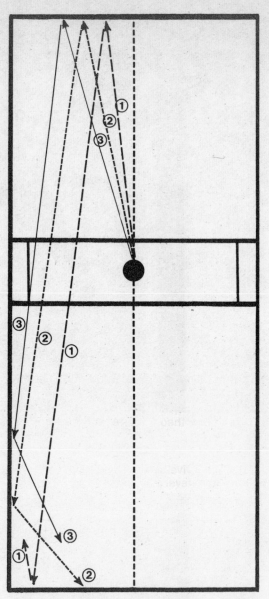

Fig. 10-19—Radioactive particles in random motion? No, these are three basic paths of the drive serve to the backhand. (Dotted line is midpoint between side walls.) Serve #1 rebounds off the back wall close to the side wall and is acceptable. Serve #2 catches left side wall within 3 feet of back wall and is acceptable. Serve #3 ricochets off the side wall early, comes out to center court for a plum and is unacceptable.

Fig. 10-18—The *perfect* drive serve would "crack out" at the left wall-back wall-floor juncture (arrow).

from the back wall. The reader may wish to dispose of this verbosity by just aiming through the box.

The fundamental explanation of the low hard serve is completed. It was alluded to earlier that the *controlled* drive is probably the most effective selection of all racquetball services. The grounds for this claim are that the low hard serve causes far more eventual set-ups for the server anxious to generate a slam-bang kill shot style of play. You will quickly appreciate, as your level of skill advances, that the staple return off most serves is a ceiling ball. But it is a task indeed to smite an accurate *ceiling ball* (figure 10-21) off a drive serve. Therefore the return off the low serve is necessarily more offensively oriented—possibly a drive or attempted kill.

All this is well and good . . . provided one is able to put the ball consistently through the mental cardboard box.

Now that the execution and substantation of the "best" serve in racquetball have been covered, it is again time for the "most common error" offering. The most frequent problems encountered by beginners attempting the drive serve are: 1) Contacting the ball too high, in excess of our maximum height recommendation of knee level. 2) Walloping the sphere

Fig. 10-20—"Box theory" on the drive serve.

Marty Hogan's drive serve is one of the best. Notice the wrist cock, step forward and below-knee-level contact.

Fig. 10-21—It isn't easy to go to the ceiling against Hogan's low screaming drive serves.

as though it were your worst enemy's eyeball, thus sacrificing control for speed. Strike the serve with no more than 80 percent power. 3) Serving from right of center. Most players discover that this wider angle of incidence in relation to the front wall begets two problems: one, it produces more "wrap-around" or side-wall-to-back-wall set-ups. Two, it allows the receiver a split second longer to view the ball as it courses completely unobscured past the server's body. 4) Serving up too many drives to the forehand. Many novices have a methodical though illogical propensity for dishing out one to the left, one to the right, left, right—do not do this. As stated previously, drive mainly to the backhand. 5) Straying from the normal forehand drop-and-kill motion. Remember, the two motions are practically identical. In addition, many court upstarts forget to snap their wrists forcefully on their low drive serves. There goes the power. This would not transpire if the usual forehand kill shot motion were adhered to.

Do you want immediate gratification from a well-placed serve? Then fling a barrage of low hards at

your next practice rival. If they are accurate and go through the box, expect to get a plum ball back. But if they miss the mark, do not expect the rallies to last past the service return.

Z-SERVE

To attempt to picture the Z-serve solely through words is necessarily wordy, and often reveals little more than a hazy image of weird angles and something about the ball's flight path resembling the last letter of the alphabet. An instructor may as well try to teach yoga's pretzeled lotus position via pure rhetoric—a task equally as formidable. Nevertheless, once the skill is acquired, the Z-serve is probably one of the easiest to execute and most effective serves ever unearthed by the game's "fight-from-the-seat-of-their-britches" paper technicians.

Boasting these virtues, the Z forms an integral part of any service regime. At least once every week, some disgruntled hacker approaches this author for some "freebee" info: "How can I improve my game by

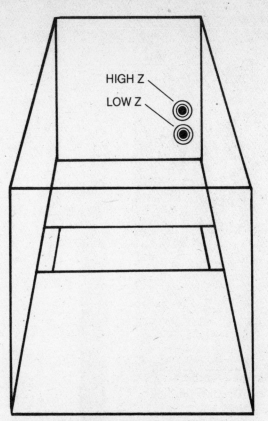

Fig. 10-22—Target area and bullseye (about 3 feet high and 1-2 feet to the left of right side wall) for low reverse Z-serve. The higher mark is for high reverse Z (5'-6' x 1'-2').

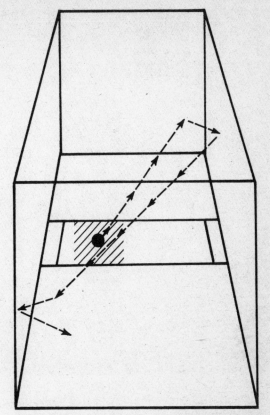

Fig. 10-23—Low reverse Z: starting position in service box and path to backhand.

five points in just 10 minutes?'' they ask. Not an unreasonable query; I demonstrate the *reverse Z-serve*. Actually there are *two* types of Z's, which we will attempt to learn now. Study figure 10-22 before continuing.

These two types of Z-serves are the *reverse Z* which is served to the receiver's *backhand*, and the *normal Z* which is directed at the *forehand*. (Again assuming both participants are right-handed.) The more effective of these two ploys is the reverse to the backhand, and this is the one I throw back at those hopeful rookies who slink out of the concrete walls inquiring, ''How can I improve my game by five points in just 10 minutes?''

The *reverse Z* is to be dealt with first and primarily. In order to execute this properly, the server must initially station himself within the shaded area of the service zone, as indicated in figure 10-23. That is, he must start by standing in the center or to the left of center within the service box. Before the reader plunges further, he may wish to experiment with this range of starting stances in the court by himself. To

do this, first think back to the Z-ball (not to be confused with this chapter's Z-serve which contacts the front wall-side wall-*floor*) from Chapter 7 on the defensive shots. The keen student may recall from that chapter that the closer one stands to the side wall the easier it becomes to produce an acceptable Z-ball. This also holds true for the Z-serve.

(Note: it is a matter of frustrating paradox, however, in regard to this initial positioning business. The farther to the left of center within the service box the player moves, the easier the Z-serve execution becomes; simultaneously the farther to the left of center service box the player moves, the more he telegraphs his intentions.) Experiment with serving from all positions within the figure 10-23 shaded area and discover which spot works best for you.

There are two variations of the reverse Z to the backhand: the lower (harder) version and the higher (softer) version. To serve up the *low hard reverse Z*, commence from the correct position within the service box and bounce the ball next to your lead foot (after stepping into the stroke), as though you were

Fig. 10-24—Brumfield (left) and Serot await service in National Doubles tourney in St. Louis in 1973. How would *you* serve to the game's best right- and left-handed forehands?

Fig. 10-25—The LOW Z-SERVE to the backhand . . .   is struck exactly like . . .

going to make a kill shot in the right front corner. In other words, this low Z to the backhand is stroked just like the drop and kill, only at a different angle.

Contact the sphere at *knee level* or lower and aim for a bullseye on the front wall about *3 feet up from the floor and 1 foot in from the right side wall.* After a few solitaire trial runs on the court, you will find the more significant dimension here is the latter, 1 foot in from the right side wall. As with most of the other services presented in this chapter, whacking a sweet Z is an elementary matter which entails beginning from the correct position and hitting a certain front wall bullseye.

You have just learned to hit a *low hard Z to the backhand* . . . and, if you can consistently duplicate this maneuver, you have just improved your game by five points in 10 minutes. The flight course of this Z serve is plotted in figure 10-23. As can be seen from this graphic representation, the struck sphere hits the front wall bullseye, ricochets into the right side wall and then travels cross-court (duck if you have to, but do not let the ball collide with your carcass) toward the left rear corner. After a floor bounce the ball rebounds sharply off the left side wall near the back wall and, due to tremendous English garnered from previous wall encounters, cuts with startling spin and steam right into the potential returner's bod. For the receiver to solidly place his quivering racquet upon a thusly wildly gyrating orb is akin to swatting at a housefly suffering from conniption fits with a vibrating hotcomb.

Hotcombs and *Musca domesticas* aside, if you do not direct the low reverse Z accurately, it is gloom and doom time. The ball will either carry too deep and rebound off the back wall, or it will come off the left side wall too early, for a routine set-up. While this serve is virtuous when struck right on, it is suicidal if inaccurate. Study the action sequence in figure 10-25 at this time.

There is no box theory parallel here, but suffice it to say that after the ball goes front wall-right side wall-floor, it should contact the *left side wall* next within the following tolerances: the height of contact is not especially significant as long as the racquetball strikes the left side wall *1 to 4 feet from the back wall.* If one serves outside these limits—closer than a foot to the back wall or farther forward than 4 feet— he may expect a strong return. Figure 10-26 displays these boundaries.

That completes the low hard reverse Z. The second

the forehand drop and kill exercise . . .

only it hits a different front wall bullseye.

Fig. 10-26—*Boundaries* in left rear corner for the low hard Z-serve.

Fig. 10-27—The high Z-serve to the backhand corner hits the front wall 5 to 6 feet high and about a foot from the right side wall.

variation of the reverse Z is the *high soft Z-serve to the backhand*. The starting position is the same as outlined above for the low hard variation. The point of string-on-racquet contact is raised slightly to about waist height. The ball is not hit "hard," with 80 percent power as before, but instead is firmly stroked with about 50 percent speed. The bullseye on the front wall is *1 foot from the right side wall* (as before) and *5 to 6 feet up from the floor*. See figure 10-27. The soft reverse Z flight path corresponds to that of the previous harder one, but obviously travels higher up from the hardwood terrain. After taking its floor bounce, the sphere contacts the left side wall *2 to 5 feet out from the back wall*, and its height of contact with said side wall is slightly higher than before. Figure 10-23 charts this flight path, while figure 10-28 portrays the soft reverse Z execution.

Ruminate for a while on these angles and heights and ball velocities, and it becomes apparent that the high soft reverse Z is essentially an elevated, slower traveling low hard reverse Z. And vice versa. By way of emphasis, it is mandatory that both these service variations strike the *left side* wall prior to back wall.

Heretofore we have considered the two types of reverse Z's. With a little imagination, the low hard reverse Z is similar to a drive serve with a few added angles and walls. And the high soft reverse Z is similar to a garbage serve with a few added angles and walls. The proverbial question now is, which of the two is the superior point fetcher? The low hard Z forces more set-ups, but because of the same rationale applied earlier in this chapter to the low hard drive serve, it is decidedly more difficult to execute. On the other hand, the high soft Z is safer and easier to hit but, like the garbage, does not extract as many serve return set-ups. The choice is a crux of complex compensations to be deciphered by each reader in accordance with his individual whims.

With the two reverse Z-serves to the backhand now surveyed, we will undertake a brief appraisal of the *normal Z's* to the *forehand* (right) side of the court. For these, the angles and walls involved are displayed in figure 10-29.

The proper serving spot is given in the shaded zone of figure 10-29. Note that this shaded zone does not carry as correspondingly far to the right side wall as does the previous reverse Z zone to the left side wall.

Fig. 10-28—I hit the high Z to my opponent's backhand . . .

with a head-high three-quarter overhead swing . . .

which I strike hard enough to prevent the receiver from charging the serve.

This is because the normal Z is facilitated by the extension of the server's right arm toward the right side wall. That is, the arm's reach supplants the body movement to the right of center. On the other hand, for a *southpaw* serving a normal Z (for him) to left rear court, the natural anatomical extension of his racquet arm to the left of center replaces any body movement to left of center when considering the lefty's starting service position. Forgive any temporary confusion on this subject and refer to figures 10-30.1 and 10-30.2.

Let us take up again with a right-hander serving a *normal Z* to another right-hander's forehand. Place your gym shoe treads in service box *center court*. The ball is bounced, struck at its peak from about the *waist* and sent flying into the front left corner. As before, the bullseye is on the front wall approximately *1 foot in from the left side wall* and *3 to 6 feet up from the floor.* (Figure 10-31.) The precise height of front wall contact, assuming the starting stance is constant, hinges upon the power of the stroke. The more force applied to the ball, the lower the front wall elevation contact point. Illustrations in figure 10-32 portray

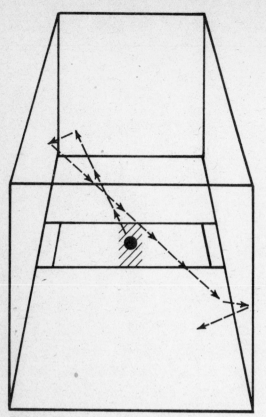

Fig. 10-29—Normal Z to forehand: starting position and flight path.

the ideal motion for the normal Garfinkle serve to the forehand.

A strategic point to ponder: Experience among quality players has proven that the low hard normal Z to a rival's *forehand* is overly risky. Unless the ball is divinely placed, an alert receiver will probably rifle back a cross-court drive or down-the-line kill. Therefore, it is this author's contention, as well as the noncognizant practice of other court virtuosos, that the percentages lie with a higher softer version of the Z-serve when said serve is directed to the forehand.

As with the high reverse Z, this normal Z should course back to the right rear corner and, following its floor bounce, should contact the right *side wall first* before the back wall. The height of side wall-ball collision is a fairly arbitrary 4 to 6 feet up; the side wall contact distance from the back wall is a more significant dimension of *2 to 4 feet* from the rear court plaster.

Although the Z to the forehand is not quite as effective as its mirror to the backhand (because the latter is directed at the receiver's weaker stroke), it is a safe change-of-pace weapon. In addition, due to the intrinsic angles involved, this shot is tailor-made for a lefty serving to a righty, or vice versa. A case in point occurs when pro Steve Serot plays pro Steve Strandemo. Southpaw Serot's service mainstay is the

Fig. 10-30.1—From exact center court, the right hander's anatomic extension to the right facilitates Z-serving into the right rear corner.

high soft Z to his rival's backhand. But right-handed Strandemo is no gymshoed slouch either, and his staple serve is the soft Z hit to Serot's backhand. Thus when the two Steve's take up racquet armaments, it makes for an interesting cat-and-mouse confrontation of one normal Z followed by another.

In summary of this section on Z-serves, we have presented two types of Z's to the backhand—the low hard and high soft, and two variations to the forehand—the low hard and high soft. Recall that the low hard Z to the right side is rarely employed unless one's opponent is a portsider. All this becomes less muddled when provided in outline form:

Z-serves
    A. To the backhand (reverse Z's)
        1. Low hard reverse Z
        2. High soft reverse Z
    B. To the forehand (normal Z's)
        1. Low hard normal Z—not recommended
        2. High soft normal Z

(Note: This outline is for right hander vs. right hander.)

Once you acquire insight into the above Z potpourri, you may wish to attempt to combine the positive aspects of more than one. However, this author in

Fig. 10-31—The Z-serve bullseye to the right rear corner is about a foot in from the left side wall and 3-6 feet high.

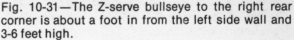

Fig. 10-30.2—For the same reason, a southpaw's bread-and-butter serve could be a low or high Z into the *left* rear corner.

Fig. 10-32—Z-SERVE TO THE RIGHT SIDE

Fig. 10-33—Ever serve an ACE?

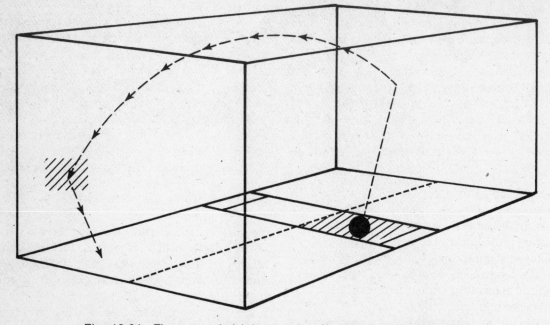

Fig. 10-34—The outmoded lob serve is effective only if the server possesses pinpoint accuracy. Ball should brush side wall (shaded area) on downward trajectory.

the past has diligently endeavored to make such incorporations, with the firm conclusion that it is best to stick to just one of the four basic Z-serves. Whatever you choose to serve up, get one service or service combination in mind the instant you tromp into the service box. During the delivery of that premeditated serve, do not get involved in the mental mixing of a low hard with a high soft, or the disastrous product will be a service which defies written description.

LOB SERVE

The fourth and final fundamental service is the lob, and allow me to preview this concise survey by pointing out that we have reserved the *worst* for last.

As with the garbage serve, the lob involves a gentle, upward directed stroke which contacts the ball *navel to chest high* at the *apex* of the bounce off the floor. But that is where the similarities between the two services cease.

The lob serve is commonly propelled into flight from the center of the service box, but its chances for success are greatly enhanced by edging *closer to the*

right side wall (when lobbing to the left rear corner—backhand). Refer to figure 10-34. The closer you plant your Buster Browns to that right side wall, the more effective the serve becomes. This is because the lob must *catch the left side wall* during its descent into the left rear corner, and when one moves to the right in the service box in order to lob cross-court to the left, the sphere is more easily angled into the side wall. This wall-ball brush is absolutely mandatory due to the energy dissipating action of the left wall. On the other hand, observe what transpires when a lob is lofted into the rear corner *without* side wall encounter: Any court habitué slinging a mean backhand will perfunctorily roll off the back wall set-up. A lob service sequence of photographs is shown in figure 10-35.

The front wall bullseye for the lob is about *three-quarters of the way up* (give or take 3 feet, depending upon the force given the served sphere) and if one serves from exactly center court, *1 to 2 feet left of center*. This latter mark will vary in accordance with the server's initial serving station. The nearer he cheats to the right side wall, the farther to the right on the front wall the bullseye moves; but the height of front wall contact remains an approximate three-quarters up. See figure 10-36, and keep in mind that this serve calls for ardent personal experimentation for more precise dimensional guidelines.

Also maintain in those mental saddlebags another fact: The overshadowing feature concerning the lob is the dampening *brush* with the side wall as the ball sails in downward plummet. Depending upon the server's initial station, this contact will be in a very generalized area about 6 to 8 feet from the back wall and 6 to 8 feet from the floor. Other than this, the key to the lobbed serve is to keep it as high and soft as possible. This is accomplished by always lobbing *cross-court* to ensure side wall contact and less back wall rebound.

To issue a lob to the opposite (right) corner, the server need only tippy-toe a little to the left of center and perform the same stroke mechanics as described above. Arch those lobs to the right side only if your court antagonist is a southpaw, or, if by rare instance your rival's forehand is inept beyond reproach and your sadistic mania is to immediately emphasize that foible to the scrutinizers in the gallery.

I feel the lob itself is a weak link in any server's repertoire, at least among higher caliber players. Inaccuracy on the lob serve is a rule rather than exception, and unfortunately the smallest error in serving often yields the biggest plum set-up imaginable. Use of this service among the professionals is sparse since its control exceeds the capabilities of even these par excellence performers. Do you recall the earlier remarks in Chapter 7 on the use of the lob during the course of play? Well, the lob *serve* is tantamount in ineffectuality to the defensive lob. The two are related forms of court philanthropy which none of us can afford.

Hopefully the reader is now aware of how and where to put the racquetball into play. Subsequently, it is only natural for questions of a more strategically oriented nature to arise. One of the most common along this line is "*which* service should I use?"

The novice racqueteer is encouraged to experiment with all four serves and their variations (making slight alterations if desired) for a period of not less than three months before resolving which one or two will be his bread-and-butter services. I made this resolution early in my court career, confidently determining that my opponent could expect a steady diet of drives and low hard reverse Z's to his backhand. All went well for a couple of years until the general quality of racquetball play increased nationwide to such a degree that when I pounded out those Z's and V's, my rivals began chewing them up and spitting

them back at me like a kid trying out his first mouthful of spinach. At this point in time I initiated a crash program on the softer serves—garbages and high Z's—and this continues to influence my overall service plan to this day.

Therefore, the greenhorn with the wooden framed racquet, as well as the intermediate with his color-coordinated outside threads, is advised to explore a *variety* of serves, subconsciously recording which ones force the most set-ups and points the majority of the time. And do not be surprised if you periodically idle in a mental quagmire as I often did, pondering to yourself: The only thing I'm completely sure of is I'm not sure which serve to use.

As you non-calloused rookies transform into hardened veterans with accordingly greater service proficiency, I believe you will eventually conclude that there is no *one* best serve. (Especially, there is no such animal as the universal serve for the universal player.) Each method of putting the ball into play boasts its strong and weak points. That is what makes the game both fascinating and frustrating at the same time.

Knowing *which* serve to use is still a fool's notion unless the knowledge is marinated in heavy concentration. Visualize the following scene. You are in the annual local tournament, right there in center court hopping nervously over the back red service line. Very aware of family and friends watching from above, you expertly call in a deep voice, "Heads, ref," for the coin toss. George Washington peers directly into your eyes and the referee directs you to serve 'em up. Please, do this chapter mild credit and do *not* step into the service box with the sole objective of simply batting the ball over the back service line and then breathing a deep sigh of relief. First *think*, . . . then serve.

Concentrate. Whether in casual play or tournament competition, develop the habit of engaging in 3 seconds of purposeful mental activity prior to whacking the orb into official play. During this 3 seconds recall the relative scores, remember your opponent's weaknesses as well as your strengths, and think where are you going to hit the ball with what type of serve. It was touched upon earlier in the chapter that one tell-tale sign of absence of concentration during service is to prance excitedly into the service area and indiscriminately start to pulverize a low hard serve. You change your mind in mid-swing and decide to switch to a gentle lob . . . and you end up clobbering a high hard lob that goes out of the court over the referee's head. Your family and friends in the gallery do not approve. I know all this from personal experi-

Fig. 10-35—LOB SERVE

ence. The chagrin can only be compared to getting caught de-linting your navel during a time-out.

Write only one serve on your mind's blackboard and then execute it methodically; only in this manner is the serve racquetball's most potent weapon.

SERVICE PRACTICE DRILLS

Practicing your services is utterly boring in the same way that Chinese water torture is utterly boring. But do not despair. With a little time, a dash of applied concentration, and a few cardboard boxes, a couple of intense one-half hour solo practice sessions should significantly bolster most players' service games. And since improvement in service is the mother to enhanced overall racquet play, the time spent drilling on serves will be well worthwhile.

This being your introductory pep talk, now hit the hardwood and practice each of the four serves. Hit and chase . . . hit and chase. Better yet, employ a bunch of balls. A friend of mine used to enter the court with a racquet slung from one hand and his motorcycle helmet full of balls in the other. He would practice serves until the motorcycle helmet was emptied and refilled ten times.

Keep at each of those serves until the motion develops into a fluid, mechanical groove. It will come in time. For example, smack two dozen drive serves to the backhand (or any number of drives until you are confident you could consistently perform the same movement upon cue in a game situation). *Then* go on to tap a couple dozen garbages, then Z's and so on. Do *not* hit one drive followed by one garbage,

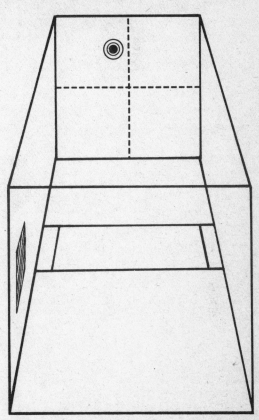

Fig. 10-36—Lob serve: front wall bullseye is 1-2 feet left of center and about three-quarters of the way up to the ceiling. Left side wall "dampening" bullseye is 6-8 feet from floor and 6-8 feet in from back wall.

then a Z, and so on. Grooves are formed through repetition.

As you practice, *innovate*. Does it help to hit a garbage serve higher up on the front wall than this text recommends? Or perhaps when serving a reverse Z you find you attain more side wall action by adding a zestful slice to the ball with the racquet face. In short, it will not hurt to toy with the model serves presented in this text.

Finally, obtain *outside criticism* of your service game if possible. The oft shouted quotation, "If only we could see our serves as other people see them" is particularly applicable here. You may wish to practice serves with a buddy who wants to practice his serve returns. No better mate is possible. While doing this criticize each other's play. An excellent alternative to this mutualistic form of drilling is to recruit a

willing wife (husband) or girl (boy) friend to shag your serves. This obviously hastens the Chinese water torture.

If four-walled low-leaguers spent one-tenth the amount of time on serves and serve returns that they devoted to practicing their other shots, the high-leaguers would come closer into view.

SERVICE RETURN

CHAPTER 11 SUMMARY

I. Serve return is second in importance only to serve

II. Initial position 3-4 feet from back wall and center or slightly left of center court

III. Service return and concept of center court
   A. Closely interrelated
   B. Prime objective—force the opponent from center court and occupy area yourself

IV. Five possible returns
   A. Three high percentage—ceiling ball, drive and around-wall-ball
   B. Two low percentage—lob and kill shot

V. Ceiling ball return
   A. Safest and most logical service return
   B. Jibes perfectly with concept of center court positioning
   C. Direct at opponent's backhand
   D. Execution previously detailed in Chapter 7
   E. Is comforting shot and thought—can be used in rebuff to any serve

VI. Drive return
   A. Second most widely used return
   B. Is both, and neither, offensive and defensive
   C. Usually directed cross-court (V-ball pass)
   D. Use against moderately good and weak serves presented at waist height or lower

VII. Around-wall return
   A. Underused, especially among lower caliber players
   B. Best utilized against "softer" serves (garbage and high reverse Z)
   C. Usually struck with backhand; always cross-court

VIII. Lob return—totally discounted except as desperation ploy

IX. Kill shot return
   A. Use only against weak serves—e.g. serves presented at waist level or lower
   B. Generally think conservative on service return—this dictated by logic and center court concept
   C. If you do kill return: forehand into forehand corner and backhand into backhand corner

X. Drills
   A. Especially practice drills from Chapter 7 on defensive shots; offensive shots needed too
   B. Ultimate drill: server vs. returner
   C. See drills in Chapter 10 on the service

XI. Summary

Fig. 11-1—Stand to receive service about a racquet and arm's length from the back wall.

SERVICE RETURN

After the serve comes the serve return. By now the overwhelming importance of the service and its rebuff should be drilled permanently into the bottomboard crevices of the reader's four-cornered cerebrum.

First a sound piece of advice, and then on to the concrete specifics of service returns. As with the server, the receiver must *think* and, especially, keep his cool. For example, upon receiving a low hard drive, it definitely ain't cool to tense up that pencil throat, let loose a strident ALLEY OOP yell and attack the little sphere with gladiator ferocity. No-no. The service return must be carried out in a confident and perfunctory manner, usually stroking the ball with 80 percent power and with a definite shot in mind. And hang loose.

Let us commence with the stark basics, progress into semi-muddled sophistications, and then return to earth with the possible types of service returns.

The ideal position for return of service is approximately *three to four feet from the back wall.* I "sense" this distance by occasionally taking up my potential position, swiveling my upper body at the hips such that the top half of me is looking at the back wall, while the bottom half of me is fixin' to run toward the front wall, and waving my racquet with an extended arm at the rear wall plaster. If I am rooted at the correct distance from the back wall, my outreached racquet will barely scrape the plaster as I wave. (See figure 11-1.) I tell beginners to stand in the *center* of the court because this is easy to remember. Actually, a station slightly to the *left of center* is per-

missible if the receiver expects most serves will be fired at his melancholy backhand, as is usually the case. Figure 11-2 displays this general receiving zone.

The correct stance within this zone has no strict limitations. For the uninitiated whose natural posture leans toward the elephantine, it is beneficial to imitate the tennis player's ready position for receiving service: knees bent slightly, eyes forward and racquet ready. Not to knock tennis, but I actually feel that a more relaxed stance is indicated for the intermediate to advanced four-wall aficionado. This is because, unlike in tennis, the racquetball serve loses energy on the front wall ricochet, arrives in rear court at a lesser velocity and is generally presented within fairly easy reach. Therefore your receiving stance should be somewhere between loosey-goosey and board-rigid. Note the serve returner's initial posture in figure 11-3.

Now on to those semi-muddled sophistications mentioned above. Although service return is an autonomous concept in itself, it is also a tight strategic associate with the theory of *center court position.* In other words, the idea of service return is one wing and the concept of center court position is another wing; and without both of these in working order your game will not get off the ground.

As you ponder the following rationalization, augment the text by examining the diagrams in figures 11-4 and 11-5. At the instant that you receive a decent serve, you are in the *worst* court position possible—in deep rear court. Simultaneously your opponent, stationed in exact center court, is in the *best* strategic position possible. Obviously, if you make a slight

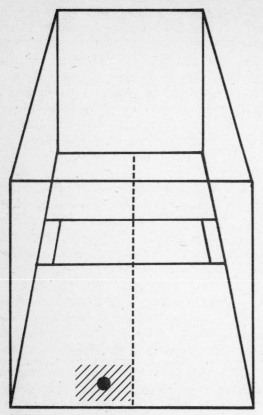

Fig. 11-2—The usual service receiver's starting stance is a racquet's swing from back wall and slightly off center to the left.

Fig. 11-3—Be ready but relaxed when awaiting the serve.

error *now* you will not have another chance until a point later when the next ball is served up.

Therefore, your first objective as service receiver is to return the ball in such a way as to *force your opponent out of center court position.* Unless the serve is outrageously muffed—for example one which rebounds high off the back wall for an appetizing set-up—do not go for the kill shot. Rather, force your rival into back court with a defensive shot and subsequently assume center court position yourself. The opening moments of each racquetball rally are remarkably similar to chess in that whoever controls the middle of the court/board will most often emerge the ultimate victor.

If all this is acceptable, then exactly how is one to best utilize strategic positioning in making strong service returns? There are five ways. That is, the receiver of the serve has *five possible returns.* However, let's simplify this on the grounds that percentage racquetball dictates only *three optimal returns* taken from the basic five. They are the ceiling ball, drive

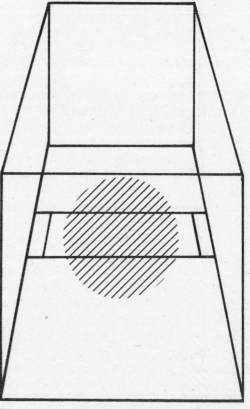

Fig. 11-4—A liberal schematic representation of center court position (shaded area).

and around-the-wall-ball. These three we will take up immediately; the remaining two lower percentage possibilities are the lob and kill shot, and they will be dealt with briskly later on. (Note: The Z-shot is unlikely as a return off of a good serve, due to the receiver's striking position in very deep court.)

CEILING BALL RETURN

Rank having its priority, the ceiling ball is presented first here as the *safest and most logical service return* of all. Remember that when the opposing player is serving, he is in control of center court, and your number one thought as service receiver is to shoo him the heck outa there. Bullet balls to the kidneys or ear lobe shots being illegal, return the sphere so as to oblige him to retreat posteriorly, concurrently allowing you to occupy the coveted center court station. The ceiling ball suits this occasion in a most appropriate fashion.

The rub is that the ceiling shot necessitates veteran patience and poise; a beginner is often overly eager to get things rolling with a more offensive return. The most convincing advice to offer such early zealots is to have them analyze a few points between a couple of pros, or at least "A" players—with a pencil and paper. Take note of the types of shots utilized to return the first 30 serves. If at least half of them are not ceiling balls, then either the serves are rotten to the ball's core or the subjects under surveillance are of sub-"A" ranking. Patience is especially a virtue on the service return, and the ceiling is the path to patience.

Since the execution of the all-important ceiling shot has already been detailed in Chapter 7, it will be reviewed only briefly now. Note the photo portrayal in figure 11-6. Recall that the properly struck ceiling ball initially contacts the ceiling, then front wall, then floor, and ultimately bounces high and deep into back court. It is pretty much impossible to cut off this shot prior to the leapfrogging bounce toward the back wall, thus the opponent (server) has to backpedal and then swat at the shot from shoulder height in deep court. Under these circumstances, the back-

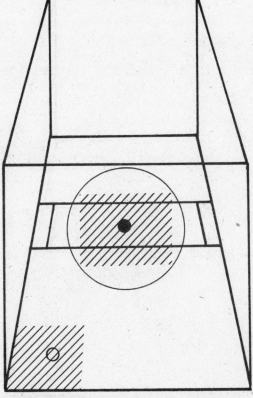

Fig. 11-5—Initial server's and service receiver's positions (after the serve) with respect to center court position. Should your serve return be a kill?

Fig. 11-6—THE main service return: CEILING BALL.

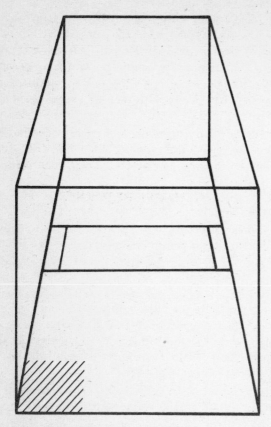

pedaling returner of the ceiling ball usually has no feasible choice but to come back with a similar defensive ploy (i.e. another ceiling ball).

Direct your ceiling returns to the server's *backhand* (figure 11-7), a process which generally entails hitting with your backhand stroke down the left line (against a right-hander). Keep the rubber orb a-huggin' that left side wall but, at the same time, do not allow the type of side wall contact which will send the ball squirting out into open air.

If, during a game, you suddenly experience difficulty in keeping your ceiling service returns close and parallel to the side plaster for near wallpaper balls, do not be afraid to change tactics just a tad. Scope in on a ceiling bullseye more toward the *center* of the court. That is, guide the sphere in a slight cross-court direction. True, this may result in a service return to the server's forehand, but this is of little consequence provided the shot carries deep enough in the court.

Fig. 11-7—Basic rule of service return: Direct most of your service returns to the opponent's weaker stroke, the backhand in deep court (shaded area).

Fig. 11-8—BACKHAND DRIVE RETURN . . .

This sequence also illustrates the proper form for . . .

240

The main mission of a service return off of a strong—or at least adequate—serve is to spew back anything which cannot be offensively attacked by the server.

At the risk of throwing this whole line of thinking out of kilter, it is compulsory to add that a *weak* serve should not be answered defensively, but should be assaulted with a pass or kill attempt. Unfortunately I see few weak serves coming my way these days.

To me, the ceiling ball is a *comforting* shot to maintain within my strategic repository as I stand there on shaking, spindly legs with racquet clutched in trembling hand about to absorb the feared rival's primo serve. Why comforting? Because the ceiling shot can be used to send back *any service* that hamburger could offer. If he lobs me, I can either step up and volley the ball to the ceiling or go to the ceiling after the floor bounce. If he low hard serves me, I do my best to flail the speeding sphere upward at the ceiling target area. A served Z, reverse or normal? I still look to the ceiling, perhaps aiming slightly toward center court to prevent the ball's English-spawned antics from eliciting an unwelcome encounter with the left side wall. Too, the ceiling ball is my 100 percent rebuff for a good garbage, unless I opt to

rush the thing for a volley shot. And when that sly humpty-dumpty catches me leaning left during his drive serve to the right, I reverse, scramble right, cast out my strings quick as a lizzard's tongue and flick the ball toward the court heavens, praying for deep deliverance. It *is* a comforting shot and thought, isn't it?

Review the ceiling ball coverage provided in Chapter 7. Then hit the courts for ceiling ball drills as outlined in Chapter 7 and at this chapter's conclusion.

DRIVE RETURN

Next to the ceiling ball, the drive (pass shot) is probably the most widely utizlied service return. The pass is much more offensively geared than the ceiling play, yet less offensively oriented than the risky kill attempt. Therefore it is neither, and both, an offensive and defensive return of service.

The drive return is advocated by the player who desires to initiate a rapid-fire, reflex type of rally. This was alluded to earlier in the book. In fact, an entire chapter (6) has been dedicated to the drive shots, their variations, executions and strategic implications. The reader is strongly advised to bone up

the backhand kill return.

Fig. 11-9—FOREHAND DRIVE RETURN . . .

on these aspects prior to attempting any drive serve returns. For a visual review of the pass shots in action, refer to figures 11-8 and 11-9.

Witness a cement coop standout during a serious game and you will doubtless observe that when that player does bash a pass shot off the serve, the ball is usually sent *cross-court*. (Figure 11-10.) This is because the cross-court drive allows for greater margin of error—an overused term signifying your shot can stink and there is still a good chance you will come out smelling like a rose—than hitting straight up and down the alley. The down-the-liner should not be discounted entirely as a potential service return (from the backhand side), but it is potent only when pinpointed with great precision, which is a tall order for a racquetballer of any stock. All in all, the pros favor the V-ball when they choose to drive return the serve.

A rather self-evident tidbit of advice for the would-be practitioner of drive service returns: if you are presented with *any well-placed serve*, play it safe and go to the ceiling rather than ripping off a V-ball. If you are given a *moderately good serve* which has some potential for offensive return, a drive may or may not be made. *Bad serves* deserve strong returns, such as riproaring drives.

Specifically, do not drive back a good garbage or similar soft style serve (e.g. high reverse Z) which must be contacted at shoulder height. But, do try drives off of ill-placed garbages which either pop off the side wall in shallow court or carry off the back wall. Do drive return low hard services which either wrap around the left rear corner for set-ups or rebound straight off the back wall. Do slash out with a vicious cross-court drive off any serve presented to your forehand, provided you are able to set up for the shot and it may be contacted at waist height or lower.

In short, the drive return uproots the opponent lounging within the service box (center court position) in a manner which forces an immediate point or, at least, a weak return.

AROUND-WALL-BALL RETURN

The around-the-waller is relied upon sparsely today as a service return; for that matter, its use during the course of normal play is also scarce. This is probably due to lack of recognition. There are a multitude of talented court club players who do not even realize the A.W.B. exists. If the reader is among this shel-

This sequence also illustrates the proper form for . . .

the forehand kill return.

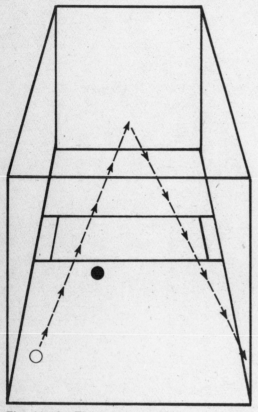

Fig. 11-10—The cross-court drive is a good aggressive service return.

the height of presentation of the softer serves. For me, the defensive ploy is an acceptable response to a garbage or high reverse Z-serve (figure 11-11).

Thus the A.W.B. is more frequently issued from the *backhand* side of the court, and is directed upward and cross-court into the right front corner at the appropriate right side wall bullseye. Re-skim through Chapter 7. And to point out two things which should never occur, but often do: First, do not allow your own around-the-wall ball to descend and strike your lumbering person. Second, do not let the server trample you during his random tramp in pursuit of the elusive orb.

LOB RETURN

If this book had been written in the very early 1970's, when racquetball was just crawling out of the catacombs and into the airy glass-walled fishbowls, a good deal of this chapter on service returns would have been dedicated to that floating, frustrating return known as the lob. However, in these days of our sport's semi-maturity, the lob is certainly outmoded due to the advent of more lively balls and modernized racquets. I touch here upon the lob as a service return only out of finicky methodicalness.

How to lob, where to lob, and why not to lob were all discussed in Chapter 7, and 'nuff said then and there on those subjects. I find myself forced into a lobbing situation only once or twice per tournament, and these are always desperation flick-of-the-wrist circumstances where no other shot is physically possible. But even in these rare instances I try to send the lob as high as possible without touching the ceiling, cross-court and strive for side wall contact on the ball's downward trajectory.

Avoid lobbing the serve return if at all possible.

KILL SHOT RETURN

The kill shot return of service is bold and flashy when successful, humiliating and demoralizing when skipped in. As a service return weapon off of a *sound* serve, it is a double-edged sword which could just as easily cut the receiver as the server. As such, the kill is an illogical choice of return.

The wizard of logic, Mr. Spock, of television's "Star Trek," would rarely go for the bottom board of the spacebound court within the steel bowels of the Starship Enterprise. He might relect that "The feasibility of shooting the serve is a fascinating possibility, but hardly one worthy of actual practice."

Another self-proclaimed logistician, Charlie Brumfield (Ceiling ball Brum) once sagely penned with

tered many hiding out in the back woods of antiquity, page back this instant to Chapter 7 dealing with the defensive shots. Review in particular the around-the-wall ball.

Got it squared away? Now throw an around-the-waller in retaliation to your opponent's next garbage, reverse Z or lob serve, and see if you are not pleasantly surprised by the other dude's shock and surprise. This multi-angled, multi-walled return should literally drive your competitor up the right side wall, his sense of equilibrium sent topsy-turvy by the ball's aerial antics. Meanwhile, you waltz up to center court with mouth watering and await the lame return.

As a service return, the A.W. ball functions best against the "softer" serves, as opposed to the lower harder drive serves and low hard reverse Z's to the backhand. The reason for this is the around-the-waller is usually contacted *above* the waist, which is

Fig. 11-11—The around-the-wall serve return may be used to rebuff any soft, shoulder-high service.

tongue in cheek: "So why try it (the service return kill)? How many balls are you going to hit for absolute winners off your opponent's best shot, his serve? I can't hit very many percentage-wise, and if you can, send me your name and I'll bet on you in the next international tournament."

This author is less fanatical about the situation than Mr. Spock or Mr. Brumfield. I do concur that a strong propensity for the *defensive* should occupy the player's mind as he awaits service. But—and this is a big but—the kill shot *is* a definite percentage possibility, as well as a quick rally-ending ploy, for returning a *weak* service. So administer the offensive punch on a languid serve by shooting the ball. To not do so would breach the "Offensive theory of play," besides removing the keep-on-your-toes pressure from the server who normally backpedals nonchalantly into back court after serving the ball.

When you do go for the death stroke on the service return, it is generally wise to place forehand kill attempts into the forehand corner, and backhands into the backhand corner. (See figure 11-12.)

Repetition spawns remembrance. So excuse any redundant emphasis which ensues, because the following concept is worth a heapful of points per game. When one goes for a kill off a *good* serve, all the cold and calculating center court theory in the court world is working against you.

Does it make sense to shoot for the roll-off from three-quarter court when your nemesis is stationed in front of you in perfect center court position? If you skip the ball in, your rival picks up a point without expending an iota of energy; and if you leave the ball up even slightly on the front wall, your opponent will be right there in two daddy-sized steps ready to gratefully pounce on the plum. This time he gains the point by outlaying but few milliergs of energy. Of course, it is true that if your shot is a flat roll-out then you win the side-out (not the point) along with the admiration of the spectators, but I can almost guarantee this will transpire a low percentage of the time. Save your kill shots for riper times, which are sure to arise during the course of the rally.

(It must be clear that the above paragraph assumes the serve to you, the receiver, is a good-to-moderately good one. But again, if the serve is weak, then inhale, grunt and tee off offensively with a kill or pass.)

But, you cry in rebuttal, it feels *so* fine to smack those solid flat rollers which send the server into vocal fits of self-condemnation. True. Just observe a pro take another pro's weak serve and handle it adeptly with a kill shot return. The faces of the server and returner are respective masks of agony and ecstasy: "I've been had by that lucky sonofaduffer!" the pro server fumes internally as he snails with weighted shoulders to rear court. "That'll show that pea-brained court scum!" his jubilant peer inwardly leers as he moseys to the service area. The latter casts a knowing eye at the bleachers, dramatizing his temporary stroke of proficiency. Two plays later, our man with the up-turned eyes and up-turned nose is a picture of humility and frustration. His eyes look inward, avoiding contact with all others, for he has just skipped in three service return kill attempts in a row.

I can identify with the above fantasized (?) anecdote. Back when I was a pure court rat, flaunting freak balls, enthusiasm and jockstrap headbands, I often found myself in the same movie. I wanted to display my flash, power and ignorance to the sprinkling of mini-skirted dumplin's in the gallery. I did this by pouncing regularly on every other service and flailing for the bottom board. Won their hearts, but not the game.

Let's assume, contrary to this, that you are after *points.* Want to unfurl a paragon of patience, poise and savy to the grizzled court veterans in the stands? Then send your service returns elsewhere than the bottom board.

SERVICE RETURN DRILLS

When practicing the various *defensive shots*, you automatically groom your skill in the area of service return. Therefore apply yourself to the defensive shot exercises, as outlined in Chapter 7. Keep in mind that most balls being put into play will be directed at your *backhand*, and train accordingly. The fly in the soup is that the offensive game is also an integral component of the receiver's consideration. Hence, some

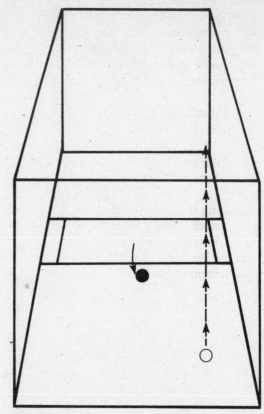

Fig. 11-12—A weak serve to the forehand may be killed in the right front corner.

skill for being able to bury the ball low into the corners is needed. It is a tough order, but drill for the service return by keeping up on all the defensive (especially) and offensive shots used in racquetball.

The ultimate way to practice the return of service is to find someone who wants to work on his serves. In this case he serves, you return and the ball is caught. Repeat and re-repeat. A more elaborate practice plan incorporating both the serve and its return was espoused upon at the closing of Chapter 10 on serves. Refer to this now, or innovate your own training methods, and put them into practice.

The summary of a chapter on service return is easily written:
1) The principal service return is the ceiling ball.
2) To a certain degree, the type of serve will dictate your type of response.
3) Be patient when responding to a good serve, and be alert for offensive possibilities when given a poor serve.
4) Mix up your returns if you have not yet dis-

covered anything that is especially effective against an individual server (e.g. at the beginning of the game).

5) If a specific service rebuttal does prove to be the antidote against a particular opponent, importune him without variation with that shot.

6) Next to the serve, the service return is the most overshadowing facet of racquetball play.

By way of further summary, the most *common errors* department is extensive:

1) Assuming an initial stance too anterior in the court. Start with heels about 3 feet from back wall.

2) Following the return stroke, not moving up to seize center court position. Do not lollygag in back court, but follow in your shot.

3) Not aiming for a specific shot. Do not spray your returns at random.

4) Forgetting the prime objective of neutralizing the server's positional advantage. Drive him posterior.

5) "Running around" the ball to take what should have been a backhand stroke with the forehand. This is strategically sacrilegious, positionally suicidal and leads to inferior development of the backhand.

6) Indiscriminately shooting of the ball off the serve. Get hep with a conservative train of thought when receiving service.

7) Not employing the "fifth wall" enough. The ceiling is not there solely to keep the raindrops out and the racquetballs in.

8) Hitting ceiling shots on balls presented to the receiver below waist height. Recall that a weak serve at knee level or lower should be assaulted with offensive intent.

9) Not hitting ceiling shots on balls presented to the receiver above waist height.

section III
RACQUETBALL APPENDICES

chapter twelve

OFFICIAL RACQUETBALL RULES

OFFICIAL U.S.R.A.-N.R.C. FOUR-WALL RULES

PART I. THE GAME

Rule 1.1—Types of Games. Racquetball may be played by two or four players. When played by two it is called "singles;" and when played by four, "doubles."

Rule 1.2—Description. Racquetball, as the name implies, is a competitive game in which a racquet is used to serve and return the ball.

Rule 1.3—Objective. The objective is to win each volley by serving or returning the ball so the opponent is unable to keep the ball in play. A serve or volley is won when a side is unable to return the ball before it touches the floor twice.

Rule 1.4—Points and Outs. Points are scored only by the serving side when it serves an ace or wins a volley. When the serving side loses a volley it loses the serve. Losing the serve is called a "hand-out."

Rule 1.5—Game. A game is won by the side first scoring 21 points.

Rule 1.6—Match. A match is won by the side first winning two games.

PART II. COURT AND EQUIPMENT

Rule 2.1—Court. The specifications for the standard four-wall racquetball court are:

(a) Dimension. The dimensions shall be 20 feet wide, 20 feet high, and 40 feet long, with back wall at least 12 feet high.

(b) Lines and Zones. Racquetball courts shall be divided and marked on the floors with 1½ inch wide red or white lines as follows:

(1) Short Line. The short line is midway between and is parallel with the front and back walls dividing the court into equal front and back courts.

(2) Service Line. The service line is parallel with and located 5 feet in front of the short line.

(3) Service Zone. The service zone is the space between the outer edges of the short and service lines.

(4) Service Boxes. A service box is located at each end of the service zone by lines 18 inches from and parallel with each side wall.

(5) Receiving Lines. Five feet back of the short line, vertical lines shall be marked on each side wall extending 3 inches from the floor. See rule 4.7(a).

Rule 2.2—Ball Specifications. The specifications for the standard racquetball are:

(a) Official Ball. The official ball of the U.S.R.A. is the black Seamco 558; the official ball of the N.R.C. is the green Seamco 559; or any other racquetball deemed official by the U.S.R.A. or N.R.C. from time to time. The ball shall be 2¼ inches in diameter; weight approximately 1.40 ounces with the bounce at 68-72 inches from 100 inch drop at a temperature of 76 degrees F.

Rule 2.3—Ball Selection. A new ball shall be selected by the referee for use in each match in all tournaments. During a game the referee may, at his discretion or at the request of both players or teams, select another ball. Balls that are not round or which bounce erratically shall not be used.

Rule 2.4—Racquet. The official racquet will have a maximum head length of 11 inches and a width of 9 inches. These measurements are computed from the outer edge of the racquet head rims. The handle may not exceed 7 inches in length. Total length and width of the racquet may not exceed a total of 27 inches.

(a) The racquet must include a thong which must be securely wrapped on the player's wrist.

(b) The racquet frame may be made of any material, as long as it conforms to the above specifications.

(c) The strings of the racquet may be gut, monofilament, nylon or metal.

Rule 2.5—Uniform. All parts of the uniform, consisting of shirt, shorts and socks, shall be clean, white or of bright colors. Warm-up pants and shirts, if worn in actual match play, shall also be white or of bright colors, but may be of any color if not used in match play. Only club insignia, name of club, name of racquetball organization, name of tournament, or name of sponsor may be on the uniform. Players may not play without shirts.

PART III. OFFICIATING

Rule 3.1—Tournaments. All tournaments shall be managed by a committee or chairman, who shall designate the officials.

Rule 3.2—Officials. The officials shall include a referee and a scorer. Additional assistants and record keepers may be designated as desired.

Rule 3.3—Qualifications. Since the quality of the officiating often determines the success of each tournament, all officials shall be experienced or trained, and shall be thoroughly familiar with these rules and with the local playing conditions.

Rule 3.4—Rule Briefing. Before all tournaments, all officials and players shall be briefed on rules and on local court hinders or other regulations.

Rule 3.5—Referees. (a) Pre-Match Duties. Before each match commences, it shall be the duty of the referee to:

(1) Check on adequacy of preparation of the court with respect to cleanliness, lighting and temperature, and upon location of locker rooms, drinking fountains, etc.

(2) Check on availability and suitability of all materials necessary for the match such as balls, towels, score cards and pencils.

(3) Check readiness and qualifications of assisting officials.

(4) Explain court regulations to players and inspect the compliance of racquets with rules.

(5) Remind players to have an adequate supply of extra racquets and uniforms.

(6) Introduce players, toss coin, and signal start of first game.

(b) Decisions. During games the referee shall decide all questions that may arise in accordance with these rules. If there is body contact on the back swing, the player should call it quickly. This is the only call a player may make. On all questions involving judgment and on all questions not covered by these rules, the decision of the referee is final.

(c) Protests. Any decision not involving the judgment of the referee may on protest be decided by the chairman, if present, or his delegated representative.

(d) Forfeitures. A match may be forfeited by the referee when:

(1) Any player refuses to abide by the referee's decision, or engages in unsportsmanlike conduct.

(2) After warning any player leaves the court without permission of the referee during a game.

(3) Any player for a singles match, or any team for a doubles match fails to report to play. Normally, 20 minutes from the scheduled game time will be allowed before forfeiture. The tournament chairman may permit a longer delay if circumstances warrant such a decision.

(4) If both players for a singles, or both teams for doubles fail to appear to play for consolation matches or other play-offs, they shall forfeit their ratings for future tournaments, and forfeit any trophies, medals, awards or prize money.

(e) Referee's Technical. The referee is empowered, after giving due warning, to deduct one point from a contestant's or his team's total score when in the referee's sole judgment, the contestant during the course of the match is being overtly and deliberately abusive beyond a point of reason. The warning referred to will be called a "Technical Warning" and the actual invoking of this penalty is called a "Referee's Technical." If after the technical is called against the abusing contestant and the play is not immediately continued within the allotted time provided for under the existing rules, the referee is empowered to forfeit the match in favor of the abusing contestant's opponent or opponents as the case may be. The "**Referee's Technical**" can be invoked by the referee as many times during the course of a match as he deems necessary.

Rule 3.6—Scorers. The scorer shall keep a record of the progress of the game in the manner prescribed by the committee or chairman. As a minimum the progress record shall include the order of serves, outs, and points. The referee or scorer shall announce the score before each serve.

Rule 3.7—Record Keepers. In addition to the scorer, the committee may designate additional persons to keep more detailed records for statistical purposes of the progress of the game.

Rule 3.8—Linesmen. In any U.S.R.A. or N.R.C. sanctioned tournament match, linesmen may be designated in order to help decide appealed rulings. Two linesmen will be designated by the tournament chairman, and shall, at the referee's signal either agree or disagree with the referee's ruling.

The official signal by a linesman to show agreement with the referee is "thumbs up." The official signal to show disagreement is "thumbs down." The official signal for no opinion is an "open palm down."

Both linesmen must disagree with the referee in order to reverse his ruling. If one linesman agrees and one linesman disagrees or has no opinion the referee's call shall stand.

Rule 3.9—Appeals. In any U.S.R.A. or N.R.C. sanctioned tournament match using linesmen, a player or team may appeal certain calls by the referee. These calls are 1) kill shots (whether good or bad); 2) short serves; and 3) double bounce pick ups. At no time may a player or team appeal hinder, avoidable hinder or technical foul calls.

The appeal must be directed to the referee, who will then request opinions from the linesmen. Any appeal made directly to a linesman by a player or team will be considered null and void, and forfeit any appeal rights for that player or team for that particular rally.

(a) Kill Shot Appeals. If the referee makes a call of "good" on a kill shot attempt which ends a particular rally, the loser of the rally may appeal the call, if he feels the shot was not good. If the appeal is successful and the referee's original call reversed, the player who originally lost the rally is declared winner of the rally and is entitled to every benefit under the rules as such, i.e., point and/or service.

If the referee makes a call of "bad" or "skip" on a kill shot attempt, he has ended the rally. The player against whom the call went has the right to appeal the call, if he feels the shot was good. If the appeal is successful and the referee's original call reversed, the player who originally lost the rally is declared winner and is entitled to every benefit under the rules as winner of a rally.

(b) Short Serve Appeals. If the referee makes a call of "short" on a serve that the server felt was good, the server may appeal the call. If his appeal is successful, the server is then entitled to two additional serves.

If the served ball was considered by the referee to be an ACE serve to the crotch of the floor and side wall and in his opinion there was absolutely no way for the receiver to return the serve, then a point shall be awarded to the server.

If the referee makes a "no call" on a particular serve (therefore making it a legal serve) but either player feels the serve was short, either player may appeal the call at the end of the rally. If the loser of the rally appeals and wins his appeal, then the situation reverts back to the point of service with the call becoming "short." If it was a first service, one more serve attempt is allowed. If the server already had one fault, this second fault would cause a side out.

(c) Double bounce pick-up appeals. If the referee makes a call of "two bounces," thereby stopping play, the player against whom the call was made has the right of appeal, if he feels he retrieved the ball legally. If the appeal is upheld, the rally is re-played.

If the referee makes no call on a particular play during the course of a rally in which one player feels his opponent retrieved a ball on two or more bounces, the player feeling this way has the right of appeal. However, since the ball is in play, the player wishing to appeal must clearly motion to the referee and linesmen, thereby alerting them to the exact play which is being appealed. At the same time, the player appealing must continue to retrieve and play the rally.

If the appealing player should win the rally, no appeal is necessary. If he loses the rally, and his appeal is upheld, the call is reversed and the "good" retrieve by his opponent becomes a "double bounce pick-up," making the appealing player the winner of the rally and entitled to all benefits thereof.

Rule 3.10—If at any time during the course of a match the referee is of the opinion that a player or team is deliberately abusing the right of appeal, by either repetitious appeals of obvious rulings, or as a means of unsportsmanlike conduct, the referee shall enforce the Technical Foul rule.

PART IV. PLAY REGULATIONS

Rule 4.1—Serve-Generally. (a) Order. The player or side winning the toss becomes the first server and starts the first game, and the third game, if any.

(b) Start. Games are started from any place in the service zone. No part of either foot may extend beyond either line of the service zone. Stepping on the line (but not beyond it) is permitted. Server must remain in the service zone until the served ball passes short line. Violations are called "foot faults."

(c) Manner. A serve is commenced by bouncing the ball to the floor in the service zone, and on the first bounce the ball is struck by the server's racquet so that it hits the front wall and on the rebound hits the floor back of the short line, either with or without touching one of the side walls.

(d) Readiness. Serves shall not be made until the receiving side is ready, or the referee has called play ball.

Rule 4.2—Serve-In Doubles. (a) Server. At the beginning of each game in doubles, each side shall inform the referee of the order of service, which order shall be followed throughout the game. Only the first server serves the first time up and continues to serve first throughout the game. When the first server is out—the side is out. Thereafter both players on each side shall serve until a hand-out occurs. It is not necessary for the server to alternate serves to their opponents.

(b) Partner's Position. On each serve, the server's partner shall stand erect with his back to the side wall and with both feet on the floor within the service box until the served ball passes the short line. Violations are called "foot faults."

Rule 4.3—Defective Serves. Defective serves are of three types resulting in penalities as follows:

(a) Dead Ball Serve. A dead ball serve results in no penalty and the server is given another serve without cancelling a prior illegal serve.

(b) Fault Serve. Two fault serves results in a hand-out.

(c) Out Serves. An out serve results in a hand-out.

Rule 4.4—Dead Ball Serves. Dead ball serves do not cancel any previous illegal serve. They occur when an otherwise legal serve:

(a) Hits Partner. Hits the server's partner on the fly on the rebound from the front wall while the server's partner is in the service box. Any serve that touches the floor before hitting the partner in the box is a short.

(b) Screen Balls. Passes too close to the server or the server's partner to obstruct the view of the returning side. Any serve passing behind the server's partner and the side wall is an automatic screen.

(c) Court Hinders. Hits any part of the court that under local rules is a dead ball.

Rule 4.5—Fault Serves. The following serves are faults and any two in succession results in a hand-out:

(a) Foot Faults. A foot fault results:
(1) When the server leaves the service zone before the served ball passes the short line.
(2) When the server's partner leaves the service box before the served ball passes the short line.

(b) Short Serve. A short serve is any served ball that first hits the front wall and on the rebound hits the floor in front of the back edge of the short line either with or without touching one side wall.

(c) Two-Side Serve. A two-side serve is any ball served that first hits the front wall and on the rebound hits two side walls on the fly.

(d) Ceiling Serve. A ceiling serve is any served ball that touches the ceiling after hitting the front wall either with or without touching one side wall.

(e) Long Serve. A long serve is any served ball that first hits the front wall and rebounds to the back wall before touching the floor.

(f) Out of Court Serve. Any ball going out of the court on the serve.

Rule 4.6—Out Serves. Any one of the following serves results in a hand-out:

(a) Bounces. Bouncing the ball more than three times while in the service zone before striking the ball. A bounce is a drop or throw to the floor, followed by a catch. The ball may not be bounced anywhere but on the floor within the serve zone. Accidental dropping of the ball counts as one bounce.

(b) Missed Ball. Any attempt to strike the ball on the first bounce that results either in a total miss or in touching any part of the server's body other than his racquet.

(c) Non-front Serve. Any served ball that strikes the server's partner, or the ceiling, floor or side wall, before striking the front wall.

(d) Touched Serve. Any served ball that on the rebound from the front wall touches the server, or touches the server's partner while any part of his body is out of the service box, or the server's partner intentionally catches the served ball on the fly.

(e) Out-of-Order Serve. In doubles, when either partner serves out of order.

(f) Crotch Serve. If the served ball hits the crotch in the front wall it is considered the same as hitting the floor and is an out. A crotch serve into the back wall is good and in play.

Rule 4.7—Return of the Serve. (a) Receiving Position. The receiver or receivers must stand at least 5 feet back of the short line, as indicated by the 3 inch vertical line on each side wall, and cannot return the ball until it passes the short line. Any infraction results in a point for the server.

(b) Defective Serve. To eliminate any misunderstanding, the receiving side should not catch or touch a defectively served ball until called by the referee or it has touched the floor the second time.

(c) Fly Return. In making a fly return the receiver must end up with both feet back of the service zone. A violation by a receiver results in a point for the server.

(d) Legal Return. After the ball is legally served, one of the players on the receiving side must strike the ball with his racquet either on the fly or after the first bounce and before the ball touches the floor the second time to return the ball to the front wall either directly or after touching one or both side walls, the back wall or the ceiling, or any combination of those surfaces. A returned ball may not touch the floor before touching the front wall. (1) It is legal to return the ball by striking the ball into the back wall first, then hitting the front wall on the fly or after hitting the side wall or ceiling.

(e) Failure to Return. The failure to return a serve results in a point for the server.

Rule 4.8—Changes of Serve. (a) Hand-out. A server is entitled to continue serving until:

(1) Out Serve. He makes an out serve under Rule 4.6 or

(2) Fault Serves. He makes two fault serves in succession under Rule 4.5, or

(3) Hits Partner. He hits his partner with an attempted return before the ball touches the floor the second time, or

(4) Return Failure. He or his partner fails to keep the ball in play be returning it as required by Rule 4.7(d), or

(5) Avoidable Hinder. He or his partner commits an avoidable hinder under Rule 4.11.

(b) Side-out. (1) In Singles. In singles, retiring the server retires the side.

(2) In Doubles. In doubles, the side is retired when both partners have been put out, except on the first serve as provided in Rule 4.2(a).

(c) Effect. When the server on the side loses the serve, the server or serving side shall become the receiver; and the receiving side, the server; and so alternately in all subsequent services of the game.

Rule 4.9—Volleys. Each legal return after the serve is called a volley. Play during volleys shall be according to the following rules:

(a) One or Both Hands. Only the head of the racquet may be used at any time to return the ball. The ball must be hit with the racquet in one or both hands. Switching hands to hit a ball is out. The use of any portion of the body is an out.

(b) One Touch. In attempting returns, the ball may be touched only once by one player on returning side. In doubles both partners may swing at, but only one, may hit the ball. Each violation of (a) or (b) results in a hand-out or point.

(c) Return Attempts. (1) In Singles. In singles if a player swings at but misses the ball in play, the player may repeat his attempts to return the ball until it touches the floor the second time.

(2) In Doubles. In doubles if one player swings at but misses the ball, both he and his partner may make further attempts to return the ball until it touches the floor the second time. Both partners on a side are entitled to an attempt to return the ball.

(3) Hinders. In singles or doubles, if a player swings at but misses the ball in play, and in his, or his partner's attempt again to play the ball there is an unintentional interference by an opponent it shall be a hinder. (See Rule 4.10.)

(d) Touching the Ball. Except as provided in Rule 4.10(a)(2), any touching of a ball before it touches the floor the second time by a player other than the one making a return is a point or out against the offending player.

(e) Out of Court Ball. (1) After Return. Any ball returned to the front wall which on the rebound or on the first bounce goes into the gallery or through any opening in a side wall shall be declared dead and the serve replayed.

(2) No Return. Any ball not returned to the front wall, but which caroms off a player's racquet into the gallery or into any opening in a side wall either with or without touching the ceiling, side or back wall, shall be an out or point against the players failing to make the return.

(f) Dry Ball. During the game and particularly on service every effort should be made to keep the ball dry. Deliberately wetting shall result in an out. The ball may be inspected by the referee at any time during a game.

(g) Broken Ball. If there is any suspicion that a ball has broken on the serve or during a volley, play shall continue until the end of the volley. The referee or any player may request the ball be examined. If the referee decides the ball is broken or otherwise defective, a new ball shall be put into play and the point replayed.

(h) Play Stoppage. (1) If a player loses a shoe or other equipment, or foreign objects enter the court, or any other outside interference occurs, the referee shall stop the play. (2) If a player loses control of his racquet, time should be called after the point has been decided, providing the racquet does not strike an opponent or interfere with ensuing play.

Rule 4.10—Dead Ball Hinders. Hinders are of two types—"dead ball" and "avoidable." Dead ball hinders as described in this rule result in the point being replayed. Avoidable hinders are described in Rule 4.11.

(a) Situations. When called by the referee, the following are dead ball hinders:

(1) Court Hinders. Hits any part of the court which under local rules is a dead ball.

(2) Hitting Opponent. Any returned ball that touches an opponent on the fly before it returns to the front wall.

(3) Body Contact. Any body contact with an opponent that interferes with seeing or returning the ball.

(4) Screen Ball. Any ball rebounding from the front wall close to the body of a player on the side which just returned the ball, to interfere with or prevent the returning side from seeing the ball. See Rule 4.4(b).

(5) Straddle Ball. A ball passing between the legs of a player on the side which just returned the ball, if there is no fair chance to see or return the ball.

(6) Other Interference. Any other unintentional interference which prevents an opponent from having a fair chance to see or return the ball.

(b) Effect. A call by the referee of a "hinder" stops the play and voids any situation following, such as the ball hitting a player. No player is authorized to call a hinder, except on the back swing and such a call must be made immediately as provided in Rule 3.5(b).

(c) Avoidance. While making an attempt to return the ball, a player is entitled to a fair chance to see and return the ball. It is the duty of the side that has just served or returned the ball to move so that the receiving side may go straight to the ball and not be required to go around an opponent. The referee should be liberal in calling hinders to discourage any practice of playing the ball where an adversary cannot see it until too late. It is no excuse that the ball is "killed," unless in the opinion of the referee he couldn't return the ball. Hinders should be called without a claim by a player, especially in close plays and on game points.

(d) In Doubles. In doubles, both players on a side are entitled to a fair and unobstructed chance at the ball and either one is entitled to a hinder even though it naturally would be his partner's ball and even though his partner may have attempted to play the ball or that he may already have missed it. It is not a hinder when one player hinders his partner.

Rule 4.11—Avoidable Hinders. An avoidable hinder results in an "out" or a point depending upon whether the offender was serving or receiving.

(a) Failure to Move. Does not move sufficiently to allow opponent his shot.

(b) Blocking. Moves into a position effecting a block, on the opponent about to return the ball, or, in doubles, one partner moves in front of an opponent as his partner is returning the ball.

(c) Moving Into Ball. Moves in the way and is struck by the ball just played by his opponent.

(d) Pushing. Deliberately pushing or shoving an opponent during a volley.

Rule 4.12—Rest Periods. **(a) Delays.** Deliberate delay exceeding ten seconds by server, or receiver shall result in an out or point against the offender.

(b) During Game. During a game each player in singles, or each side in doubles, either while serving or receiving may request a "time out" for a towel, wiping glasses, change or adjustment. Each "time out" shall not exceed 30 seconds. No more than three "time outs" in a game shall be granted each singles players or each team in doubles.

(c) Injury. No time out shall be charged to a player who is injured during play. An injured player shall not be allowed more than a total of 15 minutes of rest. If the injured player is not able to resume play after total rests of 15 minutes the match shall be awarded to the opponent or opponents. On any further injury to same player, the Commissioner, if present, or committee, after considering any available medical opinion shall determine whether the injured player will be allowed to continue.

(d) Between Games. A 5 minute rest period is allowed between the first and second games and a 10 minute rest period between the second and third games. Players may leave the court between games, but must be on the court and ready to play at the expiration of the rest period.

(e) Postponed Games. Any games postponed by referee due to weather elements shall be resumed with the same score as when postponed.

PART V. TOURNAMENTS

Rule 5.1—Draws. The seeding method of drawing shall be the standard method approved by the U.S.-R.A. and N.R.C. All draws in professional brackets shall be the responsibility of the National Director of the N.R.C.

Rule 5.2—Scheduling. (a) Preliminary Matches. If one or more contestants are entered in both singles and doubles they may be required to play both singles and doubles on the same day or night with little rest between matches. This is a risk assumed on entering both singles and doubles. If possible the schedule should provide at least a one hour rest period between all matches.

(b) Final Matches. Where one or more players have reached the finals in both singles and doubles, it is recommended that the doubles match be played on the day preceding the singles. This would assume more rest between the final matches. If both final matches must be played on the same day or night, the following procedure shall be followed:

(1) The singles match be played first.

(2) A rest period of not less than ONE HOUR be allowed between the finals in singles and doubles.

Rule 5.3—Notice of Matches. After the first round of matches, it is the responsibility of each player to check the posted schedules to determine the time and place of each subsequent match. If any change is made in the schedule after posting, it shall be the duty of the committee or chairman to notify the players of the change.

Rule 5.4—Third Place. In championship tournaments: national, state, district, etc., (if there is a playoff for third place), the loser in the semi-finals must play for third place or lose his ranking for the next year unless he is unable to compete because of injury or illness. See Rule 3.5(d)(4).

Rule 5.5—U.S.R.A. Regional Tournaments. Each year the United States and Canada are divided into regions for the purpose of sectional competition preceding the National Championships. The exact boundaries of each region are dependent on the location of the regional tournaments. Such locations are announced in *National Racquetball* magazine.

(a) Only players residing in the area defined can participate in a regional tournament.

(b) Players can participate in only one event in a regional tournament.

(c) Winners of open singles in regional tournaments will receive round trip air coach tickets to the U.S.R.A. national tourney. Remuneration will be made after arrival at the Nationals.

(d) A U.S.R.A. officer will be in attendance at each regional tournament and will coordinate with the host chairman.

Awards: No individual award in U.S.R.A.-sanctioned tournaments should exceed value of more than $25.00.

Tournament Management: In all U.S.R.A.-sanctioned tournaments the tournament chairman and/or the national U.S.R.A. official in attendance may decide on a change of courts after the completion of any tournament game if such a change will accommodate better spectator conditions.

Tournament Conduct: In all U.S.R.A.-sanctioned tournaments the referee is empowered to default a match if an individual player or team conducts itself to the detriment of the tournament and the game.

Professional Definition: Any player who has accepted $200 or more in prizes and/or prize money in the most recent 12 calendar months is considered a professional racquetball player and ineligible for participation in any U.S.R.A. sanctioned tournament bracket.

Amateur Definition: We hold as eligible for amateur racquetball tournaments sanctioned by the U.S.R.A. anyone except those who qualify as professionals under current U.S.R.A.-N.R.C. rules.

Pick-A-Partner: The essence of the "Players' Fraternity" has been to allow players to come to tournaments and select a partner, if necessary, regardless what organization or city he might represent.

Age Brackets: The following age brackets, determined by the age of the player on the first day of the tournament are:

Open: Any age can compete.

Juniors: 18 and under.

Seniors: 35 and over.

Masters: 45 and over.

Golden Masters: 55 and over.

In doubles both players must be within the specified age bracket.

ONE-WALL AND THREE-WALL RULES

Basically racquetball rules for one-wall, three-wall and four-wall are the same with the following exceptions:

ONE-WALL—Court Size—Wall shall be 20 ft. in width and 16 ft. high, floor 20 ft. in width and 34 ft. from the wall to back edge of the long line. There should be a minimum of 3 feet beyond the long line and 6 feet outside each side line and behind the long line to permit movement area for the players.

Short Line—Back edge 16 feet from the wall. Service Markers—Lines at least 6 inches long parallel to and mid-way between the long and short lines, extending in from the side lines. The imaginary extension and joining of these lines indicates the service line. Lines are 1½ inches in width. Service Zone—floor area inside and including the short side and service lines. Receiving Zone—floor area in back of short line bounded by and including the long and side lines.

THREE-WALL—Serve—A serve that goes beyond the side walls on the fly is player or side out. A serve that goes beyond the long line on a fly but within the side walls is the same as a "short."

chapter thirteen
GLOSSARY OF TERMS

"A" Player—Racquetball participant whose tournament skill level is excellent. With this type of classification a competitor becomes an "A" player by winning a "B" tournament. Next step is "super A" or professional.

Ace—Legal serve that goes untouched by receiver. One point is scored.

Amoeba Man—A player whose sluggish court locomotion approaches the speed of the singled-celled amoeba.

Anterior—In front of. Toward the front wall.

Anticipation—Practice of reading an opponent's body movement, gaining prior-to-game knowledge of his court habits and "reading his mind" in order to predict shots and cover them accordingly.

Apex—Highest point in bounce of the ball. Zenith. Peak.

Around-the-Wall Ball—Defensive shot that first hits high on the side wall, then the front wall, then rebounds in the air to the other side wall before finally striking the floor at three-quarter court.

Avoidable Hinder—A hinder or interference, not necessarily intentional, which clearly hampers the continuance of a rally. Results in loss of serve or point.

"B" Player—(See *"A" Player*) tournament skill level is average. One becomes a "B" player by winning a "C" tournament.

Back Court—Court area behind the short line.

Backhand—Fundamental stroke hit on the side of the body opposite the hand with which one plays.

Backhand Corner—Area of the court where the side wall and back wall join on the same side as the player's backhand.

Backhand Grip—Position of gun hand on racquet when stroking the backhand.

Back-Into-Back Wall Shot—Ball that is driven into the rear wall and travels on the fly to the front wall.

Backspin—Rotation of the ball hit with bottom or reverse spin. Usually due to contacting the ball with an open-faced racquet.

Backswing—Initial step in any stroke whereby the racquet is brought into the ready position.

Back Wall—The rear wall.

Back Wall Shot—Shot taken on the rebound from the back wall.

Blinkus of the Thinkus—To falter mentally. To lose

Body Surfing

one's head or let the mind wander during play. See *Paralysis via Analysis*.

Block—Maneuver done to prevent the opponent from viewing or getting to the ball. Constitutes a hinder; avoidable or unavoidable.

Body Surf—The diving and subsequent sliding of a sweaty player on the court floor.

Bottom Boarder—A rolloff or perfect kill shot (off the "bottom board") off the front wall.

Bottom Spin—Rotation of the ball hit with reverse or back spin.

Box Theory—A teaching, practice and/or game aid whereby the player utilizes an actual or imagined

The "Box Theory utilizes an imaginary 1-foot-square box for kill shots during play, a real one during practice.

box to direct his kill shots or serves to a general rather than exact target area.

Buildups—Conditioning exercise consisting of beginning with a slow jog and increasing speed over a short distance to a sprint, and then immediately back to a jog again.

Bullseye—Specific target area on the front wall which must be hit for a proper serve to result.

Bumblebee Ball—Ball mishit or struck by the rim of the racquet head. The sphere gyrates wildly enroute to the front wall.

Bumper—Protective covering on the rim of most metal racquets for proper distribution of head weight and/or protection of court walls.

Bumper Ball—Ball mishit on the racquet's bumper. Frequently results in a bumblebee ball.

Butt—The enlarged terminal bump of the racquet handle.

"C" Player—Skill level is novice. Usually the lowest classification level in tournament play. Sometimes synonymous with novice.

Ceiling Ball—Defensive shot which strikes the ceiling first, then the front wall and then rebounds to the floor with top spin that propels ball into deep back court.

Ceiling Serve—Serve that hits the ceiling. If the ball contacts the ceiling first it is a side out; if it hits the front wall prior to the ceiling it is only a fault.

Center Court—That floor area of the court generally described as starting from the front short line and extending posterior to about 5 feet behind the short line.

Center Court Control—Maintaining position in center court and thereby forcing one's opponent to retrieve and make shots in deep court.

Change-Up—A shot hit softer than normal to throw the opponent's timing off.

Choke—1) To psych out during play. 2) To move the grip on the racquet handle toward the head.

Closed Face—Racquet face is not parallel with front wall, with the top of the head tilted forward. May cause ball to skip continually into the floor on kill shots.

Club Play—Informal competition at local facilities.

Cock Position—Ready position of the racquet on the backswing with wrist cocked and prepared for snapping upon ball contact.

Control—Ability to consistently place the ball to intended spots.

Controller—Player whose game strategy involves hitting more passes and defensive shots than kills. (As opposed to a *Shooter.*)

Corner Shot—A kill shot that hits at or near the front right or front left corner.

Court Hinder—Interference of a normal rally by an obstacle that deflects the ball. For example, a light fixture, door latch, etc. This is an unavoidable hinder and the point is replayed.

Crack Ball—Shot which strikes the juncture between the side or rear wall and the floor. Ball squirts out irretrievably.

Cross-Court Drive—A relatively hard hit shot that strikes the front wall and passes the opponent on the opposite side from which the shot originated. V-Ball. V-Pass.

Crotch—Juncture of two playing surfaces. For example, the front wall-side wall crotch.

Crotch Ball—Shot that strikes the front wall-floor juncture. This is a skip ball.

Crotch Serve—Serve that strikes the juncture of the front wall and the floor or ceiling. This is a side out.

Crowding—Intimidating the opponent through playing too close. This is an avoidable hinder.

Cutthroat—Racquetball game with three players. Each player during his serve plays against and scores points against the other two. Triples.

Dead Ball—1) Any ball that goes out of play or causes a hinder situation. For example, when a shot hits a player en route to the front wall. 2) A racquetball that does not bounce as high as normal.

Defensive Position—Player's station in rear court.

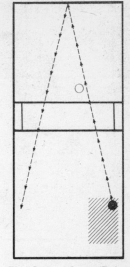

The Cross-Court Drive

An undesirable area for an offensive shot or for controlling play.

Defensive Shot—A conservative shot usually made to continue the rally rather than terminate it. Examples: ceiling ball, around-the-wall ball, Z-ball.

Delay Tactics—Stalling shenanigans. For example: wiping up a dry floor, arguing with referee or opponent, adjusting clothes or equipment.

Die—Verb applied to a ball which barely reaches the front wall and then rebounds with little or no bounce.

Dig—To barely retrieve a low kill shot before it hits the floor twice.

Donkey Kick—With the ball coming to the player's

Crowding

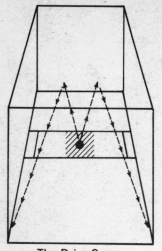

The Drive Serve

(usually forehand) side, he dives and hits the shot, simultaneously entangling his legs with his opponent's causing the latter to trip.

Donut—Zero points scored in a game. For example, to give the opponent a donut.

Doubles—Racquetball game where two teams composed of two players each compete.

Downswing—Downward pendulum movement of the racquet following the backswing and prior to ball contact.

Down-the-Line Drive—A shot hit from near a side wall directly to the front wall and rebounding back along that same wall past the opponent.

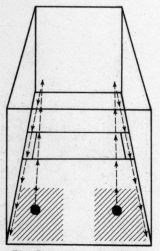

The Down-the-Line Pass

Down-the-Line Pass—R.A.W. ball. Down-the-Line Drive.

Drive Serve—Relatively hard hit service that strikes low on the front wall and rebounds in a straight line to the right or left rear corner.

Drop Shot—A softly struck ball, usually used to return a retrievable kill shot, aimed low into the front wall. Dump Shot.

Dump Shot—A Drop Shot.

Error—To muff the return of an apparently playable ball.

Exchange—The termination of the rally which results in a point or side-out.

Fatigue Factor—The element of extreme tiredness which often emerges in the third game of a strenuous match. This numbs the court senses and hampers shot accuracy.

Fault—Illegal serve or other infraction of the serving rules which allows the server one more chance to legally put the ball into play. For example, a short serve.

Fishbowl—Descriptive term applied to a court having one or more glass walls.

Five-Foot Line—Painted line 5 feet posterior to the short line which dictates the Five-Foot Rule (below).

Five-Foot Rule—Safety regulation stating that the receiver must stand behind the Five-Foot Line when receiving the serve. (For a more detailed interpretation, see the Official Rules.)

Flat Roll-Out—The perfect kill where the ball strikes the front wall so close to the floor that it rebounds with no bounce.

Floater—Shot mishit or struck with excessive backspin such that the ball drifts very slowly toward the front wall.

Fly Ball—Shot played directly on the rebound from the front wall before it contacts the floor. For example, a Fly Kill Shot. Volley Shot.

Follow-Through—Completion of the stroke after racquet contact with the ball.

Foot Fault—Illegal placement of a foot before or during the serve. This is a simple fault.

Footwork—Movement of the feet in correct relationship to the body and ball.

Forehand—Fundamental stroke hit on the same side of the body as the hand with which one plays.

Forehand Corner—Area of the court where the side wall and back wall join on the same side as the player's forehand.

Forehand Grip—Position of gun hand on racquet when stroking the forehand.

Four-Wall Racquetball—The most popular variety of the game where four side walls and a ceiling are utilized in indoor play.

Freak Ball—Out of the ordinary shot hit from an out-of-the-ordinary position for a winner. For example, the three-quarter court backhand overhead reverse rolloff.

Front-and-Back—See the *I-Formation* of doubles play.

Front Court—Area of the court in front of the short line including the service box.

Front Line— See *Service Line*.

Front Wall-First-Ceiling Ball—Infrequently employed defensive shot that strikes first the front wall, then the ceiling and then the floor.

Front Wall Kill—A kill shot that strikes and rebounds directly off the front wall (with no side wall contact).

Front Wall-Side Wall Kill—A kill shot that first hits the front wall, then the side wall.

Game—One racquetball contest to 21 points.

Gamesmanship—Use of unusual court tactics such as the psych-out, crowding and similar dubious ploys to secure points or psychological advantage.

Garbage Serve—(Synonym: Half Lob) A half-speed service which presents itself to the receiver at shoulder height. This deceptive serve is almost always returned to the ceiling.

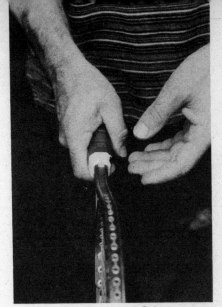

The Forehand Grip

Garfinkel Serve—Forehand cross-court or Z-serve to the opponent's forehand.

Golden Masters—Age group division in tournaments in singles and doubles for players 55 years and older.

Gravity Ball—Intended kill shot which is struck so softly that the force of gravity causes the ball to skip into the floor prior to contacting the front wall.

Grip—Manner in which the racquet is grasped for forehand or backhand strokes.

Ground Ball—A skip ball.

Gun Hand—That hand employed to wield the racquet.

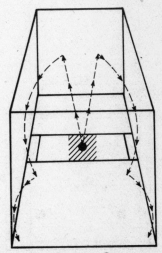

The Garbage Serve

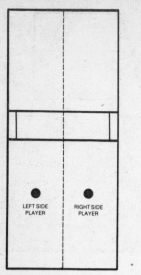

The Half-and-Half Formation in doubles

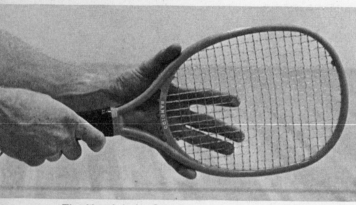

The Handshake Grip

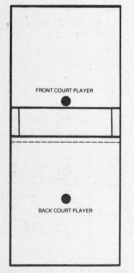

The I-Formation in doubles

Half-and-Half—One means of dividing court responsibilities between two players of a doubles team. Here, an imaginary line is drawn down the middle of the court with one player generally covering balls on the right, his partner covering balls on the left.

Half-Volley—To stroke the ball on the short hop from the floor.

Hand-Out—Loss of the service by the first partner serving for his team in doubles play.

Handshake Grip—Common method of holding the racquet in the handshake manner.

Head—Hitting surface of the racquet. The strung face plus the rim.

Hospitality Room—Refreshment room at tournaments where, typically, ten percent of the players consume 90 percent of the food.

Hypotenuse Shot—Kill shot traveling from either the left rear to right front corners, or the right rear to left front corners.

I-Formation—One means of dividing court responsibilities between two players of a doubles team. Here, an imaginary line is drawn to split the front and back courts: one player covers the front and his partner the back.

I-Pro—Professional division of the IRA organization.

Inner Game—The mental or psychological aspect of racquetball play. (As opposed to the *Outer Game.*)

Inning—A complete round of play in which both players (or teams) serve.

Interval Training—Rigorous method of physical training whereby periods of stress are interrupted by rest intervals for partial recovery.

IRA—International Racquetball Association, a major national organization.

Isolation Strategy—In doubles, the strategy of hitting consecutive shots to one player and very few to his partner in order to tire the former and cause the latter to get ''cold.''

Juniors—Age group division in tournaments in

singles and doubles for players 18 years and younger.

Kill—Shot that hits low on the front wall and rebounds with so little bounce that a legal return is impossible.

Let—A fault, hinder or similar interruption of play.

Live Ball—1) Any ball in play. 2) A racquetball that bounces satisfactorily or one which bounces too high.

Lob—A serve or infrequently used defensive shot which is directed softly, with a high arc and usually cross-court into a rear corner.

Long Serve—Any serve that carries to the back wall on the fly (before striking the floor). This constitutes one serving fault.

Masters—Age group division in tournaments in singles or doubles for players 45 years and over.

Match—A complete racquetball contest consisting of best two out of three games to 21 points.

Mercy Ball—Unwritten rule of court etiquette where one player holds back his swing because, had he hit the ball, that shot or his racquet would have struck his opponent. This is a simple hinder play.

NRC—National Racquetball Club, a major national organization.

Nonfront Serve—Any serve that hits any surface before initially striking the front wall. This serve is illegal and results in a side-out.

Novice—An unskilled player. A beginner.

Odor Hinder—Self-explanatory; not claimable in tournament play.

Offensive Position—Approximately center court, a superior court station.

Offensive Shot—An aggressive shot (usually kill or pass) intended to either terminate the rally or put the opponent in poor court position.

Offensive Theory—Certain school of strategic thought which advocates the use of offensive rather than defensive shots whenever feasible.

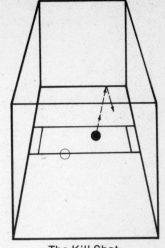

The Kill Shot

Off Hand—The free or non-gun hand not being utilized to wield the racquet.

One-Grip System—Infrequently utilized among better players, a method of grasping the racquet with the same grip for both forehand and backhand strokes.

One-On-Two—Game with three players in which one person versus the other two as a team for the entire game. As an additional handicap, the single player may have only one serve to the team's two.

One-Wall Racquetball—Variety of the game where only a front wall is utilized in outdoor play.

Open Face—Racquet face is not square (parallel) with the front wall, with the top of the head tilted backwards. Causes slicing of the ball.

Out—Loss of service due to an illegal serve.

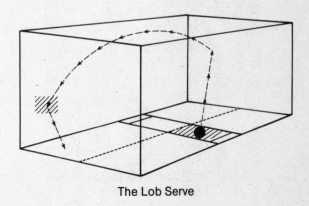

The Lob Serve

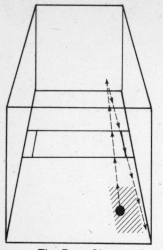

The Pass Shot

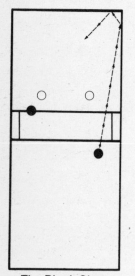

The Pinch Shot

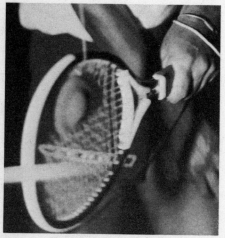

The Point of Contact

Outer Game—The physical aspects of racquetball play, including shot selection, covering, quickness (as opposed to the *Inner Game*).

Overhead— Pass or kill shot that is struck over the head.

Paddleball—Predecessor of modern racquetball where a wooden paddle and deader ball with pinhole are employed under same rules as racquetball.

Paralysis via Analysis—To "choke" or mentally seize-up due to over-examination of a situation.

Pass Shot—Down-the-line or cross-court shot hit out of the opponent's reach. A drive shot.

Pendulum swing—Basic building block motion for racquetball strokes.

Photon—An extremely hard hit shot. Bullet. Powder Ball.

Pinch Shot—Kill shot which goes side wall-front wall. A "wide" pinch ricochets off the side wall at some distance from the front, while a "short" pinch makes side wall contact within 3 feet of the front wall.

Plum Ball—An extraordinarily easy set-up.

Point—Unit of scoring. Only the server may score points. A tally.

Point of Contact—The exact spot of racquet and ball rendezvous.

Portsider—A left-hander. Southpaw.

Powder Ball—An extremely hard hit shot. Bullet. Photon.

Power Grip—Incorrect forehand grip whereby the racquet face is closed at the point of contact.

Psych Out—To mentally falter during a shot or contest. Choke.

Psych Up—To mentally prepare for a contest.

Pushing Off—Illegal shoving or touching the opponent (as in basketball) to gain superior court position. Results in a point or side-out.

Racquet Face—Strung hitting surface of the racquet head.

Rally—Time during which the ball is in play.

R.A.W. Ball—Acronym for run-along-the-wall ball, a wallpaper shot which clings closely to a side wall.

Reading—Practice of observing the opponent as he takes his shots to pick up signals that may aid one's anticipation.

Ready position— 1) Stance taken by receiver awaiting the serve. 2) Set or cock position at top of the stroke backswing.

Receiver—Person to whom the serve is hit.

Receiving Line—The 5-foot line.

Referee—Person who controls and makes all judgment calls in a tournament match.

Reverse Corner Kill—Kill shot made from the right side into the left front corner, or vice versa.

Reverse Garfinkel— See *Garfinkel Serve.* A crosscourt Z-serve sent into the left rear corner.

Rim—The fiberglass, metal or woodhead frame of a racquet.

Roadrunner—Player whose forte is retrieving and hustling as opposed to shooting the ball.

Rollout—A flat, irretrievable kill shot.

Safety Hinder—Interruption of play when further action could result in injury. For example, a mercy ball or foreign object in the court.

Sawdust Ball—A skip ball, short shot, oilwell ball, splinter ball, dirt ball, ground ball.

Screen Ball—Visual hinder either on the serve or during the rally. Play goes over.

Self-Waffle—To hit one's own body with one's own racquet.

Seniors—Age group division in tournaments in singles or doubles for players 35 years and over.

Serve—Act of putting the ball into play. Service.

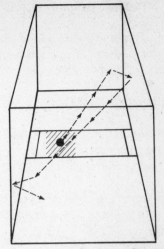

The Reverse Garfinkel Serve

Server—Player who puts the ball into play.

Serve Return—The receiver's initial shot after the ball has been served.

Service Box—1) The court area between the front and short lines from which the server initiates the serve. 2) Area where player of a doubles team must stand when his teammate is serving.

Service Line—The front line, parallel to and 5 feet anterior to the short line.

Set Position—The ready position or initial stance in preparation for the stroke.

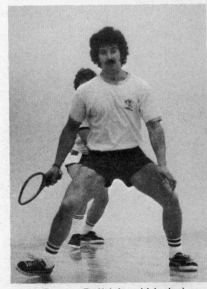

A Screen Ball (visual hinder)

Setup—A shot that is easily returned. A plum ball.

Shooter—An aggressive player whose game strategy revolves around attempting to kill a high percentage of setups. (As opposed to a *Controller*.)

Shoot the Ball—To try a kill shot.

Short Line—Line halfway between and parallel to the front and back walls past which the served ball must carry before hitting the floor.

Short Serve—Serve that fails to carry beyond the short line. This constitutes one service fault.

Side-By-Side— See *Half-and-Half*.

Side-Out—Loss of service with the server and receiver exchanging positions.

Side Wall-Front Wall Kill— See *Pinch Shot*.

Singles—Racquetball game where two players compete, one against another.

Skip Ball—Ball that hits the floor before reaching the front wall.

Southpaw—A left-handed player. Lefty, portsider.

Spin—Intentional or unintentional English imparted to the ball by the racquet strings.

Splinter Ball—Skip ball.

Straddle Ball—Ball which passes through the legs of one of the players on the front wall rebound. This may or may not be a hinder.

Straight Kill—See *Front Wall Kill*.

Super Pinch—Usually accidental kill shot that results when the ball is hit into one side wall, ricochets into the opposite side wall and then rolls off the front wall.

Sweet Spot—Center hitting surface of the racquet head which provides the most power and control.

Swish—Sound made by racquet strings traveling swiftly through the air when the wrist breaks at the point of contact (during practice strokes without the actual use of a ball).

Target Area—1) See *Bullseye*. 2) On the serve, that area to which the server intends the ball to travel to following the front wall rebound.

Technical—Call made by the referee during tournament play usually due to unsportsmanlike antics. The player responsible for the infraction has one point subtracted from his score at the time of the technical.

Tension—Amount of pressure at which the racquet is strung. Normal tension ranges from 26-32 pounds.

Thong—Strap attached to the butt end of the racquet handle and looped around the player's wrist as a safety precaution.

Three-Quarters and One-Quarter—One means of dividing court responsibilities between two players of a doubles team. Here, an imaginary line is drawn diagonally from one front corner to the opposite back corner with one player generally covering balls on the right side of the diagonal and his partner covering balls on the left.

Three-Wall Racquetball—Variety of the game where a front and two partial or full side walls are utilized in outdoor play.

Three-Wall Serve—Serve that strikes three walls on the fly. This is illegal and results in one serving fault.

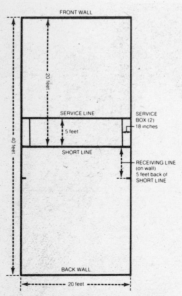

The Service Box, Service Line and Short Line

Time-Out—A legal, short (30 seconds or 1 minute) interruption in play called by one player or team usually for the purpose of regrouping physically or mentally.

Top Spin—Rotation of the ball hit with over spin.

Touch—Superb racquet control, especially on soft shots.

Tournament Play—Formal competitive play under scheduled and supervised conditions, as opposed to less formal club play.

Tour of the Court—A drawn-out rally where one player exerts little effort in controlling the play and runs his opponent all over the court.

Trigger Finger Grip—Normal method of grasping the racquet as if it were a pistol.

Turning Point—Specific time during a game or match that is considered crucial, often due to a shift in momentum.

Two-Grip System—Most often utilized among better players, a method of altering the hold on the racquet handle when changing from the forehand to backhand and vice versa.

Unavoidable Hinder—An interference of normal play brought about unintentionally or uncontrollably by the players, the court, the equipment or other hindrance.

Undercut—To apply backspin to the ball via an open racquet face.

USRA—The amateur division of the NRC organization.

V-Ball—Cross-court pass shot. V-Pass.

Veteran—Player with many years of court experience.

Veteran Hinder—Interference of the opponent's shot which is actually an avoidable hinder but, due to subtle body movement and often theatrics of innocence, is interpreted as unavoidable hinder.

Volley—1) See *Rally*. 2) To take the ball out of the air on the fly.

Waffle Face—Action of one player hitting his opponent in the face with the racquet.

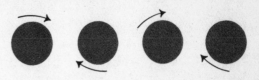

Top Spin

The Trigger Finger Grip

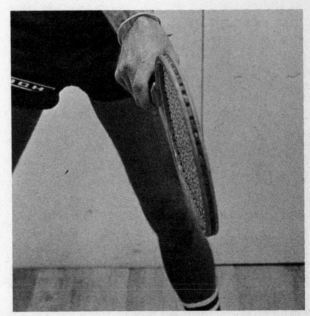

An Undercut

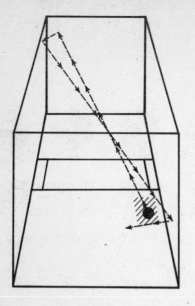

The Z-Ball

Wallpaper Ball—Shot that hugs a side wall so closely it is difficult to return. See *R.A.W. Ball*.

Windshield Wiper Play—An extended rally during which one player runs from one side wall to the other, etc. in retrieving a series of cross-court drive shots.

Winner—A successful kill shot.

Wrist Snap—Anatomical flexion of the wrist on the forehand and extension on the backhand which occurs at the point of contact and is a main source of power on the stroke.

Z-Ball—Considered a defensive shot by most, this ball hits high up on the front wall in either corner, ricochets quickly into the near side wall, then travels to the opposite side wall before finally striking the floor.

Z-Serve—See *Garfinkel* and *Reverse Garfinkel* serves.

PORTRAIT OF A TOURNAMENT

A Spectator's-Eye View of Racquetball Today

Photos by Arthur and Dick Shay at The Court Club, Burlington, Vermont.

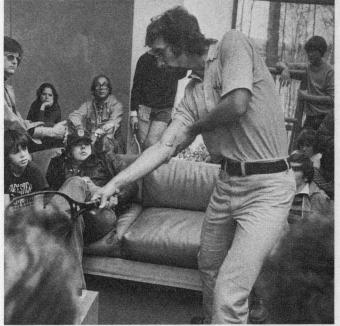

A POCKET GUIDE TO RACQUETBALL

COLLECTED SUMMARIES OF INSTRUCTIONAL CHAPTERS

CHAPTER 2 EQUIPMENT

I. Introduction—"court equipment ain't what it used to be."

II. Shoes and socks

III. Shorts and supporters

IV. Shirt and warm-ups

V. Sweatbands and gloves
   A. Sweaty palm is due to emotion and perspiration from arm
   B. Use one or two wristbands
   C. Use of the glove
   D. Most sticky sprays and powders are ineffective
   E. The mini-towel is universal solution to the racquet slippage dilemma
   F. Headbands effectively combat the "beady forehead syndrome" and hair-in-eyes problem

VI. Eyeguards and safety lenses
   A. Highly recommended—the singular major injury common in racquetball is related to the eye
   B. Test protective efficacy with "roll test"
   C. Test range of peripheral and vertical vision
   D. Superior solution is safety lenses. Ensure that present glasses are safety lens equipped
   E. Contact lenses okay if are soft type

VII. The racquet
   A. Descendant of the wooden paddle—history
   B. Three price ranges
   C. Question of which frame material to buy: plastic or metal?
      1. Plastic frame summary
      2. Metal frame summary
   D. Question of racquet length: standard or extra length?
      1. Standard length summary
      2. Extra length summary
   E. Question of racquet strings
      1. Material: usually silicone coated, braided monofilament nylon
      2. A quality racquet usually has quality string
      3. Tension: optimal range is 26-34 pounds. More specifically, 28-30
      4. Novices often prefer tightly strung and veterans more loosely strung tensions.
      5. String will settle in first week of play, i.e., lose 2-4 pounds tension
      6. Strings usually not guaranteed
      7. Restringing: acquire full restringing rather than patchwork. $5 to $8 for quality nylon
   F. Question of grips: rubber or leather?
      1. Rubber grip summary
      2. Leather grip summary
   G. Grip size
      1. Racquetball stroke more comparable to golf than tennis stroke

2. Tennis grips usually oversized for racquetball
3. Try out a small grip; it may be built up with tape
4. Overriding factor is comfort

H. Miscellaneous racquet information
1. Test run tentative racquet prior to purchase
2. Mail in guarantee card
3. Most court faults due to strokes rather than racquet itself

VIII. The ball
A. Two problems at present
B. Pepping up pooped spheres; two methods

IX. The court

CHAPTER 3 THE GAME

I. The teaser
A. Brief overview of racquetball
B. An individual sport
C. One-time test run is a hooker
D. Racquetball's mass appeal all-encompassing
E. Common denominator—healthy fun

II. The game
A. The serve
1. Must hit front wall first
2. Must carry past short line but not to back wall
3. Concept of faults—two successive faults cause a side-out
4. Side-out also results when serve does not initially hit front wall, or if serve touches server's body on the fly

B. The serve return
1. Return must be made before ball hits floor twice; ball may be taken on fly
2. Any combination of walls or ceiling is permissible on return

C. The volley
1. Is the alternate hitting of ball by players
2. Shots must be made before ball hits floor twice; ball may be taken on fly
3. Any combination of walls or ceiling is permissible

D. The exchange
1. Terminates the volley
2. Occurs when either player:

a. Lets ball hit floor twice prior to hitting
b. Lets his shot hit floor en route to front wall

E. Point scoring system
1. Each exchange results in a point or side-out
a. Exchange in favor of server is a point
b. Exchange in favor of receiver is a side-out
2. Only server may score points
3. One game is to 21 points
4. Best two out of three games is a match
5. At 20-20, the next point scored wins that game

III. Additional suggestions
A. Hinders—disruptions of play: two types
1. Unavoidable hinders
2. Avoidable hinders
B. Ball out of court: two circumstances
1. After ball hits front wall: a simple hinder
2. Before ball hits front wall: a point or side-out

IV. The chocolate freak

V. Doubles
A. Methods of court coverage
1. Half-and-half
2. Front-and-back (I formation)
B. Center court exchange—the team not hitting the ball has the right to front court positioning
C. Keys to doubles strategy
1. Center court control
2. Patience
3. Ceiling rallies
4. Kill shots—side wall-front wall
5. Cross-court pass to the left
6. Strong serves and serve returns necessary
7. The inner game
8. Isolation factor
D. Eschew the madness

VI. Basic singles strategy
A. Strategy on the service
1. Low and high zones of ball contact
2. Variety is the spice of service
3. After serving, retreat along this diagonal toward corner at which one served
4. Watch the wall during play
B. Strategy on the service return
1. Strategy revolves around center court position
2. Usual return is a defensive shot
3. Take the serve on the fly if possible

C. Strategy on the rally
  1. Know your own and your opponent's capabilities
  2. Use of complementary shots
  3. Offensive vs. Defensive play
  4. Three different hitting areas on the court
  5. Kill shot strategy and areas of shooting
D. Strategy on miscellaneous situations
  1. Game plan formulation prior to game
  2. Warming up: Stretching and circulation stimulants
E. Summary

CHAPTER 4 FOREHAND

I. Forehand grip
  A. Handshake grip
  B. "V" positioning
  C. Trigger finger
  D. Heel-in-butt

II. Forehand stroke
  A. Basic three elements
    1. Pendulum swing
    2. Wrist cock set position
    3. Step forward
  B. Set position—wrist cock
  C. Point of contact
    1. For passes—knee high; for kills—ankle high
    2. Away from body
    3. Off lead heel
  D. Break wrist upon contact
  E. Level follow-through
  F. Hit ball with 80 percent effort
  G. Killing the ball—same stroke; ankle high
  H. Baseball sidearm swing

III. Forehand drills
  A. Practice is mandatory
  B. Exercises
    1. Drop and hit—3 positions
    2. Set-up and hit—3 positions
    3. Drop and kill
    4. Set-up and kill
  C. Obtain feed back
  D. Stave off boredom

CHAPTER 5 BACKHAND

I. Backhand grip
  A. Rebuttal of the one-grip system
  B. Start with forehand grip
    1. Rotate handle ⅛-turn in hand. (Top of racquet toward front wall)
    2. Racquet face should be parallel with front wall
    3. Juncture of thumb and index finger should be on edge of handle
  C. Use of 'off' hand to facilitate grip change and set position

II. Backhand Stroke
  A. Two main differences from forehand
    1. Grip change
    2. Point of contact—slightly more anterior with backhand
  B. Assume athletic position facing left side wall
  C. Three-step procedure—without, then with ball
    1. Pendulum swing—imitation of left-handed golfer
      a. Backswing
      b. Body weight transfer in conjunction with hip rotation
      c. Uncoil hips
      d. Racquet handle passes nearly parallel with floor
      e. Follow-through—dictated by rest of stroke
      f. Strive for fluid movement
    2. Wrist snap
      a. Wrist cocked at top of backswing
      b. Wrist broken at bottom of downswing at potential ball contact point
      c. Listen for swish sound
      d. Point of contact near lead toe
      e. Backhand wrist snap is essentially forehand wrist snap in reverse motion.
    3. The step forward
      a. Ensures proper body momentum and weight transfer
      b. Toe will point direction of shot
  D. Combine the three steps for fluid backhand
  E. If backhand stroke becomes ungrooved, revert to left-handed golf analogy and three-step procedure
  F. Reminder points from forehand chapter
    1. Get into set position quickly
    2. Point of contact in relation to floor: knee high for passes, lower for kills

3. Kill and pass strokes basically the same
4. Point of contact in relation to body—about 2 feet away
5. Body momentum important
6. Eye on ball (mental concentration)
7. Hit with approximately 80 percent effort

III. Backhand drills—identical to forehand
   A. Drop and hit
   B. Set-up and hit
   C. Drop and kill
   D. Set-up and kill
   E. Three-quarter court random set-ups
   F. Work on weaknesses. Practice what you know to discover what you don't know

CHAPTER 6 PASSES

I. Pass shots
   A. Definition
   B. Four types of passes
     1. Backhand down-the-line
     2. Forehand down-the-line
     3. Forehand cross-court
     4. Backhand cross-court

II. Down-the-line passes
   A. Backhand utilized more frequently than forehand
   B. Use model stroke
   C. Point of contact knee to navel high
   D. Contact front wall 2-4 feet, 1-3 feet high from sidewall
   E. Use top or back spin

III. Cross-court passes
   A. Forehand utilized more frequently than backhand—is bread-and-butter shot
   B. Point of contact knee to waist high
   C. Contact front wall 2-4 feet, 1 foot left of center
   D. Pool table analogy

IV. Pass drills
   A. Drop and hit
   B. Set-up and hit
   C. Perpetual drives
   D. Practice with partner

V. Common errors
   A. Hitting too hard—use 80 percent effort

B. Hitting too high—aim low on front wall
C. Not enough angle on cross-courts
D. Contacting too high—strive for knee level

CHAPTER 7 DEFENSIVE SHOTS

I. Three defensive shots
   A. Z-ball
   B. Around-the-wall ball
   C. Ceiling ball—most important one
   D. Discount use of lob as defensive shot

II. When to hit a defensive shot
   A. Rule of thumb—when it is unacceptable to hit offensive shot
     1. When out of position
     2. When off balance
     3. When in deep rear court
   B. Use defensive shot to recover center court position and to limit opponent's shot selection

III. Z-ball
   A. History
   B. Is an exotic shot—difficult to hit
   C. Important features
     1. Must be anterior in court and next to side wall to hit
     2. Always driven cross-court
     3. Always hits front wall first
   D. Bullseye—3 feet down and 3 feet in on front wall

IV. Around-the-wall ball
   A. History
   B. When to use—when in deep court, especially off of soft service and ceiling ball
   C. Hit it cross-court and strike side wall first
   D. Bullseye—3 feet down and 3 feet in on side wall
   E. Ball must not strike ceiling

V. Ceiling ball
   A. The major defensive shot
   B. Neutralizing shot—only return off it is another ceiling ball
   C. Bullseye—1 to 5 feet on ceiling from front wall
   D. Avoid contact with side wall
   E. Forehand ceiling ball
     1. Baseball pitcher analogy

2. Tennis serve analogy
3. Two swings—three-quarter overhead (recommended) and full overhead
F. Backhand ceiling ball
  1. Golfer analogy
  2. Baseball hitter analogy
  3. Rotation and de-rotation of hips
  4. Regular backhand shot analogy—waist high contact
G. Backhand more significant than forehand ceiling balls
H. Common errors
  1. Healthy stride
  2. Forehand—snap wrist; backhand—body into ball
  3. Contact at proper height
  4. Avoid side wall contact
  5. Most important—1- to 5-foot striking bullseye
I. Front-wall-first ceiling ball—nonpercentage

VI. Defensive shot drills—use lively ball
A. Z-ball drills
  1. Drop and hit
  2. Set and hit
B. Around-the-wall drills
  1. Drop and hit
  2. Set and hit
  3. Ceiling set and hit
  4. Perpetual around-the-wall balls (with partner)
C. Ceiling ball drills—spend most practice time on these, majority on backhand
  1. Drop and hit
  2. Set and hit
  3. Perpetual ceiling drill (solo)
  4. Perpetual ceiling drill (with partner)
  5. Perpetual cross-court ceiling drill (with partner)

VII. Center court-control important
A. Occupy center court position following defensive shot
B. Defensive shots can be offensive shots

CHAPTER 8 BACKWALL PLAY

I. Back wall play
A. Footwork is the key
B. Player's directional movement same as ball's

C. Two styles of playing ball off back wall
  1. Stop-and-step
  2. Jog-and-hit (stop-and-three-step)
D. Sideways shuffle when pursuing ball to back court

II. Back wall drills
A. Shadow play—start 3 feet behind service box
B. Toss and hit
C. Hard set and hit—start 3 feet behind service box
D. Soft set and hit—start 3 feet behind service box

III. Three common back wall errors
A. Point of contact off lead foot—retreat close to back wall prior to stepping into ball
B. Healthy step into ball to generate momentum
C. Watch the ball

IV. Back wall variations
A. Front wall to back wall to floor—return with offensive shot
B. Front wall to back wall to floor to front wall—return with "dump"

V. Shot selection off back wall—usually offensive
A. Drive shot
B. Kill shot

CHAPTER 9 OTHER SHOTS

I. Volley
A. i.e. Taking the ball out of the air; on the fly
B. Difficult to execute
C. What shot to use off of volley—usually offensive
D. When to take ball on volley—complex
  1. Volley if you expect ball to die at back wall
  2. Do not volley shots above head
  3. Volley soft serves
E. Stroke mechanics
  1. Use normal forehand or backhand
  2. Knee to waist contact height
  3. Do not tap or push ball
F. Exercise—set-up and volley

II. Half-volley
A. i.e. Taking the ball on the short-hop
B. Stroke in same manner as the volley
C. Practice is difficult and not mandatory

III. Drop shot
   A. Exclusive execution by forehand
   B. The stroke
      1. Stride forward with left foot
      2. Catch ball on short hop
      3. Stiff wrist with racquet rolling motion
      4. Push ball into near corner
   C. Is difficult play whose mastery is not mandatory

IV. Overheads—two types
   A. Overhead kill
      1. Hit cross-court generally
      2. Hit side wall first generally
   B. Overhead drives
      1. May be hit cross-court or up and down line—former allows greater margin of error
      2. Bullseyes: apparent—1 foot high on front wall; actual—about 3 feet high
   C. Stroke—the overhand forehand; forehand only
      1. Similar to ceiling ball overhand swing
      2. Full overhand or three-quarter overhand
   D. Degree of difficulty of control of overheads—easiest to hardest
      1. Ceiling ball
      2. Drive
      3. Kill
   E. Overheads rarely employed by pros; more common among beginners and intermediates
   F. Practice—off ceiling balls, solo and with partner

V. Ball-into-back-wall ball
   A. Employed only in emergency when no other shot is possible
   B. Often is an addiction which must be bucked
   C. Return of the B.I.B.W. ball
      1. Rush ball and volley it in mid-air
      2. Kill into near corner
   D. Do not practice B.I.B.W. ball. Its return may be practiced.

CHAPTER 10 SERVICE

I. Importance of the serve

II. Four basic services
   A. Garbage (half-lob)
   B. Drive (low hard)

C. Z-serve
D. Lob

III. Purpose of serve
   A. Simply putting ball into play
   B. Striving for weak return

IV. Three basic recommendations
   A. Serve from centralized position
   B. Majority of serves to the backhand
   C. Quality as opposed to variety

V. Garbage serve
   A. Starting position—central service box
   B. Height of contact—navel to chest
   C. Stroke is a "push" or "put"
   D. Front wall bullseye—1 foot left of center and about halfway up front wall
   E. Rear court bullseye—3-foot cubic box theory; ball bounces into top of box
   F. Garbage also possible to forehand, though not as effective
   G. Avoid side wall contact, unless within 3 feet from back wall
   H. Forces ceiling ball return

VI. Drive (low hard) serve
   A. Most effective serve when accurate; is difficult to control
   B. Avoid aiming for "crack"
   C. Starting position—center or just left of central service box
   D. Height of contact—knee level or lower
   E. Strike with gusto—80 percent power
   F. Front wall bullseye—1 foot left of center and about 3 feet high
   G. Rear court bullseye—through a 3-foot cubic box
   H. Stroke is normal drop-and-kill motion
   I. Initiates reaction—kill-pass game style

VII. Z-serve
   A. Easy to execute and highly effective
   B. Four types of Z-serves
      1. Low hard to backhand—a reverse Z
      2. High soft to backhand—a reverse Z
      3. Low hard to forehand—a normal Z
      4. High soft to forehand—a normal Z
   C. Low hard reverse Z to backhand
      1. Starting position—center or left of center
      2. Height of contact—about knee level
      3. Front wall bullseye—3 feet high and 1 foot from right side wall
      4. Stroke is normal drop-and-kill motion
      5. Ball must contact left side wall (1 to 4

feet from back wall) prior to hitting back wall (after floor bounce)

D. High soft reverse Z to backhand
  1. Starting position—left of center
  2. Height of contact—about waist level
  3. Front wall bullseye—5-6 feet high and 1 foot from right side wall
  4. Ball must contact left side wall prior to back wall (after floor bounce)
  5. Approximately 50 percent power on stroke

E. Low hard normal Z to forehand—not recommended

F. High soft normal Z to forehand
  1. Starting position—center service box
  2. Height of contact—waist level
  3. Front wall bullseye—3-6 feet up and 1 foot in from left side wall
  4. Approximately 50 percent power on stroke
  5. Right side wall contact prior to back wall (after floor bounce)

VIII. Lob serve
  A. Starting position—right of center
  B. Height of contact—waist to chest level
  C. Stroke is a lofting "push"
  D. Front wall bullseye—(depending upon starting position) three-quarters up and 1 foot left of center
  E. Ball must brush side wall—about 6-8 feet in from back wall and 6-8 feet up from floor
  F. Always lob serve cross-court
  G. Use of lob discouraged

IX. Miscellaneous
  A. Which serves to use
    1. Beginner—experiment with all
    2. Advanced—acquire 2 or 3 bread-and-butter serves
  B. Temper service knowledge with concentration
  C. Do not change serves in mid-swing

X. Service practice drills
  A. Concept of practicing each serve a number of times before progressing to next
  B. Innovate and experiment
  C. Obtain outside criticism
  D. Drill with a helper in court
  E. More practice time should be devoted to serves and serve returns

CHAPTER 11 SERVICE RETURN

I. Serve return is second in importance only to serve

II. Initial position 3-4 feet from back wall and center or slightly left of center court

III. Service return and concept of center court
  A. Closely interrelated
  B. Prime objective—force the opponent from center court and occupy area yourself

IV. Five possible returns
  A. Three high percentage—ceiling ball, drive and around-wall-ball
  B. Two low percentage—lob and kill shot

V. Ceiling ball return
  A. Safest and most logical service return
  B. Jibes perfectly with concept of center court positioning
  C. Direct at opponent's backhand
  D. Execution previously detailed in Chapter 7
  E. Is comforting shot and thought—can be used in rebuff to any serve

VI. Drive return
  A. Second most widely used return
  B. Is both, and neither, offensive and defensive
  C. Usually directed cross-court (V-ball pass)
  D. Use against moderately good and weak serves presented at waist height or lower

VII. Around-wall return
  A. Underused, especially among lower caliber players
  B. Best utilized against "softer" serves (garbage and high reverse Z)
  C. Usually struck with backhand; always cross-court

VIII. Lob return—totally discounted except as desperation ploy

IX. Kill shot return
  A. Use only against weak serves—e.g. serves presented at waist level or lower

B. Generally think conservative on service return—this dictated by logic and center court concept

C. If you do kill return: forehand into forehand corner and backhand into backhand corner

X. Drills

A. Especially practice drills from Chapter 7 on defensive shots; offensive shots needed too

B. Ultimate drill: server vs. returner

C. See drills in Chapter 10 on the service

XI. Summary